COMPLEXITY AND THE NEXUS OF LEADERSHIP

COMPLEXITY AND THE NEXUS OF LEADERSHIP

LEVERAGING NONLINEAR SCIENCE TO CREATE ECOLOGIES OF INNOVATION

Jeffrey Goldstein, James K. Hazy, and Benyamin B. Lichtenstein

palgrave
macmillan

First published in hardcover in 2010 by PALGRAVE MACMILLAN®
in the United States - a division of St. Martin's Press LLC, 175 Fifth Avenue,
New York, NY 10010.

Where this book is distributed in the UK, Europe and the rest of
the World, this is by Palgrave Macmillan, a division of Macmillan
Publishers Limited, registered in England, company number 785998,
of Houndmills, Basingstoke, Hampshire RG21 6XS.

Palgrave Macmillan is the global academic imprint of the above
companies and has companies and representatives throughout the world.

Palgrave® and Macmillan® are registered trademarks in the United
States, the United Kingdom, Europe and other countries.

ISBN: 978–0–230–62228–9

Library of Congress Cataloging-in-Publication Data

Goldstein, Jeffrey, 1949–
    Complexity and the nexus of leadership : leveraging nonlinear science to
    create ecologies of innovation / Jeff Goldstein, James K. Hazy, and
    Benyamin B. Lichtenstein.
        p.   cm.
    Includes bibliographical references and index.
    ISBN 978–0–230–62227–2
    1. Leadership.   2. Organizational change.   3. Organizational effectiveness.
    4. Complexity (Philosophy)   I. Hazy, James K.   II. Lichtenstein,
    Benyamin B.   III. Title.
    HD57.7.G66396 2010
    303.3′4—dc22   2009044862

A catalogue record of the book is available from the British Library

Design by Integra Software Services

First PALGRAVE MACMILLAN paperback edition: April 2011

10 9 8 7 6 5 4 3 2 1

Printed in the United States of America.

Transferred to Digital Printing in 2011

CONTENTS

LIST OF TABLE AND FIGURES

CHAPTER 1

INTRODUCTION: A NEW SCIENCE OF LEADERSHIP

During the initial panic of the "Great Recession of 2009" John Chambers, the CEO of Cisco Systems, told the *New York Times* of a crucial lesson he had learned nearly a decade before from Jack Welch when he was CEO of GE.[1] Chambers had asked, "Jack, what does it take to have a great company?" Welch responded, "It takes major setbacks ... by that I mean, a near-death experience!"

Well, in 2001, Cisco nearly did die when the tech bubble burst and Chambers's leadership came under question. Yet, in 2003, when it became clear that the company had passed the test, Welch called Chambers and told him that he now had a great company. "It doesn't feel like it," Chambers replied. But at that very moment, in responding to Jack Welch, he finally understood what Welch had meant back in 1998: organizations that face and survive serious challenges can emerge stronger. This, of course, is only if they don't fail!

What distinguishes companies that emerge stronger from those that fail? The key lies in how innovation supplies additional capabilities for adroit action in the face of unexpected and rapidly changing conditions. Firms that can't innovate go the way of dinosaurs. As a major ingredient in adaptability, innovation means much more than introducing new products or services, although without those no organization can compete in this economy. Truly adaptable organizations must also innovate their practices, processes, strategies, and structures so that their internal capacities become a match for turbulent environmental conditions. Staying competitive in the twenty-first century requires a higher level of innovation and adaptability than most of us have ever seen, and the bar keeps rising. Achieving this is simply not possible through traditional top-down management fiats, nor by "shared" or "distributed" leadership that is being sold by so many books and consultants these days.

So, how can such high levels of innovation be achieved? This book provides a new answer to that critical question by showing how leaders, guided by the insights coming out of complexity science, can create *ecologies of innovation* throughout their organizations. Leaders in an ecology of innovation encourage and support "experiments in novelty," building new organizational pathways that allow these experiments to materialize into novel offerings and improvements. Complexity science thus puts leaders in a greatly enhanced position to help their organizations effectively navigate critical periods of growth and change.

A COMPLEXITY SCIENCE OF GENERATIVE LEADERSHIP

Our book presents a host of insights coming from complexity science about how ecologies of innovation can be created. Over the last decade or so, nonlinear science researchers have developed tools and concepts that more accurately explain how organizations operate, how leaders can be more effective within them, and how innovation really comes about.

In particular, complexity science shows how the typical focus on "heroic" and charismatic leaders can result in a *lack* of innovation in modern organizations.[2] In contrast, we reframe "leader" and "leadership" as referring primarily to *events* rather than to people. Through a series of interactions over time, *leadership events* alter the underlying framework of engagement. They change the rules by which individuals interact, influencing the ends to be achieved, such as where a work group is headed, as well as the means by which it gets there.

A complexity science based view sees leadership as an influence process that arises through *interactions* across the organization: leadership happens in "the space between" people as they interact. Through influential interactions, which are happening all the time in every corner of the organization, novelty emerges and is enacted in unique and surprising ways. This means that the true catalysts of innovation are the web of relationships—in the nexus of interactions—that connect members to each other and to others in the environment.

We are using the term "generative leadership"[3] to highlight that the process of innovation is not led by any one individual but emerges through an unfolding series of events at every level of the organization. Generative leadership focuses on the mutual influence that occurs within every exchange. Accordingly, rather than concentrating on how a supervisor expresses influence *over* an employee, generative leadership sees them *both* as expressing leadership. Moreover, generative leadership refers to capturing the benefits of this mutual interplay as a *generative* process—it spawns new opportunities that increase the organization's potential for novelty, flexibility, and growth. As a process that builds progressively, generative leadership tunes into *patterns* of interaction rather than specific "one-time moves" that a manager may initiate and carry out.

Generative leadership does not wait fatalistically for the unexpected to happen, but instead actively participates in and coevolves (more on this term later) with the environment and the future. *Complexity and the Nexus of Leadership* shows the usefulness of this new understanding of leadership through research findings from complexity science and through many cases and examples from a wide range of corporations, entrepreneurial start-ups, social ventures and NGOs, and governmental agencies.

COMPLEXITY SCIENCE EMPOWERS LEADERSHIP

One of the most important takeaways from this book will be just how empowering the new advances in complexity science are for leadership. What we mean by the term "complexity" is not the same as what most managers are taught to fear, and therefore try to undo. In technical terms, "complicated" describes, for example, the design and manufacture of a jumbo jet, an exceedingly difficult task involving up to two million separate parts and untold operations. In contrast, "complex" has to do with the *interactions* in the system, through which something new emerges, such as norms in a work group or a groundswell of momentum for a new enterprise. Until recently the differences between complicated and complex were not well understood; as a result they have often been treated in the same way, as if the same process should be used to "deal with" situations that are complicated *or* complex. Business schools justified this by treating organizations as if they were machines that could be analyzed, dissected, and broken down into parts. According to that myth, if you fix the parts, then reassemble and lubricate, you'll get the whole system up and running. *But this is exactly the wrong way to approach a complex problem.*

In this book we show precisely why this is wrongheaded: it misses the fact that under the right conditions a complex system can *adapt*, whereas a piece of machinery cannot. A complex system, through its own internal processes, can actually change itself so as to generate better outcomes. No one would expect an aircraft, no matter how complicated the design, to reconfigure itself so that it flies faster or operates more efficiently! And yet, organizations do these kinds of things all the time. This is a critical difference between complex versus complicated systems that traditional approaches miss entirely. Instead, they talk about performance and efficiency and then add as an afterthought, "Oh yes, you need innovation also, so do that too." Although complex systems are often intricately entangled and complicated with all sorts of factors and people and systems, it is their *complexity* and not their complicatedness that makes them adaptable.

There is one more crucial difference. In a complex system, but never in a complicated one, even a small number of people, working well together, can make a major difference that goes beyond any one of their capabilities. Complexity science empowers individuals by demonstrating how they can alter a system, collectively making new things happen. What is exciting about the advent of complexity science is that it helps explain, for the first time, why some organizations are able to adapt and change and grow, and why others fail the crucial test that Jack Welch posed to John Chambers. In this book we will tell you how you can make this critical difference.

THE ADAPTIVE POTENTIAL OF COMPLEXITY

Complexity science empowers leadership in another way: it presents an *active* and *constructional* model of leadership based on a highly engaged view of mutuality, interdependence, and shared accountability. By "active" we distinguish this book from a spate of "complexity" texts that promulgated a laissez-faire view of leadership; by "constructional" we mean the *hands-on building up* of ecologies of innovation, the construction of more effective social networks, and the search and amplification of experiments in novelty, which result in the emergence of innovations.

This sharply distinguishes our book from the so-called self-organization approach to leadership—the laissez-faire style that has only the most superficial connection to the science of complex systems. This facile notion of self-organization was linked to a somewhat absurd claim: somehow, by dismantling hierarchically directed command and control structures, the organization will spontaneously reorganize "on its own," resulting in positive directions for it. In fact, rigorous complexity science research has borne out the *opposite* conclusion, namely, that any positive result from the emergence of innovation requires both bottom-up and top-down influences from proactive leadership events. In contrast, tearing down hierarchical structures can easily lead to a morass of unanticipated outcomes, many of which are much worse than what existed before.

Finally it is important to note that organizations have always been complex. What has changed is our ability to understand them as complex systems and thereby influence them. Complexity means that "system components"—individuals, or more generally "agents"—each with a different perspective and information, interact with each other in a mode of mutual influence. In this mode complexity arises when even two agents interact, since their unique information and perspective generates *difference*, and difference leads to unanticipated and novel outcomes. Of course, this is magnified many times across the interactions of 20 or 100 or 1,000 people. Everyone who works in an organization intuitively realizes that social interactions are complex in this way, and yet business schools and most so-called leadership experts have traditionally ignored this obvious fact.

A simple example will clarify the nonlinear and non-proportional effects of this kind of complexity. In a social network with two people there are two connections, one in each direction. With three people there are six possible connections, each person to two others. Five people have 20 connections, eight people have 56 connections. Notice how this buildup of connectivity is not linear; the number of connections increases much faster than the number of individuals. For example, a social network with 100 individuals yields 9,900 possible connections, any number of which can come together to influence the outcome.

This view of nonlinearity helps explain some powerful elements of complex systems. First, as we've said, complex systems are not linear—hence the term "nonlinear" in our title—because a given cause does not lead to a proportionate result. Second, complex systems are not easily predictable, since what emerges from their interactions is something *more* than a simple aggregation of their properties. Third, although complex systems are undoubtedly stochastic (i.e. irregular), they are not random since dynamical patterns are discernible, and these can be acted upon by generative leadership. Indeed, if randomness was the final message of complexity, then this book should be about how to teach leaders to become better gamblers!

It is the very uncertainty, unpredictability, and uncontrollability of organizational processes that signal the adaptive capability of complex systems; their capacity for the emergence of novel practices, processes, and routines is at the heart of an ecology of innovation. Because of this capacity for adaptability, the complex systems that are of interest are often described as *complex adaptive systems*. Examples of complex adaptive systems include living organisms and ecologies, healthy immune systems, thriving economies, and the sustainable functioning of organizations, whether entrepreneurial start-ups, nonprofit entities, or large institutions and corporations.

In a business or other organization, a complex adaptive system is composed of individuals—semiautonomous agents—who interact according to certain rules. Each individual gathers information about the internal workings of the organization as well as the environment according to that person's own position and history. Individuals in a complex system are necessarily diverse in form, in capability, and in the information they hold and use. Moreover, each adapts more or less effectively by gathering information, learning from others, and changing their own rules or mental models when possible. Whether a group of these learning individuals somehow translates into an organization that is adaptable, though, is a different matter. This is where generative leadership can make the critical difference. In this book we show how generative leadership can build and enhance this capacity for adaptability.

THE CONTRIBUTION OF NONLINEAR SCIENCE

We are claiming that insights from complexity science have the power to reframe leadership and transform organizations, but only when these insights are properly understood. Unfortunately, most leadership or management books that have appealed to complexity science have presented a narrow understanding of complex system dynamics, on the basis of a highly stylized interpretation of a few intriguing outcomes. The result is merely a set of metaphors that fail to deliver any sustainable advice to managers and executives dealing with rapid change.

Furthermore, many previous books in this genre were insulting to the reader by aiming for a lowest common denominator of intelligence and expertise. In contrast, we are assuming that our readers are intelligent, with proficiencies based on years on hard work and difficult decision making. This means that in order to provide the accuracy and value you deserve, the material in this book requires thoughtfulness and imagination. Rather than masking the inherent complexity of organizations by using simplistic interpretations, we will take this difficulty on directly through clear descriptions and vivid examples, visual diagrams, and alternative ways of understanding.

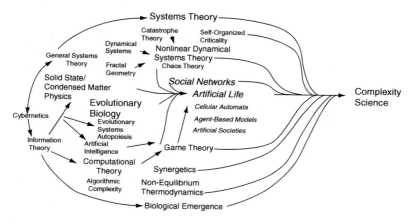

Figure 1.1   Scientific and Mathematical Fields Making Up Complexity Science

To begin, we provide a glimpse of what complexity science encompasses. The various fields making up complexity science are presented in figure 1.1. As this diagram shows, the science of complex systems is the confluence of a number of fields. On the far left we see the original systems sciences of cybernetics, information theory, and General Systems Theory, all of which originated around the time of World War II. These approaches were then extended in the 1960s, 1970s, and 1980s by new theories of nonlinear dynamics in physics and mathematics, order emergence in thermodynamics, the advent of network science, and a great plethora of computational simulation studies. For the past 20 years there has been a literal explosion of complexity research due to the availability of powerful microcomputers and the establishment of institutes and centers around the world that are devoted to the study of complexity science.

Rather than go into the history of complexity science, suffice it to say that in this book we draw on fields that are situated roughly to the right of the center of this whale-shaped diagram. Whereas virtually all other complexity books make use of perhaps one or two fields, our treatment is based on relevant insights from nearly a dozen fields of complexity science. The result is a robustness of theory and application that has a proven track record of success. We now turn to a summary of some of the key themes that are illuminated throughout the book.

COMPLEXITY AND THE NEXUS OF LEADERSHIP: CORE THEMES

To give you a sense of what's to come, we present the main themes of the book, some of which refer to specific chapters and others that are interwoven throughout the book: Ecologies of Innovation; Interaction Resonance within Social Networks; Differences, Information, and Novelty Generation; Critical Periods and their Potential for Innovation; Emergence; and Boundaries and Constraints.

ECOLOGIES OF INNOVATION

At the heart of our complexity view of leadership is the idea of an ecology of innovation. The science of ecology consists of the study of interactions between ecosystems, eco-subsystems, and their environments. By focusing on the network of interrelations making up an ecosystem within a specific area, ecology employs a whole-systems viewpoint. In an important sense, an ecosystem is the most accurate picture of what a complex, nonlinear, adaptive, and interactive system is all about. Sub-ecosystems are the components in interaction with each other and with other subsystems in the environment; these interactions supply the nutrients, building materials, wastes, and information that get transmitted from system to system in a vital exchange. No sub-ecosystem can survive on its own. Instead, the vast set of interchange and exchange that connects one to another enables the entire ecology to thrive.

It is within this vast web of interconnectivity that we see all the features of complex systems:

- Micro-level diversity supplying seeds of novelty
- Experiments that move parts of the system away from normal routines
- Intricate networks connecting interdependent subsystems to one another
- Innovations conferring new functionalities that enhance adaptability to unexpected changes or "jolts" from the environment
- Critical periods of instability that allow for substantive transformations of behaviors and dynamics

Recent complexity science and ecology research has uncovered some key patterns in ecologies—regularities that help sustain a thriving ecosystem within a continually changing environment—insights that we describe in detail in the next chapter.

Since ecologies are driven by all of the exchanges, interchanges, interactions, and connectivities existing between its subsystems, whatever is essential takes place at these interfaces. That is why interactions, as first spelled out in Chapter 2, are so important to our approach. This concentration on interaction should not be taken merely in the sense of distributed control, but instead highlights how innovation itself relies on the "space" between systems as where novelty has its most fertile environment.

By an ecology of innovation we recognize that every organization occupies a niche within its communities, customers, suppliers, strategic partners, and competitors, and this places constraints on the organization's choices. This means that information is being discovered all of the time, by many people in many specific situations. The information first appears in a specific context, and it is often difficult to recognize and comprehend and is easy to lose. This prompts the question of how an organization can learn to distinguish signals of imminent change from the constant level of noise inherent in day-to-day activity. That is one of the key themes of this book, and one of the main areas in which complexity science can help all of us. In chapters 2, 5, 6, and 7 we provide ways to think about this issue and tools to help individuals do exactly this.

An ecology of innovation offers one more conceptual advantage: it can be understood at many different scales of resolution. For example, a desert can be viewed at the scale of tiny lichen on shaded rocks or on the wider scale of small cactus growing near dried rivulets or on a wider scale of small rodents scurrying among the rocks on the north side of desert mountains away from the sun or on the larger scale of the slow changes in the weather that may occur as one season haltingly changes into another. The same is true of organizational ecologies. Thinking and acting can occur at many different levels of scale, and since complex systems are inherently nonlinear, what happens on a microscale may have a large impact on a macro- or even collective scale.

INTERACTION RESONANCE WITHIN SOCIAL NETWORKS

At the core of ecosystems are patterns of interactions—the vital exchanges—that connect all the subsystems together. In complexity science, interaction is a web of positive and negative feedbacks among components. Because a complex system is composed of interdependent, interacting subsystems, information about the functioning of the system is distributed throughout the networks of connection. This is why generative leadership focuses attention on the nexus of relationships linking individuals within the social network. This nexus of relations is the source of influence, the driver of innovation, and the regulator of change.

In social systems, interaction shows itself in the prevalence of social networks that connect the components of any system, a topic we explore in depth in Chapter 7. Every social network has a structure that reflects the configuration of how people are linked with one another. These networks extend not only within an organization but throughout its entire ecology, as well as into the environment. Arguably, an individual's professional success in business and in other fields is determined as much or more by the scope and quality of their network connections than by their individual competence. These networks of interaction, although largely ignored in Business Schools, are central to our view of generative leadership.

Although communication has long been an important topic in leadership practice and management education, the specific nature of how information can be enriched as it is exchanged has not received the attention it deserves. From our complexity science perspective, we are calling the process of information enrichment *interaction resonance*. It is largely through interaction resonance that the kind of micro-level diversity that we discuss in the next section expresses itself as those experiments in novelty that are at the core of innovation. Interaction resonance is described in Chapter 2, and it is a theme that winds its way through our entire presentation of innovation, particularly in Chapter 3, in which we suggest that interactions are central to "critical periods" of change, and in Chapter 7's explanations of social networks, which are the context in which interaction resonance takes place.

DIFFERENCES, INFORMATION, AND NOVELTY GENERATION

One of the hallmarks of a complex system is its heterogeneity, that is, the vast diversity of components, agents, and parts, each involved in an ongoing variety of distinct interactions with the others. These differences create novelty since the interaction of two identical things cannot generate something new. We conceive of organizations and their leadership as complex systems that operate from as well as produce great differences, which in turn allow for innovations to emerge.

In the original version of information theory, information referred to the "important" bits of a message in a communication channel, as opposed to "noise." Later, the idea of information was generalized to be patterns of redundant order mixed with elements of *surprise*, thus expanding information to include the *differences* among a range of patterns. Information in social systems plays a role similar to the role played by energy in physical systems, namely, it is the "life blood" that flows through organizations and connects them to systems in their environment. In this way information is meaningful—it literally carries meaning throughout a system.

In organizations, meaning emerges through the *differences* in members' backgrounds, skills, opinions, and perspectives; these differences help drive innovation, a theme we'll return to in Chapter 3. Our use of the term "information" throughout this book thus includes formal facts contained in textbooks and reports but also surprises from events, experience, or experiments.

Pushing this analogy further, the catalyst for innovation lies in deviations from what is expected, that is, experiments in novelty reflecting departures from the currently accepted and conventional ways of functioning. These experiments are constantly going on in organizations, although such deviations are typically unnoticed or marginalized. Complexity science has shown that this micro-level diversity, when it is noticed, amplified, and disseminated by generative leadership, can emerge as novel patterns, practices, and strategies that can improve and transform organizations. These emergent phenomena, which we discuss in chapters 3, 4, and 5, introduce new qualities into the system that are neither expected, predictable, nor deducible from the preexisting components.

An issue, therefore, for leadership working with complex systems is to determine which micro-level deviances possess a potential for significant emergent innovation. In chapters 5, 6, and 7 we describe several ways in which generative leadership can approach this issue, including a type of social network called "intercohesion" which makes it more likely that micro-level diversity with the potential for innovation is recognized and amplified.

In Chapter 6 we describe a particular kind of difference with innovative potential, termed "positive deviance," a unique framework that links the constructive term "positive" with the usually negatively term "deviance." We show that major innovations and transformations have, in one way or another, relied on radical departures from what is expected, and these are justifiably examples of "positive deviances." Leadership can use the tool of positive deviance as social intervention that helps social systems identify and amplify novel experiments that have previously gone unnoticed, but whose problem-solving and opportunity exploitation potential can be unleashed.

CRITICAL PERIODS AND THEIR POTENTIAL FOR INNOVATION

Another feature of complexity science, and an important theme in this book, is how complex systems can dramatically transform during critical periods. We use the term "criticalization" to refer to major transitional periods, which have important implications for generative leadership. Complexity science insights from criticalization are drawn from phase transitions – when matter transforms from one state into another, the emergence of new dynamics – when the connectivity structure of a social network is changed, the emergence of new order in self-organizing physical systems – when some critical parameter value is reached, and the emergence of new attractors – when nonlinear dynamical systems *bifurcate* or split into two separate stable states. We will be alluding to all of these critical phenomena in chapters 3, 4, and 7.

Customarily, criticalization is understood as a system that moves away from equilibrium or normative functioning, and in so doing leaves behind stability while opening to novel and unstable states. These conditions of disequilibrium and instability may be unsettling, but they are necessary for the complex system to undergo deep transformation. Indeed, a system ensconced in a stable condition will reject any fluctuations that may lead to novelty, and as quickly as possible it will return to its original stable state. In contrast, complexity science shows that it is only when a system is unstable—especially in a period of criticalization—that internal changes can move it to a new regime of activity.

Criticalization is the essence of the anecdote at the beginning of this chapter: as Jack Welch told John Chambers, critical periods are what define an organization. They separate the companies that are truly great from those that merely survive. It is during critical periods that the strength and proficiencies of an organization's leadership are truly tested, and it is during these periods that the organization most needs its leadership to step up to the task. Complexity science shows that the key difference between success and failure is generative leadership, which effectively guides an organization to embrace the "critical period" instead of trying to avoid its effects. In Chapter 3 we describe how this was done in the transformation of IBM under CEO Lou Gerstner[4] as well as at Targeted Marketing Solutions, Inc. and Oracle, and in Chapter 5 we describe the various strategies leading to expansion at Starbucks when it engaged several critical periods.

Change management consultants sometimes describe the need for leaders to "manufacture a crisis" as a prerequisite to a successful change management effort; however, in our experience we have found that employees and all the other stakeholders see through such artificial moves. Instead, generative leadership positions the organization so that it can recognize and take advantage of significant changes in the environment. A key task of generative leadership at every level is to enable and encourage a vital connection between an organization and its changing environment; it is only when such connections are engendered that critical periods can offer the potential for renewal and emergence that are the hallmark of long-term success.

Successful criticalization leads the organization into a stronger era—the company becomes better matched to its markets and better able to change with them in the future. It requires that the organization develop new capabilities that facilitate a new pattern of interaction between its members. If used in the right way—if one can be in a state of "surfing forever on the edge between never stopping but never falling"[5]—then the organization has the potential to engage in the unique process of emergence itself.

EMERGENCE

Emergence, one of the most exciting and relevant areas of research in complexity science, refers to the arising of novel structures, patterns, or processes in complex systems. For example, the emergence of new attractors is discussed in Chapter 3, the emergence of new structures with new properties is covered in Chapter 4, and the emergence of new forms of social cooperation in social networks is described in Chapter 7. The study of emergence in social systems is especially apt given the plethora of new kinds of organizational forms: joint ventures, strategic alliances, social entrepreneurial organizations, and other forms of collaboration.

Emergent phenomena seem to have a "life of their own," with their own rules and possibilities. Emergence is about the arising of the radically novel—unpredictable and not deducible from its components; thus, emergence is the essence of innovation in organizations. Both emergence and innovation supply additional functionalities to a complex system, providing the system with a much greater repertoire of possible actions and processes. Much of the current work in complexity research centers such as the Santa Fe Institute is built around emergence, because systems that emerge gain a significant adaptive advantage in their environment.

Emergence comes about through a recognition, amplification, and dissemination of those seeds of innovation that come from micro-level diversity or experiments in novelty. Thus, a primary objective of generative leadership in facilitating emergence is to foster and amplify novelty generation within an ecology of innovation.

Among the different prototypes of emergence found in complexity science research that we describe in Chapter 4, we are especially attentive to the "dissipative structures" model studied by Nobel laureate Ilya Prigogine through nonequilibrium thermodynamics and the German physicist Hermann Haken in his School of Synerget-ics, biological emergence such as found in Lyn Margulis's idea of "symbiogenesis," and social emergence through the formation of cooperative teams and similar phenomena.

As we have explained, earlier approaches to emergence in orga-nizations strongly coupled it with a particular notion of self-organization understood as a supposedly spontaneous process. This view, however, resulted in the mistaken belief that leaders could be passive and simply allow emergence to take place, once command and control mechanisms were relaxed. More rigorous research and experimentation have proven that emergence hardly comes about spontaneously—instead, it demands rigorous containing, constrain-ing, and constructional operations. Accordingly, our interpretation of leadership's role in emergence is not passive, but instead is active and generative.

BOUNDARIES AND CONSTRAINTS

One counterintuitive result from complexity science is that adapt-ability can emerge only if there are constraints or boundaries that consistently operate on the choices and actions of the individuals in the system. A good example comes from complexity researcher Peter Allen, whose longtime studies of fish populations in the North Atlantic showed that boundaries and constraints in the ecosystem enabled many new species to develop and persist. He called this effect "micro-diversity" and claimed it was critical to the ecosystem's ability to respond and adapt to change.[6] Certain species did better under changing conditions, whereas a previously dominant species might flag under the change. However, since one replaced the other in the food chain, the ecosystem as a whole adapted and continued to prosper, albeit with a different mix of species.

Similarly, it takes a constrained complex system to encourage and maintain the information differences within individuals. These con-straints, from external boundaries or between functions, act like the nooks and crannies in the seabed of the North Atlantic, serving to protect and nurture the ecology's most important resource, namely, informational differences.

If not for constraints of some kind, organizational members would not be motivated to organize in new and different ways, and no new structures would emerge. An example is the implementation of Sarbanes-Oxley reporting requirements, or any law or regulation that limits the degree of freedom in which the organization and its members can operate. New routines and procedures have had to emerge to address these new constraints, and these in turn have changed other aspects of the organization so that the process could be supported effectively.

In a similar vein, for adaptability to emerge in a complex system, the right *context* is also important to the mix, a topic that we discuss in Chapter 3. For generative leadership, context is as important as content. The distinction between context and content can be understood through an analogy from semantics.[7] In the *context* of everyday talk, a "daughter" is a female descendant and "left" can mean, in political discourse, the more liberal point of view. A comment such as "the daughter of that family tends to veer to the left" has a rather unequivocal meaning: the female descendant of that family has political leanings that are more liberal than conservative. But in a different context such as nuclear physics, "daughter" refers to the immediate product of radioactive decay of an element, and "left" is a direction, not a political stance. In this context, a comment such as "the daughter of that family tends to veer to the left," made by a nuclear physicist to her colleague, means that a "family" of elements undergoing nuclear decay tends to move toward the left side of the experimental screen.

Most managers learned to lead through interventions that are aimed at directing and controlling followers' activities. In contrast, generative leadership is more interested in the *context* or *parameters* of organizing, the internal and external organizational environment, and the opportunities and constraints it generates. Far more than the substance of daily tasks and goals, it is the *context* of organizational interactions that determines the potential and quality of members' contributions.

At the same time, organizations need managers and executives to take responsibility for specific business goals and outcomes. This presents the conundrum of how a manager may have an influence on their part of the system while being a generative leader who allows influence to flow throughout the entire organization. Exploring this balance is an issue that hovers within every chapter. The suggestions we make are put forward as avenues for reflection and action for the thoughtful and committed reader.

CONCLUSION

In summary, *Complexity and the Nexus of Leadership* offers a view of how individuals at all levels can make a difference in their organizations through the practice of generative leadership. The key to generative leadership lies in creating ecologies of innovation in the workplace, in which experiments in novelty lead to innovative practices, processes, and routines, enabling an organization to become adaptable to the unprecedented levels of change characterizing today's business environments.

The remainder of this book unfolds as follows: the next chapter, Chapter 2, presents a 50,000-foot view of why organizational life has become so difficult to navigate in recent years. With global supply chains and Internet connectivity, the age of the stand-alone business that runs like a machine is being replaced by one in which organizations exist in a network of partnerships that looks much more like an ecological system than a complicated machine. We draw on complexity research to explore how ecologies work, as well as the critical role played by interaction resonance—our term for effective, two-way information flow—the key enabler of adaptation within ecologies. After this high-level overview, we proceed to the core of the book, chapters 3, 4, and 5, wherein we provide a complexity perspective on what is actually happening within an ecological system when organizations collide, and why, at times, organizational life seems so difficult and uncertain. The good news is that complexity thinking provides tools to make sense of this confusion. Here, we explore the challenges—and rewards—associated with the nonlinearity of influence among individual human agents who act within organizations and ecological systems. Chapters 6 and 7 provide ideas, behaviors, and actions to empower individual human agency within complex organizations. These chapters speak from the individual's perspective and suggest specific actions that will enable the thoughtful executive to practice generative leadership and implement the insights in this book. The end of Chapter 7 brings back and again highlights the importance of interaction resonance as a key enabler of the entire process. In Chapter 8 we provide a summary of the key takeaways that the reader might have identified throughout the book. We are hopeful that this chapter can also serve as a refresher, a resource that you can return to again and again as you develop your skills in the practice of generative leadership.

We emphasize that generative leadership recognizes the folly of trying to solve organizational problems through feats of personal heroism. Instead, complexity science shows how to engage all the members of an organization through enhanced network connectivity and interaction resonance. Differences in perspective are encouraged to coexist and persist since out of them come the seeds of innovation.

This book presents the most significant findings in the field of complexity science applied to leading the dynamics of innovation.

We discuss how these approaches are already in use in the successes of Google, Apple Computer, Starbucks, and Merck, as well as many other entrepreneurial firms and nonprofit organizations. Our hope is that you'll find many ways to apply them to your company within the first week of reading the book. With that in mind, we turn to Chapter 2, which introduces the fundamentals of ecologies of innovation.

NOTES

1. Chambers, J. T., & Bryant, A. (2009). Openers: Corner office—In a Near-Death Event, a Corporate Rite of Passage. *New York Times.* August 2, 2009, p. 2 Business.
2. Hazy, J., Goldstein, J., & Lichtenstein, B. (Eds) (2007). *Complex systems leadership theory.* Boston, MA: ICSE Publishing.
3. The term "Generative Leadership" has been used in the past, but more recently in a complexity context in Surie, G., & Hazy, J. K. (2006). Generative leadership: Nurturing innovation in complex systems. *Emergence: Complexity and Organization, 8*(4), 13–26.
4. Gerstner, L. (2003). *Who says elephants can't dance? Leading a great enterprise through dramatic change.* New York: Harper Paperbacks.
5. Ibid., p. 470.
6. Allen, P. (1984). Ecology, thermodynamics, and self-organization. *Canadian Bulletin of Fisheries and Aquatic Sciences, 213*: 3–26.
7. Henning, J. (1995). *Model Languages:* The newsletter discussing newly imagined words for newly imagined worlds. 1 (4), August 1, 1995. Available at: http://www.langmaker.com/ml0104.htm#1.

CHAPTER 2

CREATING ECOLOGIES OF INNOVATION

Innovation—it's a buzzword for the twenty-first century. Creating new services, new products, new processes, new business models, new organizational forms, and new industries seems to be the key to success in this era of business. What drives innovation? Why do some companies achieve innovation more consistently than others? Is it the people? Is it the compensation? Is it the industry?

According to complexity science, innovation is not the province of any one of these content areas, nor does it lie in any strategic competency, nor within any particular department. Innovation is the outcome of a system-wide set of processes and interactions— what we call an *ecology of innovation*. In this chapter we describe the essential features of an ecology of innovation; in later chapters we show how leadership can create ecologies of innovation in the context of the many ecologies of partnerships and collaborations that link companies together across the globe.

To begin, we take up a case that is familiar to many Americans— that of the DVD rental company Netflix—to show how the creation of an ecology of innovation can transform not just one organization but even an entire industry.

THE STORY OF NETFLIX

The DVD rental company Netflix has become a household name in the United States even though it has been around only for ten years or so. Currently, it boasts of over 10 million subscribers, and assuming that most of these are families, the total number of renters is closer to 30 million. Although Netflix opened with merely 30 employees and 925 titles (which at the time covered nearly the entire catalogue of DVDs in existence), today it possesses an inventory exceeding 100,000 titles of films, television shows, concerts, educational programs, and computer games, across more than 200 genres ranging from British humor to 15 varieties of anime to steamy romance.[1]

To remain in the vanguard of firms offering entertainment for home use, Netflix is now going full steam into the instantaneous download market, in fierce competition with the "on demand" capabilities of television cable companies. This is evidently a company that has managed to succeed despite intense competitive threats from such powerful foes as the Blockbuster chain of video rental stores and even Wal-Mart.

In a world of fast-paced entrepreneurial ventures that exploit cutting-edge technological advances and niche markets, the rapid growth experienced by Netflix is no longer unexpected. Netflix's amazing success story certainly includes all the hallmarks that various theories of entrepreneurship have suggested as the enablers of success:[2] visionary/charismatic founders, technology transfer, exchange of organizational capabilities, a culture of collaboration with strong economic incentives, and a strategy built around ongoing partnering.

As helpful as each of these separate pieces might be, what has not received attention is the *systemic* dimension of innovation, more specifically the *eco-systemic* or *ecological dimension*, which explains how charisma, collaboration, capabilities, knowledge transfer, and partnering can come together synergistically. But why should modern managers care about the biological concept of ecology?

Consider the origin of the term "ecology," which stems from the Greek word "eco," meaning "household" or "community." Ecology refers to a particular kind of "community;"in biology these include ecologies of grasslands, wetlands, rain forests, and so forth. Both biologists and complexity scientists recognize that a thriving ecology is a set of subsystems embedded and nested in a community of interactions with each other and their shared environments. These cooperative, competitive, and symbiotic interactions and relationships are the basis of an ecology.

What generates a *thriving* ecology—the kind of ecology of innovation that companies are striving to create? Vital and growing ecosystems always involve sustainable exchanges of energy and resources, through the system and across its environment. These exchanges occur across semipermeable boundaries, which act as a kind of constraint on excess energy flow. For example, an organization's boundaries act as a check on strategic information flowing to competitors, just as the border between two countries helps maintain a demarcated flow of resources between the two neighbors.

It turns out that innovation is driven by the combination of energy exchange across constraints—a healthy amount of energy and resources that flows *across* semipermeable boundaries within the ecology. This combination helps generate the "micro-diversity" so crucial for the vitality of any ecosystem.[3] Moreover, this flow leads to "experiments in novelty," which, when properly nurtured, result in greater adaptability for the system—and in many cases, for the entire ecosystem. This insight is one of many ideas we'll explore throughout this chapter, as we apply an ecological perspective to innovation and leadership. Netflix, as we'll see, is an exemplar of this ecosystemic approach.

How Netflix Created and Utilized an Ecology of Innovation

Developing a vital ecology is a step-by-step process; in organizations these steps are strategic decisions involving stakeholders from across the ecosystem, leading to a scaffolding of emergent innovations. We now discuss some of these key ecological decisions at Netflix.

GETTING DVD PLAYERS INTO AMERICAN HOMES

In hindsight it might seem that renting DVDs by mail would be a great business idea. Yet in 1998 it was quite a risky move because at the time Netflix was launched DVD players were a rarity in American households. This was mainly due to their higher cost compared with very cheap and ubiquitous VHS players. If Netflix was to make a profit, it would need an abundance of customers who wanted easy access to a wide range of home entertainment on DVDs. However, in 1998 it was not at all clear whether there were enough potential customers with DVD players, let alone those interested in this new model of renting movies by mail. To make matters worse, during this same time period Blockbuster had a very large inventory of video tapes in all its stores, enabling it to rapidly become the market leader of the home movie rental business.

Thus, Netflix's first challenge was getting more DVD players into American homes.[4] This challenge could not be solved by an inward-focused strategy, like reducing the cost of shipping/receiving DVDs, or increasing the inventory of DVD titles. (In fact, this later goal was not even possible, since Netflix was constrained by the very limited number of titles that were on DVD at the time.) Instead, Netflix had to focus *outwardly,* across the ecosystem, to enable the growth of its market. It achieved this by doing something that doesn't really make sense on the surface: it entered into deals with much larger companies throughout the electronics industry. Specifically, Netflix developed partnerships with Toshiba, a major manufacturer of DVD players, as well as with HP, Apple, and other microcomputer manufacturers who were adding DVD capabilities to computers. Netflix's strategy was rather brilliant: it would offer free DVD rentals to accompany the purchase of DVD players, whether stand alone or computer based. In so doing, Netflix supported these companies in creating a market for DVD purchasers, while generating a growing list of potential customers.

Note the dual elements that correspond exactly to the complexity science of a thriving ecology. Netflix increased the flow of energy and resources in the system by developing a marketing incentive for DVD customers and by highlighting the DVD rental capability inherent in the partnerships between Netflix and the manufacturers. At the same time, Netflix recognized and even capitalized on the constraints in the system, which were amplified by the differences in size and power between this fledgling company and the giant manufacturing companies with which it forged these deals. In combination—increasing the flow of resources *across* semipermeable boundaries—a true ecology of innovation was developed by Netflix; an ecology that helped to create the company and catalyze an entire industry.

CEASING TO SELL DVDs, AND THE PARTNERSHIP WITH AMAZON.COM

In addition to renting DVDs Netflix started out by selling them, usually at a large discount—a practice directly connected to consumer demand. As one highlight of its sales business the company sold 10,000 copies of the DVD of President Bill Clinton's Grand Jury testimony in the Monica Lewinsky affair at the amazingly low price of just two cents each plus $2 for shipping and handling. The purpose here was obviously not to generate a profit on sales *per se* but rather to gain the huge free publicity this event garnered in the news media. But then in December of the same year Netflix surprisingly stopped selling DVDs altogether. Why would a struggling start-up eliminate a core component of its business model, putting an end to one of its most profitable revenue streams?

Here again, Netflix was developing an ecology of innovation through its recognition of constraints that were presented by

Amazon.com. Amazon, already a high-profile company, had just become a major competitor to Netflix by entering the DVD sales business—part of their broader goal to expand their online offerings beyond exclusively selling books. In the face of this major competitor, however, Netflix made a remarkable move that yet again increased resources and energy flow by creating a semipermeable boundary between itself and this newfound competitor. In this unique deal, Amazon.com would promote Netflix rentals on its highly trafficked site in exchange for Netflix's agreement to not sell DVDs. This innovative partnership allowed both firms to avoid head-to-head competition; Amazon.com gained a small customer base, whereas Netflix gained a huge amount of additional advertising, and in addition, became focused on a much more distinct niche of DVD rentals. With this new partnership Netflix lost a good deal of revenue but strengthened its hold on a growing niche in the ecosystem it was promoting.

ESTABLISHING A SUBSCRIPTION PLAN

In September 1999 Netflix set up a multileveled subscription plan whereby a renter would pay a monthly fee to rent a certain number of DVDs at a time. It introduced this innovation with another one— a website through which each subscriber could create a personalized queue of desired titles, receiving each successive new title as soon as Netflix had processed the one just sent back. Richard Hastings, cofounder and current CEO, has pointed out that the subscription policy only became viable once Netflix had achieved an economy of scale; by this point Netflix was processing 10,000 orders per day using its proprietary software system. The subscription plan further enabled Netflix to create rental profiles for each title and for each customer, for example, which DVDs were more popular and which were paired with other titles by renters.

This move reflects how Netflix turned toward creating an internal ecology of innovation that produced two new-to-the-world advances. Yet again, it achieved this by creating and leveraging constraints, in this case by designing semipermeable boundaries around every single customer—each renter was now treated as a separate entity with their own queue, and soon an immediate feedback system that personalized the selection process even more was put into place. Note, too, how the creation of these constraints—the need to respond to each customer individually—corresponded to the increased flow of energy and resources, as the number of rentals processed daily continued to increase beyond a certain threshold.

Finally, although establishing a business model with economies of scale is an obvious step toward more effective operations as well as reduced risk, Netflix did not see this as a goal in itself. Instead, as Hastings noted, this success was a stepping-off opportunity to allow success to build upon success. The lower cost was used to generate a new vital, interchange relationship between Netflix and its customers within its ecology.

REVENUE-SHARING AND SOLE DISTRIBUTOR AGREEMENTS WITH ENTERTAINMENT PRODUCTION FIRMS

Another crucial strategic move by Netflix was the many revenue-sharing agreements it made with entertainment production companies that produce films and television shows, which are the mainstay of Netflix's DVD rental business. For instance, Netflix has entered into special agreements with such prominent companies as Warner Home Video, Columbia Tristar, Dreamworks, Artisan, as well as with film producers in the rapidly growing film industry in India, known as "Bollywood" (Hollywood in Bombay).

Closely related is how Netflix has established itself as a very small niche-based distributor. For example, it has negotiated *sole distribution* rights with several independent film producers—a relatively outlandish concept given the constraints this places on these small film houses. Yet, this strategy seems to increase resources for both parties, as exemplified by the solely distributed film *Croupier*, which featured an obscure English actor who would later become a well-known movie star, Clive Owen.

In addition, Netflix has begun to offer prizes for aspiring filmmakers. An example is Netflix's partnering with Film Independent (FIND), the nonprofit arts organization that produces the Spirit Awards as well as the Los Angeles Film Festival.[5] Films are judged by prominent individuals from the film industry, such as the actor/director Josh Brolin. One of the winners is Phillip Flores's "Touchback," which will be produced as a feature film and will concurrently premiere at the Los Angeles Film Festival in June 2010 while being available for instant streaming from Netflix. Another example is the hard-hitting *Born into Brothels*, which was a big hit at the Sundance Film Festival, won an Oscar, and has an exclusive distribution deal with Netflix.[6]

In one sense, these moves may look like a traditional vertical integration strategy, in which Netflix seeks to own its suppliers. However, from a complexity perspective, what's happening is much more systemic and coevolutionary. The difference hinges on the nature of the relations between the organization and its suppliers. In the traditional view, vertical integration's potency rests largely on reducing the risk of access to a supplier or distributer, as well as cost reductions that come from combining operations. In contrast, the ecosystem perspective shows that Netflix has entered into mutually enhancing relations with production companies—a coevolution among linked entities within an overarching ecosystem that defines DVD production and distribution. This is a facet of ecology that we will explore in greater depth shortly.

THE WAL-MART DEAL

The last milestone we explore is the shocking entry in 2002 of Wal-Mart into the DVD subscription market, which led to a huge drop of Netflix's stock to $2.50.[7] In this case, however, the unilateral nature of Wal-Mart's business culture made those boundaries non-permeable rather than semipermeable. Nor could Netflix devise a strategy with Wal-Mart that would increase the total energy and resources in the system. Instead—and in keeping with its overall goal to pursue only those partnerships what would expand its ecology of innovation—Netflix "girded its loins" and put up with Wal-Mart as a competitor. This decision was supported by a realization of CEO Richard Hastings that Wal-Mart couldn't be as knowledgeable or focused as Netflix was in the DVD rental business. Eventually, Wal-Mart came to recognize it had a much larger opportunity in selling DVDs than mere renting could reach. Once Wal-Mart made this announcement, Hastings hosted a dinner with the CEO of Walmart.com, which formed the seed of an arrangement whereby the two companies promoted one another. As Hastings put it, "We're not celebrating victory at Netflix, though, because Wal-Mart never gave its best shot. Whereas, Blockbuster is spending hundreds of millions of dollars—When we beat them, it will be celebratory."[8]

Other milestones in Netflix's history include: its eventually successful IPO in 2002 after a first failed attempt in 2000, the expansion of its regional warehouses throughout the United States in order to decrease mail order time and expense, the tremendous boost in rentals following 9/11 due to a sharp increase in insecurity about leaving one's home, and the current strong impetus toward online streaming. But even in these milestones we can see a similar ecosystemic emphasis on exchanges across semipermeable boundaries, and increased flows of energy and resources. This dual connection creates a strong ecology of innovation for Netflix internally, and throughout its external environments.

STRATEGIES FOR CREATING
AN ECOLOGY OF INNOVATION

In the face of these environmental and competitive challenges, Netflix over and over again adopted strategies that relied on one common theme, namely, the establishment of new connections, exchanges, or interchanges with various other players in its ecosystem. The success of Netflix's ecosystemic strategy, which established new links with other entities in its environment, is an important feature of an ecology of innovation. Research into ecology has identified many of the factors that enable biological communities to flourish, particularly through *symbiotic* (we will define this term shortly) connections and synergistic interactions. This emergent order confers more behavioral flexibility as well as greater adaptability to unexpected changes in the environment.

At the heart of *Complexity and the Nexus of Leadership* is the creation of a new context for connection and creativity that goes beyond the exceptional individual—this is the starting point for an ecology of innovation. Another jumping off point for the idea of an ecosystem is the sheer size and complexity of today's organizations. Many corporations and NGOs are so large, with locations and divisions in a host of countries, that it doesn't really make sense to view these as a singular entity, whether practically or theoretically. A similar situation holds true for smaller companies, which due to globalization have had their operations sheered up into subsystems interacting with different environments of suppliers, wholesalers, manufacturing units, customer bases, government regulators, and so on.

Certainly, Netflix has not been alone in pursuing the externally directed strategies of "connecting"—we are in the midst of a great surge in joint ventures, strategic alliances, and similar new organizational exchanges coming into existence. Even competitors who were previously at each other's throats have joined together to produce mutually beneficial products and services. Even more than these external connections, building an ecology of innovation *within* an organization requires a deepening of connections between members and stakeholders close to the core of the business. But how does an ecology of innovation get created?

Unfortunately, theory has not kept pace with practice in this new arena of interaction. What is needed is a theory commensurate with the tremendous strides that have already been made and that can serve to generate even greater innovations in the years to come. Complexity science provides such a theory, grounded in the insights from ecological science. Here, we are following the famous advice of the eminent social researcher Kurt Lewin, who ushered in a new wave of practical organizational theory with his maxim that there is nothing as practical as a good theory! The best complexity theory of ecology has identified seven main features of ecosystems, each of which can be applied to organizations.

SEVEN MAIN FEATURES OF ECOSYSTEMS

In the first section of this chapter we used the Netflix experience to highlight a particular theme—the strategies it developed to cocreate ecosystems amidst rapidly changing circumstances. Each strategy reflected the creation or recognition of constraints within the ecosystem, and each involved the creation or repositioning of vital exchanges between the subsystems in Netflix's environment. We build on that theme by examining the seven main features of an ecosystem, using Netflix and several other companies as illustrations along the way.

1. Ecologies Are Systems of Difference

It is not a historical accident that the fields of ecology and complexity science have arisen at roughly the same time, since the core themes of both disciplines have developed through a healthy cross-fertilization of ideas between them. This can be seen, for example, in the key complexity theme of difference or diversity mentioned in the last chapter. As early as the mid-1950s, ecology researchers had begun investigating the correlation between diversity and stability in ecosystems.[9] One place this manifested itself was in the sometimes discrepant and oscillating rates of population growth and death among different species in an ecology. Research found that the reason for such problematic shifts was a lack of diversity in the ecosystem. Thus, the "complexity" of an ecosystem started to become measured in terms of the diversity of species, the varied relations among them, and the changing strength of these various interactions. Each of these differences was seen as a strength and ecosystem stability was found to come from the way these differing components and interactions enabled greater resilience to each of the ecological subsystems.

Diversity also includes the many microlevel fluctuations or departures from the expected, which form the seeds of innovations in new species, forms, traits, and so on. We build on this concept in Chapter 4 on emergence, and Chapter 5 on Experiments in Novelty. In relation to organizations, the Netflix example shows how the firm's leaders recognized the complexity of the ecosystem in which the company existed. Their theory of this recognition is embedded in the following three principles that we quote from the company's values statement:[10]

- Recognizing that in the midst of the increase of complexity that comes with growth, we need to increase talent density faster;
- You *challenge prevailing assumptions* when warranted, and *suggest* better approaches;
- You say what you think even if it is controversial (going beyond politics as usual).

Each of these principles expresses Netflix's commitment to the unearthing of differences. Netflix's leaders well recognize that only when such differences are encouraged will experiments in novelty emerge, leading to innovations that have a meaning—differences that make a difference.

2. Diversity is the Source of Adaptability

According to research in ecology, the greater the diversity in a system, especially at the micro-levels of individual differences and group-level heterogeneity, the higher the potential these differences can be amplified into emergent innovations.[11] Complexity science has demonstrated that the origins of these initially small variations can come from random departures from what is expected as well as from various recombinations (described in Chapter 4).

One useful model for the progression of an innovation was developed by Andrew Van de Ven and Raghu Garud, through their in-depth study of dynamics in spin-out companies.[12] They suggest that innovation accrues through a series of events, in which a novel variation is expressed through a small "discontinuity" in technology; that "event" becomes known, gets selected, and is then reinforced through a series of additional events. The whole process is repeated when another technological discontinuity arises. They suggest that what is really going on is a cumulative progression of numerous novel events and numerous reinforcements over a much longer period of time. They cite studies in mechanical innovation such as ship building in which many small novelties and recombinations cumulatively add up to the innovation, a process usually consisting of many discontinuities, and trials and errors, accompanied by a multitude of internal and external resistances. They call the latter a *generative* process; in our context of leading we have adopted the term as generative leadership as described in the last chapter.

The variations that occur within animal species in an ecology are similar to the experiments and new ideas in human organizations—they are the seeds of innovation occurring within the subsystems of an organizational ecology of innovation. In building ecologies of innovation, generative leadership shows a bias for exploration and experimentation, more than the traditional goal of efficiency, or cost reduction, measures. Micro-level diversity is possible only if there is freedom to depart from what is expected, that is, if conforming to current practice doesn't outweigh differences of opinion, and these differences are supported within boundaries or other constraints.

The leadership at Netflix actively supports diversity and differences in perspectives. The company's values statement includes the following:

- Our goal is to increase employee freedom as we grow rather than limit it as so many companies do with more and more bureaucratic red tape, streamlined lean and mean procedures, and HR policies, the result of which is usually a significant drop in innovation.
- We try to get rid of rules when we can, to avoid "rule creep" from taking over.
- You *reconceptualize* issues to discover practical solutions to hard problems.
- Avoid reacting too quickly; instead, listen well with patience in order to better understand.
- Treat people with respect independent of their status or disagreement with you.

This last statement focuses on how respect is more important than obedience to a command and control model. Here again the leaders emphasize the importance of individual voices—even dissent—which leads to great diversity and thus greater innovation.

3. An Ecology Is a *Nexus* Of Interacting Ecosystems

In an important respect an ecology is nothing but a web of relationships, in which individual nodes are subsystems that are the *intersections* of the various strands of the web. Each strand and each intersection exhibits different transport rates of nutrients, information, and wastes—the whole is a complex network of agents and linkages. In fact, each subsystem of an ecology can survive only through these vital interchanges, interpenetrations, and exchanges across and even within its boundaries.[13]

This leads to a better understanding of the term "nexus," which refers to the intricate coupling between the nodes of a network—a coupling that can become so significant that the identity of each node or subsystem becomes *interdependent* with the identities of all the other subsystems. We see this interdependence in the family system—a true nexus of relationships in which each person's identity and actions are deeply connected to those of all the others.

By including "nexus" in our title we are *de*-emphasizing a leadership of charismatic individuals. Instead, as we said in Chapter 1, both complexity science and ecology suggest that leadership events and behaviors emerge out of the nexus of relationships making up an organization and its relations with other environments. For example, although Bob Hastings is clearly a smart CEO for Netflix, the organization derives its success from a nexus of generative leadership throughout the company's network—internal and external. The ecology of Netflix embodies the actions and interactions of thousands of people, all coupled with one another via a nexus of interactions.

A "nexus" should not be understood as an "aggregate."[14] In an aggregate there is a collection of entities or subsystems, but they are not reciprocally related in the sense that their existence depends on each other, for example, on receiving nutrients from, and supplying nutrients to, each other. In a nexus as we define it, if a subsystem suddenly disappears, for example, a species becomes extinct, it might be disastrous for the other subsystems as well. Each is dependent on the others in the ecology. It is because of this interdependence that ecologists are so intent on making us aware of the dire consequences that would follow the extinction of so many species.

A nexus implies a focus on relationships between entities, rather than on the content of those individual things. It is relationships among sub-ecosystems that provide the requisite conditions for life. Further, this frame recognizes the key role of *interactions* as the seed of creative collaboration—a view expressed in the values statement from Netflix:

- Since in "procedural work" the best are two times better than average, while in creative work the best are ten times better than average, a huge premium is put on creative teams.

Netflix is not alone in this realization; as we describe in Chapter 5, Apple Computer also gives a lot of importance to relations and creative interactions. Later in this chapter we describe successful innovation at Merck, which also depends on high-quality relationships; we contrast these with a case at the "old" AT&T in which such interdependent connections were starkly lacking. Companies that are successful in bringing about thriving ecologies of innovation often point out the value of their nexus of relationships, and the value they place on creative, collaborative teams.

4. Ecosystems Require Interaction Resonance

An ecosystem thrives only when the exchanges of energy and resources among its subsystems are vital, numerous, and sustainable, which render it more adaptable to unpredictable changes in its environment. A vital interaction is one characterized by what we call "interaction resonance," which signifies a richness of information flow that is generated and maintained through interactions over time.

As executives begin to see their work from the perspective of one actor in a thriving ecology of other actors, the centrality of interactions and relationships comes to the fore. When the resources and information in an ecology are accessible only through relationships and the flows that run through them, individuals and the organization as a whole are vulnerable to these ebbs and flows of energy, and the overall quality of those interactions. With such an ecology, continuous effort is needed to strengthen, widen, and *deepen* the capacity of the relationships, so as to transport resources and knowledge more quickly and effectively.

The notion of deepening the information exchanged is captured by the term "resonance," which literally means "re-sounding"—as in a "resounding success." It has to do with a kind of "sympathetic vibration" between people; when we say we "resonate" with someone or someone's ideas we can also say, "It strikes a chord in me." Interaction resonance in organizations takes advantage of the phenomenon of "striking chords" among people interacting. When it comes to the science of music, "striking a chord" is a literal description of resonance. In fact, most musical instruments rely on the physical phenomenon of resonance to produce their beautiful sounds. This resonance occurs when the sounds produced by the musician are "re-sounded" or amplified internally through the physical space that has been constructed inside the musical instrument. In a string instrument it is the body of the instrument that acts as the resonator, so that when the musician strikes a note or vibrates a string, the instrument resonates or amplifies this sound. The master violin makers are the ones who can reliably produce an internal cavity with the greatest resonance.

One more example of physical resonance will push home the point we are trying to make about interaction resonance. Resonance is at the basis of the auscultation techniques of doctors and nurses when they listen to a person's heart and lungs with a stethoscope. What they are actually listening for is the resonance of sounds within the chest cavities that yield clues to whatever may be blocking the sound vibrations from "resounding" on themselves.

In organizations, interaction resonance speaks to a high quality of engagement and responsiveness in any given exchange. This quality is so central to the creation of an ecology of interaction that we devote an entire section to it later in this chapter.

5. Ecosystems Coevolve by Cooperative Strategies

In contrast to the traditional emphasis in evolutionary theory on conflict and competition, most recent versions of ecology and complexity science theories of evolution focus on the crucial role of *cooperation* in developing and maintaining a thriving ecology or species. In the past 25 years the idea of *coevolution* has joined the ideas of conflict and competition as common conditions that drive adaptation across multiple scales, a process that characterizes the subsystems of an ecology.[15]

Coevolution is a process of shared benefit in which all agents gain adaptability through their ongoing interdependence and interactions. A coevolutionary viewpoint also suggests that each subsystem and its interactions provide the microlevel variations or diversity that serve as the seeds of emergent innovation—we will be discussing these seeds of innovation later in this chapter as well as in chapters 4, 5, and 6. In an important sense it is the entire ecology that evolves; individual subsystems contribute to, and are affected by, the whole system's evolution. This also means that the ecosystem's various environments are also coevolving, in open exchanges with the whole ecology. This can be seen in our earlier discussion on Netflix, which thrived when it supported and was supported by other businesses in the overall environment, that is, through the coevolution of itself and its partners. Of course, coevolution is *not* a call for naïve altruism; instead, it refers to a theory about the nature of ecologies as an interwoven nexus of systems in interchange with each other, rather than one system or organization necessarily trying to get ahead of others. This idea can be understood through a powerful type of coevolution that was well displayed by Netflix, namely, symbiosis.

Beneficial Interchanges: Symbiosis

In the study of ecology attention is focused on three types of relationships among species or subsystems: predation (where one entity consumes another), competition (where some entities survive while others fail), and symbiosis (where interdependent coevolution is the main driver).[16] In this book, symbiotic relationships are the focus of our leadership perspective. We employ a complexity science approach to building ecologies of innovation since it is in *symbiosis* that we see the greatest likelihood of the emergence of innovative, adaptive organizational practices, entities, and processes. In symbiosis, different species exist in a highly mutual and highly beneficial relationship with each other, a capability for sustained open exchange with each other and their various environments that strengthens the viability of the whole ecology.[17] Symbiotic interactions are the vehicle whereby each sub-ecosystem supplies and receives nutrients and waste since it is often the case that what is waste for one species can turn out to be a nutrient for another. We can see this, for example, in waste management and recycling corporations.[18]

It is important to note that symbiosis shouldn't be taken in the sense of the nefarious Borg in *Star Trek* taking over and incorporating everybody into a "hive" mentality. That would be a type of predation as well as parasitism—with the Borg nanotechnology serving as the mechanical parasite taking over the human host. In contrast, although a symbiotic relationship may exhibit a very close style of togetherness, this very togetherness works because it is mutually beneficial and productive of greater species integrity.[19] When cooperation or collaboration is effective, each system's integrity and intactness is not torn down but is actually firmed up. In this regard, it can be helpful to envision the exchanges between sub-ecosystems as taking place across a semipermeable boundary that remains intact while encouraging a traversing of the boundary in a vital exchange of resources and information.[20]

We saw an example of symbiosis in our earlier discussion of Netflix. The company partnered with movie production companies to grow DVD content for its customers, which supported stronger distribution in very specific niches for these movies. Likewise, its partnerships with Amazon and to a lesser degree with Wal-Mart allowed it to enlarge its market while providing a less competitive landscape for the other. Of course, if Amazon and/or Wal-Mart had become competitors, Netflix may well have been consumed (destroyed), either by one of them or by some other player. Instead, Netflix successfully pursued symbiosis to survive and prosper.

The Environment Is not a Generic Background but a Nexus of Sub-Ecosystems

In coevolution the intricately connected networks of coupled sub-systems are not only in cooperative relationships with each other, but also with the multifarious subsystems that make up "the environment" of the ecology. In early systems thinking, when this idea was applied to organizations and leadership, the emphasis was on a demarcated system—one strictly bounded to keep it intact and separate from an environment understood as some sort of vague background. More recent theory has shown how coevolution operates across a much wider breadth than we had previously known.

The ecologies of innovation we have in mind contain subsystems, each with its own unique operating practices and each in vital and unique kinds of interchange with a host of other sub-ecosystems in the environment. Our emphasis on an ecology of innovation also stresses that the niches of each subsystem are not just passively generated but are cocreated or coevolved through innovation.

Later in this book, in Chapter 4, we will talk about the expansion of Starbucks through experiments in novelty. One important outcome from that discussion is the realization that the "environment" for Starbucks in Chicago, where it was expanding, was quite different from its environment in Seattle, where the firm began. Clearly, Starbucks didn't exist within a generic background. In each case, Starbucks was "invading" a distinct ecology, and in each case, it had to adapt its business model to fit in. This important lesson about coevolution within ecosystems was critical to Starbucks's long-term success.[21]

6. Ecosystems Thrive in a *Dis*equilibrium World

Considered as ecological communities, organizations do not exist within a so-called balance of nature, but instead can survive and thrive only when in decidedly disequilibrium conditions.[22] In the biological realm, plants and animals face disequilibrium conditions all the time, for example, in seasonal or yearly changes in rainfall, heat, and wind, as well as in unpredictable storms, earthquakes, and tsunami. In such a disequilibrium world, the mechanisms for survival that work well during wet periods won't necessarily be that effective during dry periods. That is why various sub-ecosystems have to continually adapt by innovating novel processes. For example, take a bird habitat ecosystem in the Great Basin of Eastern Oregon: during dry periods, vegetative patterns show a general increase in height as well as coverage in order to cover more surface area to catch the little rain and dew that exists. Moreover, the bird species living there show a general looseness in their relations with other species so that they have the concomitant freedom to exploit their environment in a more exploratory manner.[23]

More recently, the complexity science – based ecologist Robert Ulanowicz has analyzed ecosystems from the perspective of "far-from-equilibrium thermodynamics" with its notions of dissipative structures and order emergence, all of which we discuss in Chapter 4. In particular, Ulanowicz has found that the more heterogeneous an ecosystem, that is, the more varied its subsystems in terms of functionality, size, and so forth, the more likely that it reflects a dissipative model of disequilibrium.[24]

The majority of companies we study throughout the book are in disequilibrium conditions. Like the norm-shaking work that is endemic to Netflix, we explore companies undergoing rapid change and experiencing events that are far from their norm, including IBM's critical period in the 1990s (Chapter 3), Starbucks' expansion to Chicago (Chapter 4), Apple Computer's launch of the iPod (Chapter 5), and more. Disequilibrating change, not "equilibrium," is the essence of an ecology, and likewise is the ground of today's global economy.

7. Ecosystems Exist at Multiple Levels

An ecology consists of many subsystems, each operating at its own unique scale or level. For example, the ecology of a Brazilian rain forest consists of huge tropical trees, a whole realm of animal and plant life dwelling in the canopies of these giant trees, the large and small birds and insects that exchange products and wastes among their niches (subsystems), the intermediate zone of nearly human-size monkeys, the large and tiny fungi and mushrooms in the interior, and so on. Understanding ecology like this—and like organizational ecologies—therefore requires looking at it from many different scales of resolution, the macro-, meso-, microscopic and all levels in between. This is analogous to how to how a camera lens can be set at the widest angle in order to capture a sense of an entire landscape, a smaller angle to capture a specific grove of trees, a still smaller resolution to zoom in on an individual tree, and an even more microlevel resolution to capture the lichens covering the tree's bark.

Indeed, as we shift resolution from narrower to wider, we begin to realize that the whole ecology is composed of many subsystems, in varying kinds of relationship with each other. These relationships are the conduits for the exchange of vital ingredients necessary for each subsystem's survival and thereby also the survival of the whole ecosystem of which they are parts. As an analogy, the story of Netflix cannot be told without also telling the story of the evolution of the DVD industry, the competitive environment of the home entertainment sector, the individual relationships that Netflix's CEO had with other peer CEOs, and so on.

Thus, an ecological perspective requires executives and managers to make a fundamental shift of emphasis from organizations as controllable machines that can be forcibly pushed into action, to organizations as living, thriving ecologies composed of interacting ecosystems whose openness enables experimentation and innovation. These interactions provide the potential for the system to adapt and change in rapidly changing conditions.

In this view, generative leadership of ecosystems is a function of managing the nature of the interactions whose vitality is the impetus for change. Just as biological ecosystems thrive through connecting and reconnecting to subsystems—forging new bonds, breaking previous boundaries, and so on—management theory must yield to an appreciation for, and a nurturing of, the vast web of relationships that are always in flux, both in their number and in the quality or resonance that characterizes them.

This insight places the notion of interaction resonance as a central concern in the ways that ecosystems can and should be treated in generative leadership. As we show throughout this book, increasing interaction resonance within an ecosystem goes a long way toward increasing the likelihood that micro-level seeds of novelty (which we describe in Chapter 5) will eventually flourish as macro-level patterns of innovation. Thus, we turn to a deeper explanation of interaction resonance, and how it can be produced in an organization system.

THE CRUCIAL ROLE OF INTERACTION RESONANCE

To appreciate what we mean by interaction resonance in an organizational context, it can be helpful to describe interactions noticeably lacking this quality. During the early 1990s one of our authors (James K. Hazy) held the position of senior investment manager for AT&T Ventures, an internal venture capital group established to capitalize on the many burgeoning innovations in the high-tech environment of the time by investing in start-ups as well as already existing companies. My (Dr. Hazy)'s responsibilities consisted partly in searching for inventions, innovations, and potential product ideas within Bell Laboratories, the research and development arm for the company.

Looking for these opportunities, I often visited AT&T's cavernous research facility in Holmdale, NJ, a building that was called "the Darth Vader building" due to its dark glass and long open corridors circling a multistory atrium on all levels. While there, I experienced firsthand how organizations can be mired in practices that not only do *not* enable the key element of interaction for generative leadership but actually run counter to it.

On one visit to Bell Labs I met with a prominent scientist who was working on new approaches to simplify the user interface for network computing systems. To put it mildly, I was shocked to discover that this brilliant individual had only agreed to share his research with AT&T's venture capital group *if* knowledge of his progress, even what he was working on, would *not* be shared with his coworkers. In effect, this scientist was literally calling for a void of resonance.

I had to agree just so I could learn what he was up to. In the next several hours I listened to this scientist describe his fascinating, revolutionary research involving the design for a very specific central component of a graphical user interface for multiple computers hooked up in a network. Remember, we're talking about the early 1990s here and also keeping in mind that these same labs had already developed the UNIX operating system—the backbone of the developing Internet—this scientist's single invention, if complemented with others, could transform AT&T into *the* premier developer of the next generation of telecommunications and computing infrastructure.

It also must be kept in mind that this particular invention could only work if *many other components of the system,* most of which AT&T manufactured and deployed, were enhanced as well. Although this scientist did realize he was working on a piece of a bigger puzzle, not only was no one else (expect presumably his supervisor) aware of the details of his work, they were *not* working on enhancing the other pieces of this interdependent system. There was an additional factor characterizing the lack of interaction resonance: the scientist's research was *disconnected* from the language, symbols, and purpose of AT&T's businesses, including AT&T's quest to take advantage of emerging opportunities. Although some of this could be attributed to the specialized language of science, a requisite response on the part of leadership would be to insure there were appropriate channels of communication, appropriate vehicles for translating the research so that others could understand it, appropriate other avenues for bringing others into a richly resonant interaction with this scientist's revolutionary work. None of this happened, and these experiments in novelty never saw the light of day.

We can already formulate a general principle of interaction resonance: the more technical the work, the more that careful communication is needed to clarify and deepen it. Without this common language and these disciplined communication practices, information remains undecipherable and thereby devolves into mere data that cannot have much effect on an organization's objectives. We will never know, in fact, what might have happened if this researcher—and the many others like him at AT&T's research facilities worldwide—had openly collaborated, across the entire ecology with rich interaction resonant and within the frame of a common language and a common purpose, to change the future of the emerging Internet.[25]

ORGANIZATIONAL RESONANCE

Resonance is not just a physical phenomenon but has its social system counterpart within the multitude of interactions making up an organization's daily activities within and between its many environments. Both complexity science and the study of successful organizations have discovered it is the *type* of interactions and the circumstances shaping their *quality of resonance* that determine whether they lead to innovation or just more of the same old thing. It is one thing to have a new idea and still another to carry it through; resonance is the key element required for novel interactions to be elaborated, extended, and implemented. Through establishing appropriate capacities in an organization for interaction resonance, generative leaders foster conditions in which new ideas can germinate, take root, and then bear fruit through interactions.

Let's turn back to the lack of interaction resonance at the old AT&T. In our terminology, how could the work group manager have constructed a capacity for interaction resonance throughout the lab and between the lab and other pertinent areas at AT&T? Recall that the scientist *wanted* his ideas to remain a secret, and apparently no manager had been able to convince him of the value inherent in sharing his ideas. So, how could generative leadership have broken through that veil of secrecy? Is it even reasonable to suppose that establishing a *policy* requiring every discovery or invention to be shared across the organization would have led to success?

In creating an ecology of innovation at Bell Labs, generative leadership would need to start by understanding *why* this particular scientist wanted to remain secretive in the first place. This is what we mean by valuing and supporting differences. What were his reasons for not sharing his work? In what respects were these reasons valid given the context of the organizational culture at Bell Labs or AT&T in general? What cultural norms constrained his behavior, and more importantly, how could these norms be altered? Yet, having access to the kind of information that could answer such questions entails first, that such information could be forthcoming, and second, that in turn it would require a high level of interaction resonance. This was just not the case.

Interaction resonance is more than the simplistic advice covered in "Management 101" on talking, listening, and getting to know one's staff. Instead, we are suggesting that generative leadership has to intentionally *construct* the right kind of networks of exchange, through which interaction resonance can expand the quality of information transmitted. These networks of exchange would expand capacity and encourage ideas to "vibrate" within a work group, to strike enough chords that what may have started out as only a tiny seed of innovation is allowed to evolve and grow and perhaps even be implemented, if its initial promise is further proved by greater resonance. This might mean providing organizational support for an informal network, a community of practice, to grow up around the seed of novelty.

In an ecology of innovation, experiments in novelty occur through building capacities for interaction resonance. If you have resonance across your product managers, if you have resonance within your technology groups, if you establish resonance between companies from different cultures in a joint project, then you are constructing an ecology of innovation. Just as the finest musical instruments are constructed by master artisans, resonant organizations don't happen by accident. They are constructed by master executives.

Developing a high degree of resonance requires that individuals with very different backgrounds and very different sets of experiences must connect in meaningful ways. But as we all know, it is all too rare in an organization that individuals with opposing viewpoints are allowed to voice them in any meaningful manner. Traditionally, most corporate conversations are shaped around predefined goals, predefined strategies, and predefined norms of acceptable corporate behavior. Interactions are necessarily constrained at achieving consensus—an implied agreement that is often directed more by office politics than framed around market opportunities and emerging resources. Interaction resonance, though, doesn't aim at premature consensus. Instead, it aims at opening up conversations that signal a departure from what is expected. And it is executives who are masters of generative leadership who act as role models in order to spark a culture of innovation.

GENERATIVE LEADERSHIP IN ECOLOGIES OF INNOVATION—TWO EXAMPLES

A well-known organizational leader who demonstrates these capabilities is Roy Vagelos, the former CEO of Merck. He once said in a private conversation to one of the authors (James K. Hazy), that leadership is about identifying people's passions, and allowing them to pursue that passion within the context of the organization's mission; in our perspective, identifying that passion occurs in the context of interaction resonance.

Vagelos joined Merck back in 1975 as the head of research after a successful academic research career at Washington University in St Louis. Although a scientist himself with clear and definite ideas about science-driven research, Vagelos chose not to impose this thinking on others. Instead, he began by learning: "I knew I had a lot of walking around and talking to do . . . With every group I stayed as long as necessary—at least a half a day and often more—to understand each project. It was a very intense study . . . there were 1,800 people in research and development." He focused on "talking and listening on a one-on-one basis with the scientists . . .. The best way to get a researcher to stop a bad project is to convince him or her to work on something much more exciting with the prospect of making an important contribution."[26]

Vagelos found that most research groups were working on too many projects rather than too few. Their efforts were much too diffused—in the language of this book, there was no opportunity for resonance to build within those interactions that had a potential for accelerating the work. Vagelos wanted to create an ecology of innovation through building an organization of *interactive decision making*, in which working together they could decide which areas were the most promising to pursue.

According to Vagelos, "In general I found that large public meetings of almost any sort were fine for disseminating information, but very inefficient, even counter productive, for critical evaluations or decisions on strategic directions."[27] To be sure, in building interaction resonance, war rooms and large meetings can have their place. This is particularly true when one person must quickly communicate information, knowledge, and direction to many others. But if such a large setting doesn't come with plenty of opportunities for feedback between the many and the one and the one and the many, resonance cannot occur, only the transmission of often unusable data.

The resonance that grew out of Vagelos's many initial conversations began to build a capacity that spread across the laboratories. Soon other generative leaders emerged as catalysts for this process. The labs came alive with exciting new science being done and new product ideas being developed just about everyday. The unique background and experience that Vagelos brought with him helped make Merck one of the world's most successful and innovative pharmaceutical companies during his tenure. At the same time, the approach to innovation and product development he established at Merck changed the way new products were identified and developed across the industry.

No matter how impressive the efforts of a top leader such as Vagelos, interaction resonance has to be practiced across the organization. The group or the company as a whole has to learn how to resonate in order to co-construct an atmosphere of openness, expansion, and development among as many individuals as possible. This type of culture is well exemplified at eBay.

This is a company that literally runs on interaction resonance among the sellers and buyers using its services. Its founders describe it as an organizational *community* of interactions. As the former CEO Meg Whitman put it: a community "of the people, by the people, for the people."[28] In fact, eBay represents more than a website for buying and selling but also a place people can meet others with similar interests, share information, discuss topics, all using the company's chat rooms, bulletin boards, and e-mail services.

The company's internal organization is built to mirror its external interactive community. Just as sellers and buyers work out the logistics of shipping, payment, et cetera, on their own, so employees inside the firm use their interactions to develop resonance that helps them decide how to proceed in a given situation. As one of eBay's founders, Pierre Omidyar, has said: "[O]ur business depends on people conducting transactions with each other, and people won't conduct transactions with each other unless they have trusting relationships first. That trusting relationship will only occur if they treat each other well. So there is a direct correlation between how our customers treat each other and the performance of our business."[29]

Meg Whitman is a role model for interaction resonance, and she has had great success in building it deeply into the eBay culture. One way she actualized Omidyar's insights was to hold lengthy meetings in the beginning of her tenure (in contrast to common corporate standards) even if it meant taking away time from acting on "deliverables." This enabled trust to build and challenging issues to be aired, leading to quicker interactions in the future since these issues were already in the open. Indeed, Omidyar's main criterion for hiring new people clearly shows the emphasis on a community of interaction resonance:

> If I interview someone who says, "Wow. You've got a really loyal community of users. We can extract a lot of value from them." I know that's the wrong type of person. On the other hand, if that person says, "Wow. You've got a really loyal community of users. They are the real foundation of this company"—that's the right tone of respect towards our community.[30]

These remarks reveal that innovation springs forth much more from a community built around a capacity of interaction resonance than could be done from any one leader acting alone. This is the power that is unleashed when executives create and nurture an ecology of innovation.

CONCLUSION

Leading a successful, thriving entrepreneurial and adaptive organization means *setting up conditions for positive interaction and interdependence.* A generative leader needs to set up these conditions across the entire ecology of interactions: among employees, clients, partners, value-chain members (suppliers, key customers), even competitors—all of whom can gain value from the organization's experiments in innovation. We are calling for an ongoing kind of *active* construction whereby new structures are built with the full knowledge that they may be only temporarily effective, and therefore they may and probably will need to change over and over again. In the following chapters, we present the building blocks and constructional operations of how executives practicing generative leadership can create ecologies of innovation in their organizations. By doing so, they not only increase the probability that their own organization will thrive, but also that all the other complex ecological systems in which their organization participates will grow as well.

When considering one's own choices and actions within the broad sweep of ecology that we have described in this chapter, there seems to be so many moving parts and interacting components that the situation can quickly become overwhelming, even appear to be intractable. No wonder human beings simplify their decision models by assuming clear roles and well-defined objectives. As we describe in the next chapter, there are good reasons why this approach often works in the short term and when things are relatively stable and reasonably predictable within some regions of an ecological system. As the prior discussion makes clear, however, periods with this kind of stability are becoming increasingly rare. This makes the development and use of more sophisticated models an important priority in today's organizations.

Fortunately for today's executives, advances in complexity science over the last half century now enable an entirely new level of understanding about how individuals and their interactions impact human organizing within ecologies. In the next chapter we will explore some of these new discoveries and what they can tell us about the dynamics at work as ecologies change, the organizations within them are pressured to react or die, and the individuals at work within these organizations must decide what to do in the face of this complexity. In the chapters that follow we then present a model of how entirely new ways of organizing emerge, how experiments in novelty that are initiated by individuals can indeed become the seeds of change, and how these lead to innovation that spreads across the entire organization, or in some cases an entire ecology.

NOTES

1. Reed Hastings: How I Did It, As told to P. Sauer (2005). *Inc.* December, 2005. Available at: http://www.inc.com/magazine/20051201/qa-hastings.html.
2. See, for example, Baron, R. A., & Shane, S. A. (2008). *Entrepreneurship: A process perspective* (2nd ed.). Mason, OH: Thomson South-Western.
3. For example, see Allen, P. (2004, September). *Micro-diversity in evolution.* Paper presented at the ECHO Conference: Managing or Muddling Through.
4. In entrepreneurial terms this is the challenge faced by the most leading-edge technology firms, namely, of having to create an infrastructure that can support a new technology. An excellent introduction to these issues is a classic and readable paper by Andrew Van de Ven: (1993), The development of an infrastructure for entrepreneurship. *Journal of Business Venturing, 8*(3), 211–230.
5. Netflix Blog, September 2, 2009. Available at: http://blog.netflix.com/2009/09/winner-of-netflix-find-your-voice-film.html.
6. Reed Hastings: How I Did It, As told to P. Sauer. (2005). *Inc.* December, 2005. Available at: http://www.inc.com/magazine/20051201/qa-hastings.html.

7. Ibid.
8. Ibid.
9. Elton (1955) argued that communities that were more diverse seemed to be more stable. He based his arguments on his observations of the dramatic oscillations in the populations of the simple communities of the Arctic, the commonness of pest outbreaks in simplified agricultural systems, the apparent absence of pest outbreaks in complex tropical forests, and the ease with which species can invade species-poor islands. Elton, C. S. (1955): *The ecology of invasions by animals and plants*. London: Methuen.
10. Netflix Values Statement. Available at www.netflixfindyourvoice.com.
11. This led to the idea of biological diversity as a measurable trait of ecosystems. Parameters from these distributions were used as diversity indices—compact measures of the degree of complexity of the communities being described. Work in this vein continued with the development of information-theoretic measures of diversity. See Bradbury, R. H., Van Der Laan, J. D., & Green, D. G. (1996): The idea of complexity in ecology. *Senckenbergiana marit., 27*(3/6), 89–96.
12. Van De Ven, A., & Garud, R. (1989). Technological Innovation and industry emergence: The case of cochlear implants. In A. H. Van de Ven, H. L. Angle, & M. S. Poole (Eds.), *Research on the management of innovation: The Minnesota Studies*. New York: Ballinger/Harper & Row.
13. Allen, T. H. F., & Roberts, D. (1997). Foreword. In Robert Ulanowicz (Ed.), *Ecology, the ascendent perspective* (pp. xi–xiv). New York: Columbia University Press.
14. F. Bradford Wallack (1980). *The epochal nature of process in Whitehead's metaphysics*. New York: State University of New York Press.
15. Okasha, Samir (2006). *Evolution and the levels of selection*. Oxford: Clarendon Press-Oxford University Press.
16. See Bradbury, R. H., Van Der Laan, J. D., & Green, D. G. (1996) The idea of complexity in ecology. *Senckenbergiana marit*, 89–96. Coevolution means symbiosis or a cooperative relationship between sub-ecosystems.
17. Fiscus, D. A. (2001). The ecosystemic life hypothesis I: Introduction and definitions. *Bulletin of the Ecological Society of America, 82*(4), 248–250.
18. If we define waste in a more general way as what results when a particular subsystem performs a set of operations turning an input (nutrient) into an output (waste), then the output is the waste that goes on to become an input for another subsystem, with which the first subsystem is coupled.
19. Ulanowicz, R. (1997). *Ecology, the ascendent perspective*. New York: Columbia University Press.
20. Hazy, J. K., Tivnan, B. F., & Schwandt, D. R. (2004, 5). Permeable boundaries in organizational learning: computational modeling

explorations. *InterJournal Complex Systems (Online)*, Manuscript number 1063, 1–8.

21. Schultz, H., & Yang, D. J. (1997). *Pour your heart into it: How Starbucks built a company one cup at a time.* New York: Hyperion.

22. Wiens, J. A. (1984). On understanding a non-equilibrium world: Myth and reality in community patterns and process. In D. Strong, D. Simberloff, L. Abelof, & A. Thistel (Eds.), *Ecological communities: Conceptual issues and the evidence* (pp. 440–457). Princeton: Princeton University Press.

23. Ibid.

24. R. O'Neill, D. DeAngelis, J. Waide, & T. F. H. Allen (1986). *A hierarchical concept of ecosystems.* Princeton: Princeton University Press.

25. It could even be argued that Microsoft's Windows/Explorer platform would not have become the dominant platform today if one of AT&T's UNIX solutions had been developed within an ecology of innovation!

26. Vagelos, R., & Galambos, L. (2004). *Medicine, science, and Merck.* Cambridge: Cambridge University press.

27. Ibid.

28. Meg Whitman (2001) quoted in Table: eBay: Of the People, by the People, for the People. *Business Week/E.Biz*, December 3, 2001. Available at: http://www.businessweek.com/print/magazine/content/01_49/b3760603.htm?chan=sb.

29. Quoted in Bunnell, D., & Luecke, R. (2000). *The e-Bay phenomenon: Business secrets behind the world's hottest Internet company.* New York: Wiley, p. 53.

30. Quoted in Viegas, J. (2006). *Pierre Omidyar, founder of e-Bay.* New York: Rosen Publishing Company, p. 105.

CHAPTER 3

LEADERSHIP IN THE CUSP OF CHANGE

The elite sales managers at IBM in the early 1990s were proud to work at the world's leading information technology (IT) company. But more recently, something had begun to change. Slowly at first, then far more quickly, it was becoming apparent that the company's prospects had become increasingly bleak. A new technology, the microprocessor, entered the market a decade before, and IBM itself had helped define this new market when it launched the phenomenally successful IBM PC in 1981. All along, IBM's experts had continued to counsel that the PC would *never* replace the vaulted IBM mainframe computer. They were wrong. During this period, low levels of interaction resonance (the important idea we described in the last chapter) among the product developers as well as the sales and services teams were setting the company up for a crisis.

More and more frequently, previously loyal clients were now buying into this new PC-based architecture! On top of that, mainframe prices were falling. A recent quarterly report showed that the company's margins were no longer supporting the sales department's massive cost structure. Top salespeople had begun to leave the organization in search of better prospects, a previously unheard of situation. In just a few short years IBM had moved from a trajectory of stable and strong growth in sales and profits to an era of destabilization. The company was facing total system meltdown.[1]

Switch scenes: the executive team for new product launch at Targeted Marketing Solutions, Inc.—a small (60-person), highly energetic entrepreneurial service company with lots of promise and a good dose of venture capital. It had only been a year since the lead executive had left his old job as the director of a large nonprofit organization with the hopes of creating an entirely new business model for this five-year-old venture. He'd been working quite hard on this new venture—65+ hours a week—building a potential client base, leading the pre-marketing team and the print operations team, and meeting with each of the other launch team members plus the company's founders. Finally, he was at the stage of going over the initial progress reports for the launch itself. Unfortunately, the numbers weren't good. The more he learned, the queasier he became: revenue for the new service offering was 60 percent below projections, and sales were less than 20 percent of the goal.[2] Given the fact that the entire team had been working full tilt for over a year—working even harder on the same things couldn't be the solution. The new product team was in a *critical period,* trying to leverage an opportunity while facing a crisis.

The two situations—at IBM and at Targeted Marketing Solutions, Inc.—reflect the kind of rapid change that is today endemic to almost every company and organization in virtually every sector of the economy. Sometimes this rapid change presents as a straightforward opportunity but often it comes as a major crisis like it did at IBM. Other times the *critical period* reflects both an opportunity and a crisis, as it did at Targeted Marketing Solutions, Inc. Our aim in this chapter is to use complexity science ideas to provide a deeper understanding of *critical periods,* and to show how such periods can be just what are needed for generative leadership to catalyze innovation in surprising ways.

We begin our discussion by offering a conceptual model of what is happening to organizations during critical periods and why. More specifically, we will lay out the dynamics of what we are calling the "Cusp of Change" taking place during critical periods. We will show how the savvy executive can navigate through the Cusp of Change and to continued success in its wake.

CRITICALIZATION—ENTERING A CUSP OF CHANGE

Criticalization is perhaps the most difficult time in the life of any organization, as a whole or in part, since it is all about the effect of internally or environmentally generated shocks that disrupt the inner workings of the company. This disruption can show itself in a growing recognition that current operating models are not sufficient and small fixes are not enough to deal with the scope and pace of change. Criticalization often signals a time of conflict and differences of opinion, a period of cognitive dissonance and information overload. Critical periods, however, also offer unique opportunities for transforming an organization through innovation.

STABILITY AND WHEN IT BREAKS DOWN

In the prior chapter about ecological systems like those surrounding Netflix, we talked about there being regions of relative stability in which organizational life can be reasonably predictable, as well as regions of significant change and uncertainty for a given organization and the people in it. The level of relative stability or instability depends upon what else is going on within the ecological system and how these external forces both influence and constrain the organization.

Regions of stability represent the common periods of organizational life, the subject of most MBA classes and most management cases. These conditions of stability can be managed reasonably well using linear thinking, in other words, using linear approximation techniques in which an effort to increase a specific outcome, such as performance, is achieved by a *proportionate* increase of a specific input: 5 percent more sales can be brought about by hiring 5 percent more salespeople regardless of how many salespeople one starts with; or 5 percent higher quality can be achieved through a proportional increase in quality efforts across all the work teams.

However, complexity science shows that linear thinking breaks down in critical periods. Due to the complex interdependencies of organizational work, when change increases beyond a critical threshold (we will say more on this later) the system may enter a phase of criticalization in which the system undergoes a shift from stability to amplifying feedback (such as the familiar screeching sound when a loudspeaker system produces feedback) that serves to increase instability. The implications of this shift are usually impossible to predict not just due to the sheer complexity of the organization but also the complexity of its multifarious relationships with its environment. No one knows what the system will do until it actually does it. But when it does finally respond, something new about the system has been learned, and this can inform future decisions and actions of individuals.

At the onset of criticalization, the normal operations of an organization that depend on linear thinking break down and nonlinearity takes over. The nonlinearity characterizing criticalization means that causes are *not* proportional to effects, that a certain degree of effort will *not* insure the same degree of result. Sometimes a small event will become magnified and thus become disproportionately important. At other times doing more (such as hiring more salespeople at IBM when margins were already negative) can have an intensely

Table 3.1   Criticalization—What to Look for

Conditions in an organization that signal a critical period include:

- An increasing sense that what we had been doing is no longer working or appropriate;
- A sense of urgency begins to enter planning sessions and executive meetings;
- Well crafted plans for entrepreneurial expansion are not working out; targets are pushed off from one quarter to the next, expectations are continuously reframed, and the pace of internal change increases rapidly.
- Performance declines due to shifting markets and changing environments—the organization's traditionally reliance on specialized activities or offerings is no longer effective.
- Concern that all of the small changes will never add up to what is needed, that something really big is necessary.
- Competing interpretations and passionate disagreements about the meaning of external events for the organization, including which events are relevant to the organization and what should be done to address them
- Increased interpersonal conflict—constructive and destructive— puts line employees and supervisors on edge
- Increased individual anxiety, and a growing divergence of organizational goals and the individuals' best interest. This can show up as higher turnover, or generalized questioning: "Should I stay or should I go?"
- Conditions of uncertainty which persist even in the face of attempted changes, or when normal efforts to reduce their significance or credibility are resisted. Sometimes, extraordinary means such as coercion begin to be used or threatened.
- The future of the firm is called into question; calls to "break-up the firm" are heard

---

negative impact. The normal range of control is lost, and even the best-laid plans can lead to failure. A classic sign of criticalization is the recognition that what had worked in the past won't work anymore. Table 3.1 suggests other signals as well.

DRIVERS OF CRITICALIZATION—PERFORMANCE CRISIS AND ENTREPRENEURIAL OPPORTUNITY

What took place at IBM showed many of these traits of criticalization. In the high-flying success days at IBM, by increasing the sales force, executives at the company knew they could drive a commensurate increase in their sales and thus their profits. What they found in the early 1990s, however, as they entered criticalization, was that hiring more sales personnel was actually generating *fewer* profits![3] The microprocessor computing power offered by competitors was rapidly increasing since the new hardware and software that connected these processors together in new ways were getting better and better. It was becoming increasingly clear that the entire IBM business model would have to change, even radically, or the company would fail.

The IBM story represents a common theme in criticalization, namely, that critical periods are often signaled by declines in performance. These degradations are often the result of changes in the market that are not met by concomitant changes within the organization, frequently because the nonlinearities and complexities are such that no one can quite figure out what to do. Further, low levels of interaction resonance (see Chapter 2) across departments and work groups constrain the flow of information about what is happening in the market and in the organization and thus block organized change initiatives. Using the perspective of the last chapter, we can say that the organization loses its ecological edge as its position within the ecology is increasingly threatened. Change is needed but the direction of that change is unclear. Different perspectives develop, but these differences are not yet available across the organization as organizing principles that can be turned into individual action. Indications of an imminent crisis are neither recognized nor understood, often until it's too late.

For example, IBM's transformation occurred in reaction to a changing marketplace and an evolution of the buying patterns of their target customers within the IT ecology. In previous years IBM products had been purchased by MIS professionals within the customer organization, technology specialists who relished the remarkable technological advances that the IBM engineers were making. These technologists were willing to learn the rather arcane techniques that were necessary to take advantage of IBM's state-of-the-art products. By the early 1990s, however, even as PC-based systems were growing in popularity, IBM's longtime corporate clients had begun outsourcing their IT purchasing process to consulting firms. These firms, representing an invading coevolutionary force in the ecology, were not at all interested in technological advances per se. Instead, for a fee, they were offering advice to IBM's customers about ways to simplify the growing complexity of IT demands and to reduce costs, often at IBM's expense.[4]

To make matters worse, IBM's business customers were increasingly using "PCs" and various networking products, such as local area networks (LANs), in offices and on desktops that completely circumvented the MIS department that had housed IBM's mainstay individual customers. When Lou Gerstner took over at IBM in 1993,[5] one of his most important insights was that the linear thinking of the past, enmeshed in the old way of doing business via mainframes, was simply no longer good enough to navigate IBM out of its "Cusp of Change." Although it's easy to see why trying to simplify growing complexity might have seemed like an appropriate leadership strategy for IBM during that period, we claim that the increased complexity within their ecology was a manifestation of criticalization. This increased complexity signaled the breakdown of linear relationships within IBM's mainframe-centric business model. In these cases, simplified models that don't anticipate the nonlinear effects of a changing ecology simply do not work. As we describe in the next section, executives should learn to recognize the signs of critcalization and then engage in generative leadership to foster experimentation and innovation across their organization. This is what Gerstner did successfully at IBM.

THE ONSET OF INSTABILITY AND THE CUSP OF CHANGE

Recent advances in complexity science offer a conceptual model of how this process works in organizations. As happened at IBM, as the ecology surrounding an organization evolves, the interaction between two distinct and independent constraining forces brought on by these changes can cause what we call a Cusp of Change to engulf the organization. The first constraint reflects the organizing demands placed on the organization's members due to their position within a changing ecosystem. As the environment changes, so too must organizing structures. The second constraint relates to the difficulties inherent in managing the fact that information gathering and interpretation are distributed among the organization's members. These effects combine to limit the ability of those with a stake in the organization's success to recognize the specific nature of the ecosystem changes and to respond to them in an organized manner. When these two constraints interact in certain ways, for example, when an organization finds itself in a challenging environment, and when it also finds itself with a less than effective social network structure with departmental silos and poor communication across them (to be described in depth in Chapter 7), the organization will almost surely find itself in the Cusp of Change.

Opportunity tension as one driver of criticalization

Recall that in Chapter 2 we described how an organization exists as an ecosystem within an ecology consisting of other organizations, components or subsets of organizations, all of which is quite complex. For example, an organization's members must negotiate with suppliers and with customers, each of whom operates within their own web of network interactions. And they must compete in unforgiving markets for many, if not all, of the "vital exchanges" that allow them to thrive. Yet, the complexities in the environment must be met with organizing efforts of equal complexity.[6] In other words, to exploit the new opportunities or to address new problems new ways of organizing that are capable of engaging them must emerge. The resulting pressure is called *opportunity tension.*

Opportunity tension is felt as the perception by individuals in the organization that not only is there a high-potential opportunity (or problem) *out there*, there is an internally generated pressure to organize in a way so as to capitalize on (or deal with) it. Increased pressure shows up as passion for action that enacts and tests the opportunity through experimentation, making it more tangible and more understandable. Enhanced tangibility increases the entrepreneurial motivation as the team begins to see the real prospects of the opportunity. This, in turn, further increases actions that explore the opportunity leading to the formation of a positive feedback loop increasingly linking the external opportunity with internal actions and capabilities.[7] It was opportunity tension that generated the activities that led to the formation of a new service offering at Targeted Marketing Solutions, Inc. Even though it was not as successful as had been first hoped (a common theme in start-ups), the perceived sense of criticalization there—like the urgency at IBM—generated a new era of possibilities at the company.

Informational differences as a second driver of criticalization

Even with a high level of opportunity tension, a successful response to criticalization does not always occur. This is because a second constraining condition is also crucial. This second constraint comes about because information about what is happening in the system and in the ecology is widely distributed among individuals in human systems and therefore is not immediately accessible for organized solutions. If the system (the organization) is to use this information, it must be in a position to recognize, gather, interpret, synthesize, and then disseminate information effectively *as a system*. Note that information about changing conditions (e.g., increasing opportunity tension) is first apparent to individuals, but often ones who are not in a position to make or even influence decisions about what the organization should do in response to these changing conditions. And yet, it is the organization as a system that must respond, change, or even come into being if the opportunities are to be exploited. Thus, the nature and quality of the network of human connections, the communication capacity, as well as the cognitive capacity of individuals within the network together form a second independent constraining factor on successful organizing projects. The question becomes, how does connectivity among organizational members impact their ability to organize in ways that can better exploit the opportunity?

The extent to which various social network structures meet this challenge is the subject of Chapter 7. For now, however, there are two extremes to consider. At one extreme, where individuals are completely isolated, where there are no network connections, opportunity tension is irrelevant. Of what use is organizing, if there is no one with whom to organize? At the other extreme, the idealized case where connection is ubiquitous and omniscience reigns, everyone would know what everyone else knows and expects. It seems clear that under this latter condition, it is highly likely that these individuals would find a way to organize to exploit the opportunity.

It is obvious that real-world organizations exist between these extremes. In addition, as we cover in detail in Chapter 7, the challenges associated with connection and communications across networks are formidable, which is why the limitations associated with capacities for human social network connectivity are a second constraint on organizing and reorganizing efforts in the face of criticalization. This second constraint is intimately related to the nature of and capacity for information flowing within social networks. Real information (and not mere data) is *new* information, and new information comes out of differences, differences of perspective, differences in experience, differences of mental models, and so forth (described more fully in Chapter 5). This is plainly the case if we consider what is communicated among people when there are no significant differences, that is, when people are so like-minded that there is nothing new in what they can say to each other. An implication is that new information carries seeds of novelty that, as we'll show in later chapters, can bloom into system-wide innovations. In other words, informational difference can be understood as the raw material for experiments in novelty generation.

Constraints on efficacious information flow manifest themselves in performance problems. For example, as the story of IBM makes clear, the realities of the marketplace, the new information emerging about changes in the market was slow to penetrate into the organization, in particular into the product development and sales management teams. As a result, sales teams were slow to respond to changing conditions on the ground. When resource decisions must be made, when opportunity tension is high, and when what is happening in the field is not visible to other parts of the organization, performance inevitably suffers. More criticalization is the result.

Accordingly, we suggest that criticalization (as well as a successful response to it) results from a consequential combination of two independent conditions. Opportunity tension must be significant enough to motivate some individuals to choose to make a sustained attempt to organize their efforts and resources in new ways that might exploit the opportunity. At the same time, there must be a high-enough level of connectivity among individuals with different information about the opportunity to enable the vital exchange of experiences and perspectives. Only when both of these conditions exist simultaneously can the full nature of an opportunity be recognized, and an organized response implemented, usually as an experiment in novelty as we describe in Chapter 5.

Conditions in which *opportunity tension* creates the desire to organize, but at the same time *informational differences* constrain ones ability to organize, combine to create what we call *the Cusp of Change*. In the Cusp of Change outcomes are not certain, and individuals, even executives, can experience a great deal of uncertainty. Employees feel opportunity tension, but at the same time they are also limited by informational differences that appear as differences in perspectives and disagreements in interpretation. To appreciate how both opportunity tension and informational differences are important factors for generative leadership to manage during these difficult periods, it is necessary to understand how an organization becomes stable and predictable in the first place.

DYNAMICS WITHIN THE CUSP OF CHANGE

ATTRACTORS AND THE APPEARANCE OF STABILITY

To understand how to navigate through these critical conditions it can be quite helpful to appreciate the dynamical systems notion of "attractors," an abstract representation of the underlying structures within ecologies and organizations that enable stability. One of the important findings in complexity science over the last several decades was the discovery that complex systems, such as those that describe organizations, can be either stable or unstable depending on the conditions that impact them within their ecology. The former case, stability, is associated with the presence of certain "attractors" or stable configurations that relate to the particular constraints placed on the organization by its ecology.[8] We measure the impact of these constraints with *parameters* as defined later in this section. In this context, stability means that small changes or seemingly random events (e.g., a key engineer missing a day's work) do not have an appreciable effect on the overall system trajectory. These small events do not upset the currently reigning attractors. Prior to the invention of microcomputers and the invasion of IT consultants, the "IBM organizational system," with its stable sales growth and predictable profit margins, had for years enjoyed a "stable" position within its IT ecology.

When a system's behavior, or that of an organization like IBM, can be represented by an *attractor* (see figure 3.1) such as a predictable range of growth or profitability, and when it is perturbed by events, the system tends to return to configurations that are defined by its attractor. Attractors represent the organization in its stable condition, in other words, when the operative constraints are balanced and steady. Thus, the two constraints introduced earlier, namely, the levels of opportunity tension and of informational differences across the organization, plus the organization's history as embodied in the routines, norms, and functions that have developed over the years, determine the attractors that are operative in the organization. A stylized illustration of an attractor, which we will describe in more detail in what follows, is shown in figure 3.1 (this is not meant to be taken as a literally accurate representation of an attractor).

A word on our representation is in order. Typically, attractors are depicted in an abstract mathematical space called phase space that reflects the values of the organization's internal variables, and how they change over time, for example, the populations of various species in an ecology. The behavior of these variables is determined by the system's particular characteristics and history, but also by the constraints that operate on the system (like opportunity tension as we described earlier), which are mathematically represented as external *parameters*. The resulting picture in phase space is called a phase portrait, and this can be interpreted visually as a shape in this space, like the stylized shape shown in figure 3.1.

Sometimes, when a parameter's value crosses a certain threshold point like when an organization enters a period of criticalization, the phase portrait of the attractor changes. Where there had been one attractor, there may now be two distinct ones separated by a region of instability. In business, for example, increasing opportunity tension might press on the organization until, after crossing a certain threshold two attractors, two distinct patterns of organizing activities, become apparent where before there had only been one. The first might represent the continuation of the old way of doing things, while the second might reflect a different way of organizing that exploits the new possibilities signaled by the opportunity tension.

The Cusp of Change model that we describe in this chapter is a way to talking about—and visualizing—how changes to parameters like those that reflect opportunity tension and informational differences influence the attractors at work within the system. Because it is impossible to visualize graphs in more than three dimensions, in future figures we will use simplified line graphs that reflect the impact of changing parameters on an idealized relationship between the organization's internal state variables, for example, the sophistication of the organization's technology, its network structure, or its marketing savvy, and the organization's ability to realize the full potential of its external mission, for example, by maximizing shareholder value. Organizations are assumed to be "attracted" to configurations that realize their potential (represented graphically, perhaps counter intuitively, as downward pressure to minimize unrealized potential). Hence each minimum point on the line graph represents an attractor. Metaphorically, as organizations become better at what they do, they fall further into the "potential well" and stay there. Any small change that is perceived to be less effective is countered to "push" the system back toward the bottom of the well.

In figure 3.2, the line graphs in the various panels show how these minimum values change as parameters change. This applies to the line graphs on figure 3.3 as well. The folded surface that is also depicted in figure 3.3 is somewhat different, however, because each point on this surface represents a minimum for a different line graph (where the derivation of the line graph is equal to zero) as determined by the parameter values. Thus, implicitly, each point on the surface represents an attractor as described above; here the horizontal axes reflect the values for the parameters, such as opportunity tension (shown as *b*) and informational differences (shown as *a*), while the surface represents mostly smooth transitions of continuing stability even as these parameters change in value. There are points of exception, however, along the edges of the fold and at the pleat. As can be seen from the line graphs at the top of the figure, in the area that is shaped like a cusp on the horizontal plane, two minima (two attractors) coexist for the system. Changing from one of these to the other, by either moving through a region of instability within the Cusp of Change or making a sudden jump upward or downward at the edge of the cusp, is the subject of this chapter.

Since our ultimate goal is to explain how organizations can shift from one attractor to another in the Cusp of Change, we will explore the impact that a change in either parameter, either opportunity tension or informational differences, can have on the attractors at work in an organizational system. In these future figures, the reader should interpret the minimum point on the curve in the diagram as implicitly representing an attractor for the system (which actually includes the combined behavior of many possible variables that are not shown on the graph). In this way we can explore how generative leadership can change the parameters, change the *context*, in which organizing occurs. By doing this, generative leadership enables a change of attractors.

Returning now to the main discussion about attractors and the appearance of stability in organizations, an attractor represents a set range of accepted values for various organizational practices, processes, behaviors, strategies, and so on.[9] The attractor can be said to "attract" these values to the set standards, hence the term "attractor." An attractor is not some mysterious immaterial entity; it is a shorthand way of talking about what defines an organization's routines, norms, and objectives. Among other things, organizational success is based on those routines and processes that have been proven over time to allow employees to effectively carry out specific value-adding activities.[10] These routines—and the individuals' choices they represent—are the core of any business model. They lead to reliability and quality in the company's products and services. For example, IBM's manufacturing and sales process for its mainframes was organized into a series of distinct and stable routines that had developed to insure the highest-quality computer was produced and delivered with the fewest-possible errors and problems.

Underlying these "standard operating procedures" is a core set of assumptions and values that organize a company's business model, whatever it is. These core assumptions and values, and the actions they induce, lead to a "dominant logic" for how things are done around here.[11] By providing core logic for what the company does and how it does it, the dominant logic is an *attractor* for employee behavior, managerial decisions, and organizational action. In other words, every organization's business model—including the routines that get the work done, and the dominant logic that makes sense of the whole process—forms an *attractor* that draws forth a certain kind of behavior from everyone in the company to maintain a level of stability. It is important to note that much of this behavior is driven by *implicit* rather than explicit forces that tend to be tacit and not necessarily easy to surface. This is another reason why change can be so difficult.

Note, however, that the attractor is not the actual set of norms. It is the pattern that the organization adopts because of these norms. Thus, attractors are like a hidden moving target: the goal is to hit the bull's eye. As individuals get feedback from others across their social network, they must quickly use the information to adjust their next "shot." In this way actions circle around the attractor, moving closer to it, and also being brought back in line if they drift out of line, as more information is gathered. When conditions are not critical, organizations are guided by reasonably stable attractors.

The more stable the attractor, the more linear and proportional the internal dynamics, and thus the more control and predictability enjoyed by managers. During these periods, linear thinking approximates reality, and it works for each short step as long as one recalibrates (and corrects the errors) with feedback received after each step is taken. A conceptual image of an attractor is presented in figure 3.1.

Attractors then refer to the relevant quantities of the variables of interest that result from routine functions and norm-governing activities in the organization. For example, Monday morning status meetings in venture capital firms ensure that the general partners

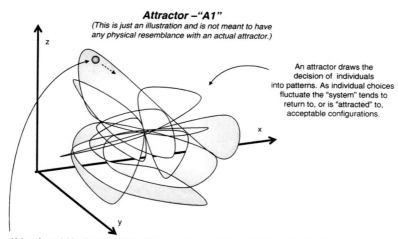

Attractor – "A1"
(This is just an illustration and is not meant to have any physical resemblance with an actual attractor.)

An attractor draws the decision of individuals into patterns. As individual choices fluctuate the "system" tends to return to, or is "attracted" to, acceptable configurations.

Values for variables (x, y, z, ...) describing the organizing system assume a constrained set of allowable configurations among various possibilities. (One such configuration is shown here as the grey ball, rolling around as events occur or individual choices are made.) The variables, like employee attendance, are drawn to particular configurations as biasing norms that constrain behavior, such as "report to work daily at 8:00 AM" versus "stay home," operate to "attract" the organization into acceptable configuration patterns. Some individuals resist, other conform.

Figure 3.1   Stylized Conceptual Model of an Attractor

come together each week for at least a few hours to stay connected about relevant quantities for their business that are associated with their pending and active deals. A deal that seems to be spinning out of an acceptable range will incite actions to bring it back in line. Marketing organizations are routinely galvanized around upcoming trade shows or new product announcements that likewise imply attractors so that everyone involved knows what to do, when to do it, and how to act to make the show come together.

Please note that in this book we are not trying to say anything negative about attractors by indicating that they represent routine functions. In fact, just the opposite is the case since attractors are what make organizations work. Rather, we argue that changing attractors can be quite difficult but can also be quite necessary during criticalization. That is why criticalization is both a crisis *and* an opportunity.

ATTRACTORS IN THE CRITICALIZATION PHASE

As figure 3.1 shows, the attractor guides decision making and organizational behavior during times of stability. However, as we mentioned earlier, if opportunity tension increases such that the system enters the Cusp of Change, what is actually implied is that suddenly there are two attractors pulling the actors in the organization in different directions—the one that continues the old ways and one that if fully elaborated would suggest a new way of doing things. The new one is associated with an emerging approach to organizing to exploit an opportunity. (We say more about this emerging new way in Chapter 4.) In other words, as individuals go about their routines, they may be conflicted about what is expected. In the IBM example that opened this chapter, sales managers were caught between their traditional sales call routines and searching for and following a new direction. When opportunity tension and informational differences interact with one another in certain ways, suddenly multiple possibilities seem to exist for the organization at once.

Within a Cusp of Change there is growing uncertainty about the normal and stable routines, whether the previous attractor representing stable times should be maintained or changed, and if changed, into what exactly. It is crucial to realize, however, that as this information about relative stability is experienced by people, it is distributed among various individuals around the organization. Another way to say this is that many individuals across the organization begin to question the prior business model, but they do this from different perspectives, that is, different information from customers, suppliers, and so forth, leading to alternate possibilities in those functions. Hence there is a need to focus on the connectivity among this disparate perspectives to recognize collectively these informational differences and their potency as a source of novelty.

For instance, back in the 1990s when an IBM mainframe sale began to look doubtful, a sales manager might have tested the boundaries of prior routines by asking the customer how a PC-based solution could possibly compete with what IBM was offering. The customer's answer would have provided information to the sales manager. Whether and to what extent this information would have flowed around the organization to product managers and others would have been determined by the organization's network structure and the interaction resonance within it.

A MODEL OF CHANGING ATTRACTORS

When the level of opportunity tension in the organization is such that a new attractor, representing a new way of organizing, is possible (in addition to the old one), the transition from the organizing attractor that is not exploiting a new opportunity to a new attractor that does exploit it is shown in figure 3.2.[12] Although we describe this process in detail later in this chapter, what we're going to see in the figure is a transition from one attractor, A1, represented as the minimum of the curve on the left, to a second attractor, A2, represented on the right as the organization becomes better at making effective use of informational differences through experimentation. The process will go through five panels from the first attractor, which is the minimum point of the graphic (Panel 1), through the emergence of a new attractor (Panel 2), while passing by a place where two attractors, A1 and A2, are equally strong (Panel 3). The process continues as the initial attractor diminishes into a small dip (Panel 4) and finally the new attractor (Panel 5) comes to dominate activities within the organization.

Let's look at this process in more detail. The system begins on the left of the figure at Panel 1 with the first attractor, A1. At this point, the information available to individuals about opportunity tension is not very available to the system; people don't talk about the changing ecology with their colleagues for whatever reason. Therefore, the old attractor dominates organized action. This may be because decision makers in the firm are so set in their ways that they don't listen, or perhaps there are no communication pathways in the network linking knowledgeable individuals to each other. Moving to the right at Panel 2, as information is better appropriated and synthesized by the

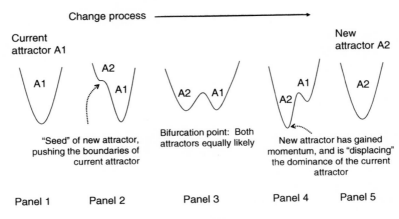

Figure 3.2   Emergence of a New Attractor

system, the organization gradually moves into the Cusp of Change as the seed of a new attractor begins to be recognized. Some people are talking about the need for change. In the figure, the new attractor becomes visible as a hitch in the side wall in the second panel.

Continuing to the right to Panel 3, as the informational differences are even further synthesized through communication and interaction resonance among key individuals, the system moves through the Cusp of Change, and a second *potential* attractor, A2, begins to equal the strength of the original attractor. As better information about the new potential opportunity is synthesized across the network, eventually the new approach, A2, has greater potential benefit to the organization members than the old one as shown in Panel 4. The new attractor, A2, then begins to govern the daily choices made by individuals across the organization as shown at Panel 5.

An example of this happened at the software powerhouse Oracle Corporation when it was faced with a diverse array of IT innovations—there were 70 different platforms and 70 different databases within Oracle's offerings. Bringing together the country managers to consider a company-wide strategy forced the organization to confront the internal informational differences that remained high due to its independent and autonomous culture. At first the company was at A1 in the figure. Recognition of these differences and a synthesis of them, however, became the seeds for its new, entrepreneurial opportunity: incorporating the Internet into its core strategy to become the first e-business of its kind, a new attractor, A2. This entrepreneurial move occurred before a crisis but nevertheless during criticalization.

Oracle's management team started early in its efforts to explore how they might leverage the Internet; each country independently bundled and sold licenses for the range of products, with an incentive structure that emphasized autonomy and country independence. As the executive team heard about the differences and possibilities being explored by different country managers, it questioned the long-term efficacy of the current attractor, A1, with the aim of potentially making a *shift* from the old attractor to a new one, A2, but as one can imagine, such a shift doesn't happen all at once.

The change at Oracle started with conversations throughout the firm, as managers and executives considered the diverse ways they had each utilized the Internet, and they brainstormed on how it could best be leveraged. The decision was to change the nature of the company from being product based to being a service provider, with an internationally consistent set of Internet-based systems that would be supported on a country-by-country basis. Further, the executives decided to do this quickly—to move through the instability as part of one team, a jump that shifted the company from one attractor, A1, to the next, A2, as shown in figure 3.2. To do this, the novel ideas of the country managers were reinforced and allowed to expand. Eventually, the organization once again became stable in its new attractor, its new organizing structure or business model.

HOW ONE ATTRACTOR CAN DISPLACE ANOTHER

Note that in the middle graphic on figure 3.2, at a point deep within the Cusp of Change, both attractors, A1 and A2, are equally beneficial to the organization's members. This represents in mathematical terms, the indeterminacy and unpredictability that a manager must face in the Cusp of Change. This is a place of great tension and stress, and of internal conflict, as both possibilities are vying for prominence and individuals are forced to choose between them or to sit on the fence, as many do. Managers in the midst of change are well aware of this tension. For example the founder at Imigatas who had introduced a new product line reflected on the challenges the company faced right at the decision point:

> It wasn't a lay-up; there were still things we needed to figure out. It was kind of like we were a big jet airplane going up the runway but we still had mechanics fixing one of the engines . . . It was not a good way of doing things. . . . We had had these nagging suspicions. Can we really pull it off? Do we have enough people, do we have enough money?

In the end, these "nagging suspicions" amplified into a full-blown organization-wide decision to drop the new service offering, and focus all attention on the original one. The organization shifted back to its original attractor, having learned from the experience.

A different example of this tension was experienced at Intel, which faced a critical period in the 1980s when Sun Microsystems, a key competitor, invented a new processing approach called reduced instruction set computer (RISC). At the time RISC was more powerful in some applications than was Intel's own processor architecture. This prompted considerable debate inside Intel as well as throughout the industry about how to proceed. One engineering manager in particular insisted on adopting the new approach, even when the emerging consensus was against it. He was so passionate in his preference, that he went so far as to reposition his RISC design as an adjunct processor that could complement Intel's own design. In the process, he pushed the boundaries of the attractor, calling into question the core technology that Intel should have been using for its microprocessors. Ultimately, he won approval for the design, which "competed" internally with the existing Intel approach.[13] In the long run the course chosen by Intel's management—to stick with the original design and stick with its original attractor—turned out to be correct, since the company's relentless and unsurpassed march toward faster and more powerful processors of its own design eventually surpassed even the temporarily more powerful RISC design. However, through the persistent generative leadership of the RISC-oriented manager, Intel did continue for a time to have a RISC design in the market as a hedge against an uncertain future.

What are the dynamics around the Cusp of Change that can either enable and grow a new attractor or suppress the new in order to retain the original? Transformation requires changes in the parameters determining the system's functioning described earlier. This means that transformation requires a high degree of opportunity tension, a pressure for others to come along, that is, to join the team and organize cooperatively, and interaction resonance such that informational differences are explored to form what in Chapter 5 we call "experiments in novelty."[14] Both the movement toward team interaction and the experimentation in novelty within the group are important because they allow the group's members to learn from one another and to move together as a team rather than as individual agents.

Thus, generative leadership encourages experiments in novelty in order to generate and share informational differences in ways that will move the organization's members from an old organizing attractor toward a new one. But for this to happen, the organization's members must first see the benefits accruing to them by making the change. They must recognize that there are two options for them, either staying with their current daily activities and thereby sticking with their earlier attractor, or choosing to band together with others to try a different strategy with an even greater promised payoff, jumping, if you will, to a new attractor. To shed light on the how individuals choose between two alternatives, in the following section we talk about another significant aspect of complexity research, Game Theory.[15] First, we'll provide some background on Game Theory. Next, we'll describe an example called the Stag Hunt Game, which is particularly relevant to the choice to jump to a new attractor. Finally, in the section that follows, we'll discuss how this applies to organizations that are in the Cusp of Change.

A GAME THEORETICAL VIEW: DECISIONS IN THE CUSP OF CHANGE

Game theory provides a simplified model of decision making that has proven to be very accurate in predicting how individual choices can affect system-wide outcomes. The most popular version of this theory is known as the Prisoner's Dilemma, in which two people are pressured to make a series of yes/no decisions that affect each other, but they do this without knowing what the other is thinking or what decision will be made. The nonlinear aspect of the game is enlightening: if both independently agree to a cooperative strategy, they each gain far more benefits, but if one player decides to go it alone, to "defect", that person receives a small "payoff," whereas the other, cooperative player who is left without a cooperating partner receives nothing or even a penalty. The issue then becomes: without being able to negotiate with your partner, what choice is the logical one to make? Do I cooperate, or do I defect?

A version of a related game, the modified Stag Hunt Game, pushes this further by including multiple people making decisions at the same time, as well as multiple rounds of decision making.[16] In this game, the decision is whether to act alone in catching a small animal that safely provides dinner for your own family, or to become "part-of-a-team" that catches a much bigger animal that can feed the entire tribe. In the first case, the "Self-Reliance Strategy", the player tries to catch a rabbit on his or her own. However, if a critical mass of players independently agree to the "Part-of-a-Team Strategy," they can band together to hunt down a stag—dinner for all of them and more. Like the Prisoner's Dilemma, anything less than a critical mass (defined as the minimum number of players needed to field a hunting party) means that no one who chooses to be on the team receives any benefits. In contrast, the less risky choice for everyone is to individually select the Self-Reliance Strategy, which yields a rabbit in every individual's pot.

The dilemma that this particular game depicts is the inherent social risk associated with committing to be part of a cooperative team. By taking the leap and adopting the Part-of-a-Team Strategy, that is, the choice to form a stag hunting party, individuals need to "give up" the type of control they would have in getting their payoffs through acting alone. To understand the role that "letting go of control" has for generative leadership in the Cusp of Change, we dig further into the dynamics of this Game Theory example.

In theory and in practice, once a strategy has been chosen by the participants and it yields a payoff, the strategy acts like an attractor—it attracts further choices for that strategy just because it pays off! In other words, after the initial choice is made and the game ensues to that payoff, there are no further incentives for any of the parties to change their strategy. In the Stag Hunt Game, there are two stable attractors: one in which all players adopt the Self-Reliance Strategy and take care of their own needs by hunting a rabbit, and the other in which a critical mass of players adopt the Part-of-a-Team Strategy, hunting the stag and achieving a larger payoff for everyone involved. Once a successful organizing plan is adopted, people stick with it as long as they continue to believe that it will work.

Thus, once either of these stable modes is adopted by the players, the choices that the players make quickly become stable as the same game is played over and over again—stable modes of behavior are the default for what we can call "choice attractors" (attractors related to choosing one behavioral option or the other) for the participating players. Once the choices are made, and they win a payoff, individuals are "attracted" to the same (winning) choices day-in and day-out.

The organizational attractors that we described earlier in this chapter are actualized in this way. Choices about how to act, what to work on, what to say to a customer, as well as how and what to communicate with colleagues, are all interacting around the reigning attractors. For instance, if a certain profit expectation is a key element of the attractor, much of the behavior and the choices made within the organization will be drawn toward actualizing that outcome. The employees make choices to support the objective because they assume it will bring a payoff to them.

Choice attractors are the "game" strategies that have worked in the past, and thus draw the players to stay within their sway. Existing strategies are stable because they work. Why should an individual jump into a newly forming group (a "stag hunting party") that is playing the Part-of-a-Team Strategy that may never work? What if a critical mass is never achieved? Many players (employees) prefer to continue doing their jobs and earning their paycheck. This is just another way of saying that they continue playing their Self-Reliance Strategy and hunting their daily rabbits.

Studies show that in most stable situations—periods not undergoing criticalization, such as the high-flying success days at IBM—employees do indeed tend to follow the Self-Reliance Strategy. This strategy is effective when linear thinking and actions prove sufficient, that is, during a period of stability. If each employee bags a rabbit, and I have 100 employees, then at the end of the work week I would have $100 \times 5 = 500$ rabbits. Not bad. This degree of predictability is highly useful for management at all levels; no wonder it is so prevalent. In the main, during periods of stability, employees strive to maintain control of their own destinies, and managers know that to change what an employee does, all that's needed is to change incentives—for example, assigning bonus payments, or setting individual objectives—such that each individual, in the context of his or her own self-interest, works a little harder or does a little more. This is, after all, what "good management" is supposed to be all about.

However, once an organization moves into a critical period, and objectives change requiring a shift into a new attractor, this Self-Reliance Strategy becomes problematic. Although it appears safe for the individual, it also resists the prospect of forming a hunting party for a new type of collective action, which is the key to making a transition from one attractor to the next. Generative leadership is partly about intervening in these choice attractors to influence individuals to make the shift from thinking just about their own personal goals to considering a collective strategy that can improve everyone's chances of success. In the language of the Stag Hunt Game, generative leadership would shift incentives away from one-rabbit-in-each-pot, and toward many stags for each department but only if we work together.

Changing from a stable strategy that pays off to a less certain one, of course, requires a good deal of trust, something that is very hard to achieve when an organization has been going through multiple rounds of downsizing as was the case at IBM. However, once a critical mass of employees make this shift, and it is clear that the Part-of-a-Team Strategy does pay off, the entire organization can begin to fall in line, adopt the Part-of-a-Team Strategy, and move forward on a pathway toward change. As we will describe shortly, this was the difficult path that IBM took on its road to change.

TWOFOLD RESPONSES TO CRITICALIZATION

INCREMENTAL AND PUNCTUATED TRANSFORMATION

A final insight from the Cusp of Change model is perhaps most surprising: just as there are many possible attractors that may emerge during critical periods, there are also always at least two distinct *pathways* toward that change. Until now we have presented the pathway of radical, punctuated change. For example, at one firm the stress and intensity that led to criticalization lasted for many months, but the actual decision to completely reorganize the company occurred in a coffee shop following a critical meeting with one of its key mentors in the industry.

Likewise, when the senior team at Oracle decided to launch a new business model that centered on the Internet—a radical redesign of the company's products, services, and international structure involving more than 40,000 employees in 70 countries—the time it took was a mere fraction of the period of stability that occurred before and after. Everyone was on board and they were all Part-of-the-Team. These punctuated pathways are risky, but they can be very effective.

However, another pathway is possible, a pathway of change in which seemingly incremental leadership events add up but in a nonlinear manner, ultimately effectuating a major shift in the attractor. Internally the dynamics may be the same, but the process of change is neither punctuated nor immediate but rather follows a more continuous path to radical change.[17] An example of this occurred at IBM at the peak of its crisis in the 1990s. At that time the price of processing power was in freefall, and its mainframe business could not be sustained. Rumors of the pending breakup of IBM into constituent parts dominated the business news when Lou Gerstner took over.[18]

Rather than choosing to break up the company, or even focusing on developing a new corporate strategy, Gerstner was remarkable in his practice of generative leadership. Famously at the time, Gerstner was quoted as saying, "[T]he last thing IBM needs right now is a vision."[19] Instead, he perceived a need to match IBM's internal operations with the rapid changes in the market. Gerstner thus engaged his management team members to set aside their current projects and instead spend time insuring that their division, and the entire company, was interacting and resonating with its environment in all possible ways, while at the same time reducing internal interdependencies that were no longer useful. In particular, they rolled out a series of "core initiatives" that linked the company to its immediate environment, especially in the areas of product development and supply chain. They also developed "enabling initiatives," which linked together a host of internal processes, including human resources, finance, procurement, and IT—and gave these functions added connection to the world outside. All of these initiatives helped bring information into the organization so that informational differences could be exploited down the line.

Rather than formulating a new vision followed by a collective jump to a new attractor as Oracle would later do, Gerstner and his team initiated a series of smaller, less conspicuous changes that were able to navigate IBM around and eventually out of the Cusp of Change. Specifically, they clearly differentiated the troubled mainframe business from the emerging service business; this reframed the business model and reduced the need for immediate radical change, effectively reducing the opportunity tension that the firm overall was experiencing. From there, a critical mass of employees with a Part-of-a-Team Strategy could be assembled in each initiative to organize into a new form intended to address its developing service marketplace. Sustaining this multiple step process is the generative leadership challenge of Pathway 2.

Both of these pathways to change—the radical punctuation and the more continuous incremental—can generate a change to a new attractor. Figure 3.3 presents this visually. Pathway 2 reflects the continuous transformation that was achieved by IBM. Beginning at attractor A1, IBM followed this pathway by focusing first on disaggregating a highly interdependent corporate structure into separate components to clarify core elements of the organization. For example, the mainframe and service businesses, as well as other core functions were modularized. This disaggregation process is shown in the figure as the arrow α. The process reduced the opportunity tension on the overall business as focus shifted to the smaller modules. Following arrow β in the figure, the practice of generative leadership in each separate group improved the exploitation of informational differences by encouraging experiments in novelty (see Chapter 5) within each module or group.

As information was uncovered through experiments, each of these subunits was able to separately adopt a Part-of-a-Team Strategy that enabled them to leap to a new attractor for their respective unit. Finally, once each unit separately adopted a new model, these were aggregated together so that the organization moved along arrow γ in the figure, increasing overall opportunity tension and once again building internal complexity to match the increasingly service-focused IT ecology. The company was now at a different attractor, A2. When this circuitous process is done well, it will indeed transform the organization from one attractor to another. But this process occurs in a more gradual way and must be sustained over several years; the IBM transformation took more than three years!

In contrast, Pathway 1 moves directly through the Cusp of Change, and thus through a period of unpredictability and uncertainty. In this pathway the organization makes a "catastrophic" change, a "big leap" to an entirely new design and business model. It does this by enlisting the entire team to discover the new future together, and everyone (or at least a critical mass) must sign up for this to work. The jump can be calculated, but the challenges along the way and the final outcomes of the change cannot be easily predicted as we describe in detail in Chapter 4. Team members have to trust each other to try experiments, to work through difficult issues, and to reach a strong new structure. Due to the nonlinearity in the system, a fair amount of taking advantage of good fortune is also needed to succeed—the risk involved may be higher than that in Pathway 2, but the rewards are more immediate.

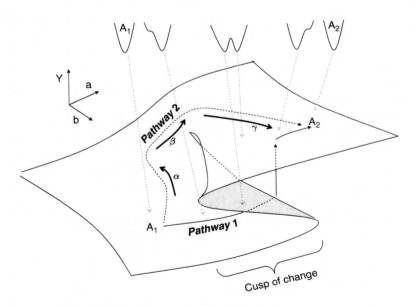

Figure 3.3   Two Pathways for Attractor Change

CONCLUSION: THE POWER OF ATTRACTORS

Attractors are not just repetitive patterns or posted rules in a business. Attractors embody the underlying system of beliefs, the core drivers of organizational culture that lead to consistent individual choices and actions. In an important sense, organizational attractors are at the basis of the *default choices* that individuals make in keeping the firm organized as it has been. For an organization to change it is the attractors that must change, not simply the organization's "design." By emphasizing the complexity science concept of an attractor, we are pushing managers to consider the factors causing stability, that is, what is *behind* organized action that leads to success. Generative leadership is always probing for what is behind the scenes, exploring below the surface phenomena, looking for difference as well as sameness. This is one of the unique perspectives of generative leadership: it doesn't take for granted the dynamics that are showing themselves but instead seeks to uncover the underlying drivers and then find the ways that these drivers need to be changed. Generative leadership therefore works on this meta-level; it *works on the level of attractors* as well as on the content level of day-to-day management.

In later chapters we explore these ideas in greater detail. Thus, in chapters 5 and 6 we move further into the process described here by focusing on the fluctuations and experiments that become the seeds of change. In Chapter 7 we describe organizational networks and how to construct them in ways that exploit the power of informational differences across the organization and its ecosystem. But before we go there, in the next chapter we present a model that builds directly on the Cusp of Change by describing what complexity science can tell us about how new and innovative ways of organizing emerge in complex systems, and in particular in human organizations.

NOTES

1. Gerstner, L. (2002) *Who says elephants can't dance: Inside IBM's historic turnaround.* New York: HarperBusiness.
2. Lichtenstein, B. (2000). Self-organized transitions: A pattern amid the chaos of transformative change. *Academy of Management Executive,* *14*(4): 128–141.
3. Gerstner, L. (2002). *Who says elephants can't dance.*
4. Ibid.
5. Ibid.

6. Ashby, R. (1962). Principles of the Self-Organizing System. In Heinz Von Foerster and George W. Zopf, Jr. (Eds.), *Principles of self-organization* (Sponsored by Information Systems Branch, U.S. Office of Naval Research). And: Uhl-Bien, M., Marion, R., & McKelvey, B. (2007). Complexity leadership theory: Shifting leadership from the industrial age to the knowledge era. *The Leadership Quarterly, 18*(4), 298–310.

7. Lichtenstein, B. (2010). Moving far from far-from-equilibrium: opportunity tension and entrepreneurial emergence. *Emergence: Complexity and Organization, 11*(4), 15–25.

8. For more on attractors we suggest a text on dynamical systems such as Hirsch, M. W., Smale, S., & Devaney, R. L. (2004). *Differential equations, dynamical systems and an introduction to chaos* (2nd ed., vol. 60). Amsterdam: Elsevier Academic press.

9. More specifically, particular attractors in models of organizations are defined for a specific set of quantities that are relevant to the organization and its members. For example, profit level, growth rate, and employee productivity might be important values that define success for a company. In this case, an attractor for the system that modeled these values would be the set of achievable and acceptable combinations of profit, growth, and employee productivity. The attractor idea means that if sales growth slowed below a certain point, for example, there would be pressure to bring growth back within the attractor. In other words, within the model of the organization that is in use,

10. Afuah, A. (2003). *Business models—A strategic analysis.* New York: McGraw Hill/Irwin.

11. Prahalad, C. K., & Bettis, R. (1986). The dominant logic: A new linkage between diversity and performance. *Strategic Management Journal, 7*, 485–501.

12. The Cusp of Change model is based upon an area of mathematics called singularity theory as well as an application of these results called catastrophe theory. Roughly, the former deals with cases, or "singularities," in which not only is the rate of change (first derivative) of a functional relationship between variables equal to zero, but the rate at which the rate of change varies (second derivative) is also equal to zero. In other words, if for whatever reason, there is a slight change in external circumstances, for example, there is a slight disturbance or fluctuation in the system represented by the equations, it is hard to predict what the relationship among variables might become. Singularities imply less predictability. The latter application of this theory, catastrophe theory, was developed by Rene Thom to describe certain of these cases where what might happen with a slight fluctuation is indeed predictable, but only if both the system's history and the external constraints on the system—described by parameters—are known. In certain of these cases, a sudden or "catastrophic change" is likely. The application of this analytic approach for predicting physical systems is

well documented. For example, E. C. Zeeman (1977) used catastrophe theory to predict the capsizing of a ship as it takes on water. When the level of water (a parameter) crosses a certain threshold, the system suddenly rolls over in a catastrophic shift in dynamic states, switching from an attractor that holds the ship upright and floating to one that finds it upside down and sinking. More about this field of research can be found in the following works: Thom, R. (1989) *Structural stability and morphogenesis: An outline of a general theory of models.* Reading, MA: Addison-Wesley; Arnold, V. I., Goryunov, V. V., Lyashko, O. V., & Vasil'ev, V. A. (1998). *Singularity Theory I.* Berlin: Springer; Arnold, V. I. (1992) *Catastrophe Theory.* Berlin: Springer-Verlag; Zeeman, E. C. (1977). *Catastrophe Theory: Selected Papers, 1972–1977.* New York: Addison-Wesley Educational Publishers. The graph in figure 3.2 is based upon the Landau equation, which is common in complexity research. For more on this equation and related theory, the reader is referred to Haken, Hermann (2006) *Information and self-organization: A macroscopic approach to complex systems.* Berlin: Springer. The graph is figure 3.3 is adapted from Zeeman, E. C. (1977). *Catastrophe Theory.*

13. Burgelman, R. A. (1994). Fading memories: A process theory of strategic business exit in dynamic environments. *Administrative Science Quarterly, 39,* 24–56.

14. See complexity science research on the emergence of participation in groups in Phelps, K., & Hubler, A. (2007). Towards an understanding of membership and leadership in youth organizations: Sudden changes in average participation due to the behavior of one individual. *Emergence: Complexity and Organization, 8*(4), 28–35.

15. Although some may not consider Game Theory to be a discipline of complexity science, to the degree it explains nonlinear thinking and action it makes important contributions to the field. It is in that spirit that we include it in our discussion criticalization. For a complexity application of Game Theory, see Hazy, J. K. (2008). Toward a theory of leadership in complex adaptive systems: Computational modeling explorations. *Nonlinear Dynamics, Psychology and Life Sciences, 12*(3), 281–310. For more on Game Theory as a general discipline, see Jones, A. J. (2000). *Game theory: Mathematical models of conflict.* Chichester: Horwood Publishing.

16. Guastello, Stephen, J. (2002) *Managing emergent phenomena: Nonlinear dynamics in work organization.* Mahwah, NJ: Lawrence Erlbaum Associates, Publishers.

17. For more on this approach, see Plowman, D. A., Baker, L., Beck, T., Kulkarni, M., Solanksy, S., & Travis, D. (2007). Radical change accidentally: The emergence and amplification of small change. *Academy of Management Journal, 50,* 515–543.

18. Gerstner, L. (2002) *Who says elephants can't dance.*

19. Ibid., p. 68.

CHAPTER 4

LEADING EMERGENCE

One of the most powerful findings of nonlinear science concerns the phenomenon of emergence: the coming into being of new structures, practices, and processes. In organizations, emergence is the basis for innovation. Emergence is a central process within the nexus of leadership, precisely because it occurs through an integration of "bottom-up" organizing and the "top-down" influences of generative leadership. Taken in combination, various processes of emergence yield true novelty, such as the creation of a new venture or a renewed organization in whole or in part. Because the resulting forms emerge from the application of changing external constraints on the system's own capabilities and history, what "emerges" can be far more adaptive than would have otherwise been possible solely through a top-down design.

An excellent context for seeing emergence unfold is the burgeoning field of social entrepreneurship—the emergence of thousands of organizations around the world that apply the expertise and vision of entrepreneurs to solve the pressing needs of local communities.[1] These social entrepreneurial ventures are formed out of a mission to ameliorate an existing social problem, while drawing in income to render these programs sustainable on their own.[2] Of course, the emergence process is equally relevant to the creation and early growth of for-profit ventures,[3] as well as the re-creation of larger companies.[4] Thus, we begin with an exemplar of emergence from social entrepreneurship—the SEED project in Indonesia, and later describe the process of emergence in a well-known entrepreneurial venture—Starbucks.

THE EMERGENCE OF THE SEED PROJECT

About two hours outside of Jakarta, Indonesia, is the small, economically depressed town of Cisondari. Although the area supports some local agriculture and small businesses, the viability of the villages has decreased in recent years, leading to a bleak situation for thousands of villagers. Rather than looking to their government for a handout, several townspeople envisioned the possibility of a project that would bring diverse players together in order to add knowledge and support to the villagers' own efforts to renew their economy.

Through a series of meetings and events, these villagers made contact with an extraordinary range of potential partners, including the Bandung Institute of Technology, the Singapore Management University, and the Asia Research Centre of the International Management Division of the University of St. Gallens, Switzerland.[5] Such a mix of disparate founders reflects a new standard for innovative organizations that employ a diverse skill set to cooperatively tackle community problems and opportunities.

The goal of SEED—Social Entrepreneurship and Economic Development—was to generate ideas for creating and improving local economic conditions in the village. Although obviously some modicum of planning went into the initial design of SEED, most of the prevailing organizational structure and processes were not planned as such but instead emerged over time as the members formed into cohesive social networks incorporating groups, subgroups, and an emergent "overseer" level. Early fieldwork and interaction with the diverse stakeholders led to a preliminary approach through which student interns would investigate current resources in the village, and use this acquired information for collaborative idea generation, ultimately turning the most promising of these ideas into business plans that would then be presented to venture capitalist companies.

The innovative ideas emerged out of an increase in "opportunity tension" within the various groups making up SEED—in important respects a type of criticalization showed itself in a sense of *disequilibrium* due to the wide range of informational differences in the form of perspectives and ideas being shared. Along the way, interaction resonance improved as concepts were sifted, combined, rejected and selected by subgroups that arose as the program progressed. Eventually, the most promising ideas were captured and summarized, the whole process starting again with another set of objectives. Although emergence can appear disorganized at first, there are patterns to the process of emergence that generative leadership can recognize and enable.

EMERGENCE AND INNOVATION IN COMPLEX SYSTEMS

As we described in the first three chapters, emergence is complexity science's term for the creation of organizational processes, structures, and practices that add greater functionality and adaptability in the face of an increasingly turbulent environment. Emergence is a crucial element in the coevolution of ecosystems, since it reveals how micro-level diversity can build up to new macro-level structures, yielding higher innovation and adaptability in dynamic environments. It is important to recognize that emergence is *not* merely a technical term for just any kind of organizational change. Instead, it refers to those kinds of changes that are deeply rooted in the organization and that significantly increase an organization's capacity to quickly adapt to environmental changes and opportunities.

Consider, for instance, this typical story told about organizational change. First, the top executives develop and describe a new "vision" for the organization; then they set about enrolling those further down in the hierarchy into this vision. In turn, this "guiding coalition" is supposed to go around coaxing key players to also buy into the vision, with the assumption that the more coherence across individuals and departments, the more successful the change will be. An all-consuming change effort now ensues, resulting in only occasional success at best, and sometimes even pure disaster.[6] "Leading change" in traditional terms is a top-down, highly controlled endeavor, with specific goals that are not always clearly linked to the motivations and interests of line employees and supervisors, and moreover, is not necessarily linked to improved organizational adaptability. Due to these limitations, such efforts do not directly enable long-run sustainability. Of course, economic development programs have often taken the same approach, bringing in external experts to analyze the situation and suggest loans or grants that are too often disconnected from the interests of the local population and are unsustainable in every respect.

In contrast to this typical narrative of change, emergence is a generative process intimately involved in the coevolution of an organizational ecosystem. It is a process that tends to engage all of the organizational members who are being affected. Far from a top-down endeavor, emergence integrates the strategic vision of top managers with the day-to-day working knowledge of line employees—or, in the case of the SEED program, the knowledge of academic experts with the expertise of local villagers. Although emergence is often prompted by long-range goals, it is at the same time open to the tactics and strategies operative at each of the levels and time spans it touches. These qualities are expressed in the SEED project, which turns economic development over to the villagers themselves, supported by a cadre of international student interns who are as invested as their Cisondari counterparts in generating useful and sustainable business innovations.

Since emergence pushes beyond the specific context in which it appears, *what* actually emerges is not known beforehand, and accordingly, is outside the direct control of any manager. In other words, unlike normal change, emergent phenomena cannot be predicted or deduced from preexisting conditions; neither can these outcomes be reduced to the elements from which they emerged. These qualities were visible in the SEED program, whose innovations have been sparked by the diversity of participation, and whose outcomes—unique business ideas that utilize existing resources in unexpected ways—have been far beyond what anyone initially envisioned. In complexity science, emergence is at the core of innovation, for both terms signify the creation of radically novel outcomes. Of course, this doesn't render emergent phenomena ineffably mysterious or supernatural. In fact, complexity research has identified a certain "logic" that the process of emergence tends to follow, a process that combines, recombines, modifies, or "complexifies" to such an extent that the outputs far exceed the inputs.[7]

Because emergence is about the coming into being of what is radically novel, it inevitably comes up against the training of even the best executives that directs them to move their organization *away from* the uncertainty associated with emergence. Even when these unstructured efforts are "isolated" in a research and development department, there are crucial moments in a company's life when an entire organization or work unit is about to undergo dramatic and radical change, moments that in Chapter 3 we call "critical periods." Sometimes these periods of criticalization are sparked by unexpected environmental "jolts." At other times, emergent events are driven by an entrepreneurial opportunity that pushes the organization outside of its normal ruts and into taking new directions. Such conditions of non-equilibrium may be present when an organization is just starting up, as in the case of SEED described earlier, or they may become operative at specific moments of high potential, as we'll see later in the Starbucks example. When the situation calls for it, the dramatic potency of emergence may be the keystone of not just surviving but even thriving in today's unprecedentedly fast-paced environment.

In this chapter, we lay out a complexity science approach to emergence derived from several complementary prototypes of emergence: "self-organization" in physical systems; aggregation in computational systems; and symbiogenesis in biological systems. Our goal is to integrate these different strands into a broad view of emergence. We will show how emergence proceeds through four phases, and how these phases can be identified in organizational dynamics and thereby expedited through generative leadership.

FOUR PHASES OF EMERGENCE

SEEING THE EMERGENCE OF ORDER

Of all the findings from complexity science, one of the most startling is the sudden appearance of unique and novel structures that emerge in a complex system when conditions are right. These new structures come into being with brand new properties and are then maintained through the open flow of energy and resources (matter) that connects an individual system to its ecosystem. This is why organization theorists describe organizations as *open* systems. The flow in and out that characterizes an open system and which is necessary for emergence, however, presents something of a paradox. On the one hand, a complex system must be open in the sense of an ecological capacity for the vital exchange of resources and information within its ecology as we described in Chapter 2. Yet, on the other hand, to exhibit emergence, a complex system must also be *contained* enough to provide a degree of *closure* and thus maintain the system's intactness and integrity. The right combination of inflow and outflow of resources within a constrained system is what enables novel emergent structures to emerge and endure when conditions are right. How can we understand this paradoxical mixture of openness and closure in emergence?

A simple experiment over a century ago helped establish the study of emergence in complexity science. Henry Benard,[8] a French chemist, set up a container filled with a viscous (thick) fluid and heated it on the bottom. Obviously, the heat flowed up through the fluid following the laws of thermodynamics. As small amounts of heat was applied at the bottom, the heat energy spread through the material via conduction. This means that energy flowed through local collisions among molecules spreading the heat upward through the liquid as kinetic energy was being transferred from fast moving molecules to slower moving ones, speeding them up through collisions.

However, when the heat was turned up beyond a certain threshold, the Benard system underwent criticalization like what we described in the last chapter. Above the threshold level of heat transfer to the system, the system was pushed beyond its capacity for dissipating the heat coming in through its normal routine of conduction. When pushed beyond its capacity for heat transfer and because the system remains constrained within its boundaries, it entered a state of *disequilibrium* or *instability*. This led to an unexpected outcome, namely, the emergence of unexpected hexagonally shaped *convection cells* resembling a honeycomb pattern. These convection cells dissipated the heat from the inflow on the bottom to an outflow on the top much more effectively way than did the overwhelmed conduction process.

Benard's findings were later interpreted by Nobel laureate Ilya Prigogine, the esteemed German physicist Hermann Haken, and others,[9] in the context of complexity science models as the emergence of novel structures in the previously homogeneous liquid, what Prigogine termed "dissipative structures" since, through a radically new emergent order, they are able to dissipate far more heat energy than was possible through the previous more disordered state of conduction. In effect, the emergence of novel organizing structures in the system was an adaptation in the face of the new environmental conditions. And, because the innovative order emerged out of the system's own dynamics and internal constraints, that is, it was not imposed in a cookie cutter fashion, it was called "self-organization" to indicate this internal locus of the reorganization.

A word of caution is in order because of potential misunderstandings from the use of the term "self-organization" in business and social science. For example, one interpretation of self-organization overemphasizes the "self" in contrast to the "organization," leading to a belief that novel structures would somehow emerge in organizations if only the "command and control" hierarchy would be dismantled in favor of individual action. This misinterpretation led to a spate of management books pushing for "self-organizing," as a form of laissez-faire leadership. This perspective held that somehow relaxing managerial control would inevitably lead to "self-organization" to solve the organization's problems. Unfortunately, these faddish applications failed to examine the science, which shows how preexisting order and structure in the system and within its ecology, such as constraints on the system and capabilities within the organization, are critical for the emergence of a new order.

Specifically, complexity researchers have found that emergence requires the presence of a substrate order that can be transformed, as well as structures that *contain* or channel the emergence processes. For example, in the Benard system, the container that holds the fluid plays a crucial role in channeling the dissipation that generates emergence. When applying these ideas to inform similar emergent processes in organizations, enabling the processes of emergence becomes an *active* not a passive leadership endeavor that requires the right conditions and constraints. Thoughtfully applied, generative leadership engages the reordering-through-disequilibrium processes directly.[10] By engaging in proactive events that "bias" a system toward the creation of a new order, generative leadership bestows greater functionality and adaptability on the system.[11]

Of course, organizations are not fluids in a container, and employees are not independent molecules! But self-organization has been documented in a host of other scientific and social fields, including biology, evolution, anthropology, cognition and psychology, and sociology, albeit sometimes with different definitions and mechanisms. Further, by relaxing the restriction that no material resources can cross the boundary of the system, as was required in the Benard system, the basic thermodynamic principles used in the original experiments have given rise to the open systems model—input-transformation-output—which forms the basic framework for operations management in business, but is also used to explain how organs work, how the body operates, and how an ecology is maintained, as described in Chapter 2. This model, which focuses on the flows of energy and resources across semipermeable boundaries, shows how all open systems thrive and adapt in disequilibrium.

Open systems—like organizations—do have the capacity for self-organization, but only when they are constrained in specific ways and when there are the requisite flows of energy, resources, and information through the system and across its boundaries. Because of this inherent capacity for order creation, a qualified type of open systems model has been used to explain the creation of groups, departments, and whole organizations.[12] More recently, management scholars have shown how the principles of emergence from this theory can be applied to the creation and re-creation of new organizations, such as Starbucks,[13] as well as the emergence of corporate strategies,[14] the reemergence (transformation) of large organizations,[15] the emergence of collaborations,[16] and the emergence of entire entrepreneurial regions.[17]

In general—and for the sake of getting down to the details—the emergence process can be understood in terms of *four phases* of activity, although these phases are not necessarily distinct, nor do they always occur in the exact order we present. These four phases are (1) **Disequilibrium Conditions**, (2) **Amplifying Actions**, (3) **Recombinations**, and (4) **Stabilizing Feedback**. We introduce each of these interrelated phases through a reprise of the SEED program, and then through a case study of the earliest days at Starbucks, Inc. We show how all four overlap and operate together to bring about adaptive emergence.

Phase One: Disequilibrium Conditions

Research into the emergence of the hexagonally shaped convection cells in the Benard experiment shows that emergent order of this kind occurs *only* when the system is in a state of criticalization or disequilibrium. In the experiment, disequilibrium conditions are reached when the heat is increased to a critical threshold, at which point the system has reached the limit of what it can accomplish by what were previously "normal" modes (for example, heat transfer via conduction). However, once criticalization is reached and the system is in disequilibrium conditions, it can no longer use the normal (currently operating) modes of functioning. These changing internal conditions reflect disequilibrium conditions, meaning stability vanishes and linear models no longer work. In the Benard system, for example, the increased heat applied to the bottom of the container soon overwhelms the normal conduction process, leading to a highly unstable and uniquely potent situation that can result in emergence.

As we said earlier, because human organizations are open systems (remember they require a kind of closure with external constraints as well as potent instability), disequilibrium conditions are the order of the day. This means that emergent order is always possible under the right conditions, as every good executive and manager knows from experience. However, as we described in Chapter 3, organizations often respond by denying this instability and enforcing a top down structure that allows them to settle into a false sense of stable functioning that can become self-reinforcing, and can act like a type of stability or equilibrium. (Of course, this is not the same as thermodynamic equilibrium, which is only possible in an idealized experimental system that artificially keeps out all environmental influences.) Instead, this type of "organized equilibrium," embodied as it is in work routines or the other choice attractors that were described in Chapter 3 can be just as resistant to a new and different emerging order as was the fluid in the Benard cell during its conduction phase. To enable emergent order in human organizations, therefore, the behavioral "normal" must be shaken into disequilibrium by generative leadership in a way that is analogous to how the Benard system was pushed into disequilibrium by applying more and more heat.

In organizations, this type of disequilibrium can be initiated in a variety of ways. First, an environmental jolt in the ecology can knock a system out of its normal equilibrium dynamics, as we saw with IBM in the last chapter, which led to our discussion of criticalization. Second, disequilibrium conditions for emergence can be initiated when leaders enact events that *intentionally* disrupt the normal functioning of their project group, department, division, or entire organization. As we describe throughout this book, generative leaders can accomplish this disequilibrium through strategies for knowledge creation, extending social networks, unlocking technological advances, among many other means. More generally, organizational complexity theorist Phil Anderson suggested:[18] "Those with influence and/or authority turn the heat up [in] an organization by recruiting new sources of energy (e.g., members, suppliers, partners, and customers), by motivating stakeholders, by shaking up the organization, and by providing new sets of challenges that cannot be mastered by hewing to existing procedures."

To be sure, this proactive method can be a risky enterprise. Sometimes the role of leadership is precisely to channel the discomfort and feelings of "unease" in disequilibrium into constructive directions. This is where a complexity science approach to leadership can prove its mettle, by showing how to turn unsettling times into opportunities for the emergence of innovative practices, structures, and processes. Likewise, entrepreneurs do this when they identify a potential business opportunity within the uncertainty of environmental change, and garner the internal passion to exploit the opportunity. We referred to this as "opportunity tension.[19] This opportunity tension *is* a disequilibrium condition that leads the entrepreneur to engage, plan, pursue, and capitalize on the potential.

Another way to trigger disequilibrium conditions is by integrating a high degree of diversity and difference, that is, informational differences, into a single program. This approach was at the core of the SEED program, which originated out of a great diversity of cultural/ethnic backgrounds, education levels, daily routines, perceptions, frames of reference, and how embedded the program was in the community. Uneducated farmers joined with research professors. Economic development specialists worked with nutritional experts. Poor villagers developed plans with wealthy funders. These differences sparked much uncertainty and disagreement about how to satisfy the diversity of needs while moving toward common goals to which all parties could commit. As the SEED founders expressed it: "[N]othing could be presumed as given, everything was subject to questioning . . . each participant's existing patterns were disrupted radically."

As we defined in chapters 1, 2, and 3, differences in information and perspective like these are the fuel for complexity, that is, for the generation of information that is central to novelty creation (a topic we will go into much more deeply in chapters 5 and 6). Further, the ability of SEED participants to engage in questioning without yet answering is a hallmark of the disequilibrium often felt by organizations that successfully initiate the kind of innovation that is required for enhanced adaptability.

Phase Two: Amplifying Actions

As disequilibrium increases, most organizations will see an increase in stress and tension, as well as an increase in experiments in novelty. As we describe in the next chapter these are departures from the normal mode that represent possible solutions to what often feels like an impending organizational crisis. Such experiments aim to resolve local tensions by increasing the system's overall capacity in some way. We briefly described various routes to experimentation in chapters 1, 2, and 3; we will go into further depth in Chapter 5. How any given experiment becomes manifest is impossible to predict, an insight clarified by one of our authors, Jeffrey Goldstein: "The role of chance relates to the unpredictability of outcomes associated with nonlinearity . . . Events take place and structures emerge that cannot be anticipated."[20]

In response to all this uncertainty, an unfortunate but common knee-jerk reaction on the part of management is to run around trying to dampen experimental deviations—but this is generally a mistake. As the system moves deeper into disequilibrium, experiments in novelty are likely to increase as people still feel the need to get things done—and this is exactly what is needed to provide the seeds for emergence that can add innovative functionalities to an organization. The key to generative leadership is to live with—and even embrace—the discomfort of disequilibrium, encouraging experiments and amplifying successes in whatever form they may come.

As stress and intensity grow, the system approaches the possibility of a state change, similar to the phase transitions that have been studied by physics. During such transitional times, fluctuations and events that were previously dampened can be amplified within the boundaries of the "container" that constrains the system, extending their impact throughout the organization.[21] As described by complexity expert Kevin Dooley, "Below a certain threshold level, change is unlikely and perturbations are dampened. Above the threshold value, change is imminent and perturbations are magnified."[22] As long as a disequilibrium condition is maintained or increases, and as long as amplifications of departures from equilibrium become rife in the system, and as long as the system in constrained to hold all of this energy, more and more experiments will be tried until a threshold is reached—an unpredictable moment when the entire system may shift.

At this point the momentum of change reaches beyond inertia and the zone where linear thinking applies, and enters into a nonlinear zone where it does not, the Cusp of Change that we described in Chapter 3. Now the system's outputs become *non-proportional* to their inputs, meaning that a great deal of effort may yield no change whatsoever while in some instances—such as the ones at Starbucks to be described below—a small input can become amplified within its container into a major system-wide emergence. A small experiment within a Starbucks work group, like the invention of the new way to package coffee (see below), grows into an organization-wide innovation that is central to the emergence of Starbucks as a nationwide chain. Although, the timing of a threshold can be unpredictable, its occurrence is unmistakable, drawing the entire system into a new level of functioning through a recombination of resources.

The amplification process we are describing was well expressed in the SEED program, as the facilitators wisely chose to utilize rather than dampen the differences in the group. They accomplished this by creating a "relational space"[23]—a safe context of what we described in Chapter 2 as *interaction resonance* in which participants could air their disagreements, share their differences, and listen carefully to how their differences could be turned into seeds for emerging opportunities. After a period of growing frustration in the process, a unique "rule" emerged amongst participants who started to preface each of their remarks with, "In my culture..." or, "In my family..." This small but significant innovation served to increase a sense of mutual respect, which in turn encouraged additional participation and more idea generation. It also led members to start classifying and comparing ideas: Mr. X said A, while Miss Y said B, while Miss Z said C. It even resulted in continuous reports from village members who were informed about the proceedings of the group meetings and responded with their own opinions and suggestions.

This is a clear example of seeds of novelty being amped up and resonated.

Phase Three: Recombinations

Once a critical threshold is crossed, the system's inertia has been overcome. The organization now enters a period when it can be influenced by forces for emergent order. In particular, at this juncture emergence is enhanced through *recombinations*, that is, reaggregations that increase the capacity of the system to operate adaptively. By leveraging resources and ideas that already exist, and by drawing on the innate connections between the organization and its environment(s), recombinations "expand the pie" in a real way for all the agents in the ecology.

Recombination is well known as a strategy for innovation in science, technology, and culture. For example, Nobel Laureate Kary Mullis, who catalyzed a crucial methodology in molecular biology, describes the importance of recombination in scientific innovation: "In a sense, I put together elements that were already *there*, but that is what inventors always do. You can't make up new elements, usually. The new element, if any—it was the combination, the way they were used".[24] Mullis' description hearkens back to the famous quip of Thomas Edison when describing the art of invention, "To invent, you need a good imagination and a pile of junk!" Likewise, recombination is at the heart of what the renowned cultural anthropologist Claude Levy-Strauss described as "bricolage," or the way that the "natives" of every culture take what is given to hand, for example, the local plants, rocks, animals, and so on, and fashion them together into emergent cultural products of art, story, ritual, symbol, rites, and ceremonies—in other words, all the chief ingredients making up the culture of any organization (bricolage has also recently been applied to organizations).[25]

Recombinations like this do not occur all at once: Emergence is a cyclic process whereby one experiment is tried, followed by another, and so on, as experiments are extended and interwoven throughout the system. In other words, seeds of emergence through recombination first become established in a local, limited regime, and only then can make onslaughts into regions that more and more cut across the whole space. In technical terms this tends toward what is called "a nucleation mechanism," since first a nucleus of innovation is generated, and then this nucleus becomes the stepping off place for further "invasions" of emergence.[26] That is why executives practicing generative leadership should expect to see a new regime of order emerge first in one particular area or activity system of the organization, then by recognizing it potential, encourage and improve on that emergent structure as it spreads and expands throughout the organization as a whole. At Starbucks, as we'll see, the invention of the new packaging for coffee started as a novel idea in one department, then was nurtured and amplified to become central to the entire project of expanding into the Midwest.

In the SEED program, recombination was exhibited through the formation and interaction of subgroups around emergent tasks, the composition of members going through many shifts as people moved around from one group to the next. This mixing of group membership served to recombine the ideas held by the individuals moving from one group to another, according to their interests and areas of expertise. Additional recombination is seen in how the subgroups mixed their tasks and topics from idea generation to amplification of the initial ideas, then a process of selection, then evaluation of what was selected, then suggestions on implementation, and so on. Certain groups would temporarily focus on one of these tasks then shift to another, then back to their initial task or topic and so forth in an unpredictable emergent fashion.

A complementary model of recombination in biological emergence is illustrated in the theory of symbiogenesis based on the diligent efforts of biologist Lynn Margulis. According to the theory, some of the novelty in evolution accrues through a symbiotic envelopment of one microorganism by another whereby each one retains its integrity through a radical interdependence that enhances the functioning of both.[27] Her theory, which represents a radical departure from neo-Darwinian models of gene-level-only variation-selection-retention, explains the emergence (origin) of primitive eukaryotic cell through the "endosymbiosis" of prokaryotic organelles.[28] Once the two systems are integrated (through absorption), the functions of both recombine, yielding an overall reduction in of the number of parts within the emergent entity. Far from a subjugation of one organism by another, which often happens in a merger or acquisition, the recombination of their respective functions and parts generates a novel form that is more adaptive in its ecology.

A similar process occurs in "gene swapping," in which DNA is exchanged in certain organisms, and out of this exchange novel traits emerge. Carl Woese, a major researcher in gene swapping has commented on the kind of novelty this process of recombination can bring about: "Novelty, of course doesn't exist in a vacuum . . . cellular evolution began in a highly multiplex fashion, from many initial independent ancestral starting points, not just a single one. Such a strategy automatically optimizes the amount and diversity of novelty generation . . .".[29]

In organizations, novel structures can emerge through any of these recombination strategies, whether a reaggregation of ideas or resources in unique ways, an entrepreneurial partnership or alliance that enhances the capacity of all participants, or an exchange that reconfigures the competencies of a venture. In most cases the reordering of system components and integration of new elements is a "middle-up-down" process, often involving those most central to the emerging system (the middle), who gain legitimacy from their managers and executive stakeholders, and then leverage this support to engage the entire system, including frontline employees, customers, and key stakeholders.[30] Far from a spontaneous process, it is adroit managers and passionate entrepreneurs who carefully identify the key issues and the necessary resources, drawing them together to reform the system.

Phase Four: Instituting Stabilizing Feedback

Finally, new emergent order, *if it is indeed creating value*, will stabilize itself in order to retain this increased capacity. This happens because the organization in its new form is working within its ecosystem as pointed out in Chapter 2, and eventually finds its new, more efficacious attractor as described in Chapter 3. Returning to the Netflix example, we would argue that the constraints in their strategies, like their agreement with Amazon.com to avoid selling DVDs and to restrict themselves to DVD rentals, stabilized the company and helped moderate its growth in the industry. As this stabilizing process takes hold, the system finds the appropriate ways to position itself for overall sustainability in the ecology.

Notice that we are describing emergent order in anthropomorphic terms as "stabilizing itself" or "finds the appropriate parameters." One of the surprising discoveries of eminent complexity scientist Hermann Haken is the notion of *order parameters*, which are macroscopic metrics of self-organization in complex systems. These values arise from the system's internal dynamics in interaction with the constraints that are placed on the system. Once order parameters arise they influence the internal dynamics that created them in the first place.[31] Thus order parameters act to stabilize new order regimes within complex systems.

Some technical details may be useful. As top-down and bottom-up emergent structures interact, self-reinforcing feedback strengthens those structures that support the system's sustainability, while negative feedback suppresses structures that don't. According to

Haken, these order parameters and the emerging structures they influence can be observed, measured, and monitored in organizations as indicators of its status and health. In this way an order parameter is a way of talking about how the stabilizing feedback from external constraints *anchors* the emergent structure by feeding the system's own outputs back into itself. If this argument sounds like circular reasoning, then you are right on target, since the stabilizing feedback that comes from external constraints refers to a kind of circular causality, which comes from the nonlinear relationships at the heart of emergence.

In effect, the nonlinear processes that became amplified into emergence in the first place, in turn help to institutionalize the change throughout the system. In organizations for example, this happens when newly created routines or emergent partnerships and coalitions help align the company into its ecology—a process we saw with Netflix in Chapter 2. Essentially, feedback from the market—both positive and negative—constrains an emerging business venture, influencing which internal processes survive and which will not. Generative leadership enables this process.

At the SEED program the creative ideas generated by the teams become stabilized through the concretely stated business plans and the evaluation of these same business plans. Moreover, the process itself became legitimized through a decision to include into each proposal a research program that would investigate what it sought to accomplish, its financial feasibility and how it would be financed, who would organize it, technical or market constraints and so on. This necessitated a growing familiarity within local constraints, insight into which the villages supplied, as well as a commitment to pursue the sustainability of the whole system, rather than simply start a flurry of projects. In these ways the program, which was initiated by a small number of villagers, became accepted and utilized by the entire town and throughout the region. The constraints that impacted the overall village thus found their way into the details of each of the projects as these in turn struggled to intermesh with one another into more stable synchronized activity.

This diffusion and emergence process holds for innovation more generally. As Everett Rogers showed, in his broadly influential research on the diffusion of innovation, only a small percentage of an organization's members are innovators, which implies that generating innovative ideas needs to cross over the barrier of the innovator's marginal status.[32] In other words, generating experiments is not enough, it is also necessary to diffuse them and then implement them. That's why successful companies ask employees to become involved in improving their workplace, and although they reward the innovators, they reward implementers as well. Next, we draw out the details of this fourfold process of emergence by exploring the emergence of Starbucks into a national firm from its roots as a local Seattle coffee shop. This example will provide specific insights into how generative leadership can facilitate the emergence of innovation in growing ventures and existing organizations as well.

EMERGENCE AND INNOVATION AT STARBUCKS

We can better appreciate how emergence links to organizational innovation by looking at a series of problems and solutions that emerged at Starbucks when it initiated its *nationwide* expansion in entering the Chicago market. Originally, Starbucks was a great idea for a circumscribed region around Seattle, hardly the large scale operation it later became. Seattle was in fact a good place to start since the culture of the Pacific Northwest was predisposed to unconventional ideas, a café-based atmosphere drawing from street traffic and a pedestrian population, and suited to the temperate climate and rugged naturalism of the community. What drove the risky foray into the mid-west was the goal to become a nationwide company, and the belief that if Starbucks could expand to an ecology as different as Chicago, it could probably be successful anywhere in the country. Chicago had a much larger and more vital downtown area than any other city on the West Coast; equally important, founder Howard Schultz knew that Chicago was a city of neighborhoods, and he was confident that the people of Chicago would be supportive of the communal, connective quality of the Starbucks stores. But that certainty was untested. The time for really testing the nationwide concept had come.

FIRST PHASE: ENTREPRENEURSHIP AND DISEQUILIBRIUM

Too often entrepreneurship is considered the special province of a select few who have exceptional skills in identifying an opportunity, articulating a vision for it, enrolling others into the vision, and being opportunistic and resourceful no matter what the environment throws at them. However, an astute reader will recognize successful entrepreneurs follow many tenants of generative leadership that we've been describing in this book. Indeed, one thing that successful entrepreneurs seem quite adept at is how they create and utilize conditions of disequilibrium as opportunities for the emergence of innovation.

Howard Schultz at Starbucks is a case in point, since he used his entrepreneurial instincts to push the fledgling Starbucks from a growing regional business to an entirely new level—the origins of a national brand. The ecology of innovation established at Starbucks provided excellent opportunities for every member to become involved, from the frontline employees including the "barristers" in the stores, to sector managers and functional executives. That friendly ecology was about to be tested as the management team prepared for the opening of their first store outside the Northwest.

The first Starbucks in Chicago faced tremendous disequilibrium from its opening day on October 19th, 1987–the same day as Black Monday, the 1987 stock market crash! Now, that's an environmental jolt! But this rapid turn in the markets was only the beginning of problems for the expansion. The distance from Chicago to Seattle is measured not only by geography and climate, but, most importantly, a difference in culture: the Mid-Western customs and traditional norms of Chicago are quite different than the easygoing, more laid back culture of the Northwest. All of these events catapulted Starbucks to such a degree of disequilibrium that it appeared the entire venture might even fail.

The disequilibrium was systemic—it went to the core of the business model itself. In fact, most people agreed that the company did not yet have the necessary infrastructure to support rapid market penetration half-way across the United States. A key example, and the most pronounced of the seemingly insurmountable problems the company faced, was how to package and distribute the coffee itself. This problem is central to the brand: freshness is a crucial element in the taste of coffee, and it was a defining aspect of the Starbucks brand experience. Unfortunately, freshly roasted coffee beans—the origin of a good fresh cup of coffee—begin to lose their flavor after just *a few hours*. Until that time, no one had figured out how to transport freshly roasted coffee beans so far from home, without losing their flavor. Instead, the only known way of keeping beans fresh was to build local roasting plants at a huge expense, and keeping operations within a several-hour radius of these plants.

This was Starbuck's solution up until their national expansion: local trucks could quickly ship freshly roasted beans throughout the Seattle area and even down to Portland, OR. But this same method of distribution would never guarantee the same degree of freshness if the freshly roasted beans had to be trucked all the way to Chicago. This huge challenge meant that the company had to do things very differently, a prospect that drove the system further into a disequilibrium state.

In addition, expanding into the Chicago region also created daunting new human resources dilemmas for Starbucks, which had already learned that the quality of its hires were another core ingredient in the company's recipe for success. Since the business concept relied on effective HR, this was another core issue to be dealt with. They could not afford a regional HR staff; expertise needed to reside in the Seattle headquarters. How to transfer the core organizational culture, values, and skills to new employees and their supervisors who were unfamiliar with the organization and who were themselves drawn from a very different culture? How were they to hire and train key managers and employees from thousands of miles away? How could they assure that the quality of these new organizational members would be up to the same level in Chicago as they were in Seattle?

SECOND PHASE: AMPLIFYING ACTIONS

Stress and Intensity. As we mentioned earlier, when an organization shifts into disequilibrium conditions, current equilibrium-based routines, systems, and ways of doing things become insufficient. At the same time, new approaches have not yet emerged to solve these inefficiencies and problems. Thus, during the transition there will inevitably be an increase in intensity and stress, as elements of the system are pushed beyond their limits.

One unexpected source of stress in the Starbuck's case was Chicago's infamous winter. During that long cold season in Chicago's downtown area, potential customers will simply not venture outside to walk for anything they don't absolutely need. This was of course well known by the retailers already in the area. But Starbucks used its corporate learning to secure a prime downtown location that, like all its stores, opened out to the street. It was not until after they signed their lease that they learned the key to success that all downtown Chicago retailers already understood: Stores must open into the lobby of sizeable office buildings, capitalizing on the large internal demand rather than on the dearth of street traffic walking by.

Stress was also increased by higher than expected costs, which went beyond budget for everything from basic supplies, to employee wages, to store leases. Worse, in a city known for Folgers and Maxwell House, Chicagoans were not eager to try this new kind of coffee experience. Even employees were voicing discontent and not supporting the overall vision. Things were not looking good.

Compounding this was a financial stress unprecedented in the company: mounting losses were overtaking the company in a severe downward spiral. Specifically, Starbucks lost more than $2.25 million in fiscal 1987, 1988, *and* 1989—adding to nearly double the entire investment into the entrepreneurial venture. As these financial losses mounted and operational problems with the Chicago expansion became more pronounced, the board of directors was compelled to ask some very tough questions. Unless the company could find its way into the black very soon, the entire project was doomed.

Schultz, however, did not always have good answers: "That was a nerve-wracking period for all of us, filled with many white-knuckle days. Although we knew we were investing in the future and had accepted the fact that we wouldn't be profitable, I was often filled with doubts." At one particularly difficult moment, several board members registered strong resistance to the entire plan, "'Things aren't working,' one of the directors said after hearing my report. 'We will have to change strategy.' . . . The pressure was on, and I had to justify those losses."

In those first two years Starbucks lost money hand-over-fist on the Chicago expansion. Bad news quickly found its way to the investment community, and when Schultz approached venture capitalists in 1989 for further funding, some of the potential investors questioned the entire Starbucks vision. In Schultz' words, "Some potential investors saw us floundering in Chicago and challenged the whole premise of my growth plan. They wondered if Starbucks . . . was [just] a fad; until we succeeded in Chicago, we couldn't prove that our idea was transportable throughout North America." In the end Schultz did raise the much-needed cash, but at a valuation that was much lower than expected. How were the other challenges met?

Experiments that amplify change. As the second phase of emergence shows, this period was met with a whole host of *experiments* that were initiated as new opportunities were recognized and amplified in the system. For example, Starbuck's ecology of innovation led to a novel method for storing and shipping coffee beans, invented by one of Starbucks' line employees at the roasting plant. This new-to-the-world invention created a simple but powerful solution—a "Fresh Pack"—which consisted of a five-pound vacuum-sealed bag with a special valve that could let out CO_2 while not allowing in any oxygen. The method was recognized as significant—its impact was amplified by generative leadership until it had become a mainstay of the company. Eventually it allowed for worldwide distribution without the cost or complications of regional roasting plants. It is important to note that this solution emerged from within the ranks of Starbucks and didn't have to be imported from an external expert.

Another critical experiment was enacted by Howard Behar, the head of retail operations who had been hired a few years before. Facing the urgent situation in Chicago, he experimented with the company's pricing and product mix by raising the prices for beverages and focusing customers' attention on cappuccinos and café lattes, which appealed to first-time buyers more than the stronger drip coffee choices. He also altered HR policies, increased employee wages, and made other changes as well. These experiments were recognized and amplified until they eventually found their way into other Starbucks across the country and thus became sparks that eventually launched Starbucks in a nationally recognized brand.

A different experiment was Starbuck's unprecedented bold commitment to use *word-of-mouth marketing* exclusively in its new Chicago marketplace. How could they even consider such a crazy strategy for a brand that no one had heard of and in an industry that didn't exist yet! This experiment represented an unthinkable defiance—and deviance—from the every well-accepted norm of marketing, as well as the dictates of all marketing textbooks. It is a remarkable fact that word-of-mouth marketing at Starbucks was recognized as a success, was replicated elsewhere and went on to become a corporate strategy that was applied to *every store opening.* By deviating from the traditional Grand Opening advertising blitz, Starbucks might have been seen as limiting potential customers to only those who happened to notice a new store in their area. Yet, Schultz believed that superior service and a unique product experience would create such a memorable impression that most of them would quickly become loyal customers. They would tell their friends to join them in this new hotspot, and the process—if it worked—would catalyze customer recognition and sales growth.

This dubious-sounding marketing experiment was combined with another unique innovation that spread rapidly during Starbucks' critical phase, namely "cluster bombing"—sighting two stores at different sides of the same intersection, or within the same block. Like their refusal to put together even a modest "Grand Opening" ad campaign, the practice of cluster bombing dramatized Starbucks' commitment to increasing customer awareness, at the expense of cannibalizing or minimizing its own business success. Seeing two Starbucks stores within several dozen feet of each other sparks a "buzz" that rapidly builds intrigue, leading to a willingness to try the product. And once inside, the customer experience was unparalleled—nearly 85 percent of Starbucks business is from repeat customers.

Starbucks also initiated a series of significant and novel initiatives that were focused on employee retention and motivation. Already Starbucks paid employees nearly double the industry's average hourly rate. Then in 1988, just as costs were soaring over revenues, Starbucks decided to spend even more money on employees by becoming the only private company ever to offer full health benefits to all part-time workers (20 hours/week or more). In addition, due to the circumstances of one dedicated employee who had been stricken with a terminal disease, Starbucks decided to pay full medical benefits for any employee in the same situation, amounting to 29 months of complete coverage before such an individual would be covered by government programs. From the point of view of the financial situation at the company, these experiments were highly questionable—the return on investment for these initiatives was unknown at the time and would remain so for at least two years or more.

It is because organizational experiments are, by definition, untried and untested, not all will work. In this regard, Starbucks tried to branch out into mail order distribution as a way to augment customer retention. However, catalogue sales never reached expectations. Likewise, in some cases store clustering was not successful. However, as can be inferred from complexity science research, if enough experiments are tried and enough of the right kind of novelty is generated, a threshold is reached, and innovation becomes the norm rather than the exception.

THIRD PHASE: RECOMBINATIONS

A key tipping point occurred in 1991, during Starbucks' high-paced and stressful expansion into yet another new market—Southern California. Like its entry into other U.S. markets the company relied on consumer's endorsements rather than advertising to initiate growth; however, this time things were different. Word-of-mouth spread quickly, and lines formed outside stores. Hollywood notables, such as director David Lynch, started frequenting the new stores. Something significant finally shifted.

According to Schultz, "Almost overnight, Starbucks became chic."[33] This "overnight" transition to critical mass was captured by Starbucks' CFO Orin Smith, who said, "We had been working for a long time, but we did not know exactly when it would bear fruit. One day it seemed that a critical mass of customers discovered

Starbucks and stayed with the company. Then virtually overnight, it just popped." What "popped" was the emergence of Starbucks as a national brand and a major player in a very broad ecology, supported by the creation of new organizing structures and systems within the rapidly growing firm.

The markets in Los Angeles, San Francisco, Chicago and other cities took off, attaining new, sustained momentum. In effect, this rapid growth represented a broader cultural change—the coffee drinking routines in the United States were undergoing a recombination. Whereas the previous culture of coffee was home based, now, through the amenities of a Starbucks store in the neighborhood, coffee drinking had become a community event. Starbucks became the American equivalent of an English pub, a place to hang around with friends and family, in effect, a new hearth warmed by a hot cup of cappuccino, some sweet cakes, and a fired-up, WiFi connected laptop.

At the same time, Starbucks also became a distributor for major corporate accounts including Horizon Air, Nordstroms, and later Barnes and Noble. Becoming a distributor of corporate accounts signified another recombination: Up until then Starbucks had been a personal customer retail-based operation, but now it began joining forces, just as with symbiosis in ecosystems would suggest, with very different kinds of organizations including airlines, book store chains and department stores! Here, what was best about Starbucks was symbiotically linked to these new initiatives from leading retailers, creating new business opportunities for both. Starbucks had become the leading edge of the growing industry, setting the pace and the rules for its competitors and for future entrants.

The outcomes of emergence at Starbucks led to a remarkable expansion of capacity. From 1990 to 1992 Starbucks nearly doubled to 154 stores and 2000 employees. In the same period, sales increased by almost 300 percent to $103 million, with net income growing 70–100 percent annually.

Propelled by this rapidly growing reputation, Starbucks also experienced the emergence of a new identity: the company recombined with financial management capabilities as they formed into a public corporation through an IPO in July 1992 that yielded $29 million in net proceeds. Finally, their dramatic expansion continued for several years; by 1995 more than 3,000,000 people per week visited Starbucks, and the average customer frequented a company store 18 times per month. In these ways, Starbucks became known as a "third place"—a location apart from home or work where people congregated for social interaction, refreshment, or a few moments of communal solitude.

FOURTH PHASE: STABILIZING FEEDBACK

In order to support and stabilize this emergence, Schultz and his team instituted new structures and systems that would allow the company to sustain itself as a national business. For example, during this time they upgraded their financial, accounting, legal, planning, and logistics operations. Other additions included the installation of an IT network that linked all stores to a central computer; the construction of a new roasting plant, and the expansion of corporate offices. These decisions laid the groundwork for future growth; the shifts in organizational design and the expansion of IT allowed for a greater flow of information, and created the potential for further changes ahead.

In an important way, many of the outcomes described above—the growing reputation, the successful IPO with its growing financial responsibilities, the emphasis on repeat customers—provided a legitimacy to the organization in the eyes of its customers, competitors, and society as a whole. This is the strongest source of stabilizing feedback of all, which allowed the system to develop into a profitable and growing company. In any organization like Starbucks that is committed to shared learning as opposed to top-down control of information, applying hard-won lessons is highly stabilizing. Feedback in this sense represents a "balancing loop"—the elements in the system work together to create a balance of positive amplification and 'negative' reductions, that is, they all balance each other. This generates a highly effective state for the organization, and over time it builds more resources, which can be used to improve efficiency in the short run, or be available for another emergence event in the long term.

CONCLUSION

Complexity science provides many clues to the dynamics of emergence that we are integrating into a four-phase process involving (1) Disequilibrium Conditions, (2) Amplifying Actions, (3) Recombinations, and (4) Stabilizing Feedback. These four overlapping and interconnected phases are useful for understanding the emergence of the SEED project for social entrepreneurship in Indonesia as well as the emergence of Starbucks, Inc. into a national brand. We would suggest that these phases, and the qualities they incorporate, operate in more micro settings as well, for example, in the emergence of new organizational routines, the innovation of new products, and in the origin of new partnerships.

At the same time, innovations—whether small scale process improvements or large-scale organizational transformations—rely on the production of new ideas that can be tried and applied in unique ways. In complexity science these ideas are called "experiments-in-novelty," and in the next chapter we show how these experiments can spell the difference between success and failure in companies as diverse as AT&T and Apple, Inc.

NOTES

1. See, for example, Brooks, A. (2009). *Social entrepreneurship—a modern approach to social value creation.* Upper Saddle River, NJ: 07458. or: Goldstein, Jeffrey, A., Hazy, James K., & Silberstang, Joyce (Eds.) *Complexity science and social entrepreneurship: Adding social value through systems thinking.* Litchfield Park, AZ: ISCE Publishing.
2. Wolk, A. (2007). Social entrepreneurship and government: A new breed of entrepreneurs developing solutions to social problems. In *The Small Business Economy—Report to the President.* Washington, D.C.: U.S. Government Printing Office. pp. 151–212.
3. Lichtenstein, B., Carter, N., Dooley, K., & Gartner, B. (2007). Complexity dynamics of nascent entrepreneurship. *Journal of Business Venturing, 22,* 236–261.
4. Plowman, D. A., Baker, L., Beck, T., Kulkarni, M., Solanksy, S., & Travis, D. (2007). Radical change accidentally: The emergence and amplification of small change. *Academy of Management Journal, 50,* 515–543.
5. Beck, Daniela, & Chong, L. Choy (2009). Creative interaction in culturally diverse groups. In Jeffrey A. Goldstein, James K. Hazy, & Joyce Silberstang, (Eds.) *Complexity science and social entrepreneurship,* pp. 487–506.
6. Kotter, J. (1995). Leading change: Why transformation efforts fail. *Harvard Business Review* (March-April): 59–67.
7. Goldstein, J. (1986). A far-from-equilibrium systems approach to resistance to change. *Organizational Dynamics, 15*(1), 5–20. Goldstein, J. (1994). *The Unshackled Organization.* Portland, OR: Productivity Press. Goldstein, J. (1999). Emergence as a construct: History and issues. *Emergence, 1*(1), 49–72. Goldstein, J. (2000). Emergence: A concept amid a thicket of conceptual snares. *Emergence, 2*(1), 5–22.
   Goldstein, J. (2006). Emergence, creative Process, and self-transcending constructions. In K. Richardson (Ed.), *Managing organizational complexity: Philosophy, theory, and application* (pp. 63–78). Greenwich, CT: Information Age Press.

8. Bénard, H. (1901). Les tourbillons cellulaires dans une nappe liquide transportant de la chaleur par convection en régime permanent. *Annales de Chimie et de Physique, 23*, 62–114.

9. Prigogine, I. (1955). *Introduction to the thermodynamics of irreversible processes*. New York: Wiley & Sons. Prigogine, I., & Glansdorff, P. (1971). *Thermodynamic theory of structure, stability, and fluctuations*. New York: Wiley & Sons. Prigogine, I. & Stengers, I. (1984). *Order out of chaos*. New York: Bantam Books.

10. Lichtenstein, B., & Plowman, D. (2009). The leadership of emergence: A complex systems leadership theory of emergence at successive organizational levels. *The Leadership Quarterly, 20*, 617–630.

11. Swenson, R. (1989). Emergent attractor and the law of maximum entropy production: Foundations to a theory of general evolution. *Systems Research, 6*(3): 187–197. Swenson, R. (1992). Autocatakinetics, yes—Autopoiesis, no: Steps toward a unified theory of evolutionary ordering. *International Journal of General Systems, 21*, 207–228.

12. Katz, D., & Kahn, R. (1966). *The Social Psychology of Organizations*. New York: Wiley & Sons.

13. Lichtenstein, B. (2000). Self-organized transitions: A pattern amid the chaos of transformative change. *Academy of Management Executive, 14*(4), 128–141.

14. MacIntosh, R., & MacLean, D. (1999). Conditioned emergence: A dissipative structures approach to transformation. *Strategic Management Journal, 20*, 297–316. Nonaka, I. (1988). Creating organizational order out of chaos: Self-renewal in Japanese firms. *California Management Review, 30* (Spring), 57–73.

15. Plowman, D. A., Baker, L., Beck, T., Kulkarni, M., Solanksy, S., & Travis, D. (2007). Radical change accidentally. *Academy of Management Journal*, 515–543.

16. Browning, L., Beyer, J., & Shetler, J. (1995). Building cooperation in a competitive industry: Sematech and the semiconductor industry. *Academy of Management Journal, 38*, 113–151.

17. Chiles, T., Meyer, A., & Hench, T. (2004). Organizational emergence: The origin and trans-formation of Branson, Missouri's Musical Theaters. *Organization Science, 15*(5), 499–520.

18. Anderson, P. (1999). Complexity theory and organization science. *Organization Science, 10*, 222.

19. Lichtenstein, B. (2010). Moving far from far-from-equilibrium: Opportunity Tension as the driver of emergence. *Emergence: Complexity and Organization, 11*(4), 15–25.

20. Goldstein, J. (1994). *The Unshackled Organization*, p. 50.

21. For more on the critical role of a container for sparking emergence, see Goldstein, J. (1994). *The Unshackled Organization*, especially Chapter.or the cases in Lichtenstein, B. (1997). Grace, magic, & miracles: A 'Chaotic' logic of organizational transformation. *Journal of Organizational Change Management, 10*(5), 393–411.

22. Dooley, K. (1997). A complex adaptive systems model of organization change. *Nonlinear Dynamics, Psychology, and the Life Sciences, 1,* 69–97.
23. Bradbury, H., Lichtenstein, B., Carroll, J., & Senge, P. (2010). Relational space: Learning and innovation in a collaborative consortium for sustainability. *Research in Organizational Change and Development.*
24. Quoted in Sutton, R. (2002). *Weird ideas that work: 11 ½ Practices fro promoting, managing, and sustaining innovation.* New York: The Free Press, p. 22.
25. See Levi-Strauss, C. (1966). *The savage mind.* Chicago: University of Chicago Press. The evolutionary biologist Ernst Mayr has suggested a similar "logic" to bricolage at work in evolution in Mayr, E. (1985). *The growth of biological thought: Diversity, evolution, and inheritance.* Cambridge, MA: Harvard University Press. For an interesting leadership application of bricolage/proximate logic, see Baker, T., & Nelson, R. (2005). Creating something from nothing: Resource construction through entrepreneurial bricolage. *Administrative Science Quarterly, 50,* 239–366.
26. Prigogine, I., & Stengers, I. (1984). *Order out of chaos.* New York: Bantam Books, p. 195.
27. Margulis (Sagen), L. (1967). On the origin of mitosing cells. *Journal of Theoretical Biology, 14*(3): 255–274.
28. Margulis, L. (1970). *Origin of eukaryotic cells.* New Haven, CT: Yale University Press.
29. Quote in de Duve, C. (2005). *Singularities: Landmarks on the pathways of life.* Cambridge, UK: Cambridge University Press, p. 185, footnote 8.
30. Nonaka, I., & Takeuchi, H. (1995) *The knowledge-creating company.* New York: Oxford University Press.
31. Haken, Hermann (2006). *Information and self-organization: A macroscopic approach to complex systems* (3rd ed.). Berlin: Springer.
32. Rogers, E. (2003). *Diffusion of innovations.* New York: Free Press.
33. This quote and the next one are in Koehn, N. (2001). *Howard Schultz and Starbucks coffee company.* Boston, MA: Harvard Business School, pp. 13–14.

CHAPTER 5

EXPERIMENTS IN NOVELTY

At the core of emergence—indeed at the core of our book—is how an ecology of innovation can produce unique experiments that have the potential to become seeds for unprecedented organizational action. This is particularly salient in the high-tech industry over the past few decades where an understanding of the workings of an ecology of innovation can explain a most baffling conundrum: why have some companies thrived while others that possess even *more* resources failed? Consider, for example, the difference between the rebirth of Apple Computer through the phenomenal success of the iPod and iPhone, compared with the unraveling of the "old" AT&T,[1] which had been a technological powerhouse at the dawn of the Internet age. Complexity science offers an incisive understanding of why an ecology of innovation took root and was enormously fruitful at Apple but at the same time ran into fatal obstacles at the old AT&T.

Some people claim that success hinges on superior technology. But the fact is that the disparity in outcomes cannot be traced to superior technology held by one firm but not the other. Although Apple had nourished a number of impressive technologies such as the iMac and PowerBook, AT&T and its famous Bell Laboratories had a far greater track record of state-of-the-art technology breakthroughs. Sparked in part by the 13 Nobel laureates who had worked at AT&T's Bell Labs over the years, including Willard S. Boyle and George E. Smith who shared the 2009 prize in physics, scientific and technological breakthroughs at AT&T were impressive and continuous, starting from the invention of the telephone in 1876 and continuing to the transistor, mobile telephony, satellite communication, fiber optics, digital photography, and more, including the first measurement of the background radiation left over from the

Big Bang![2] So, why didn't this technological prowess lead AT&T to the forefront of Internet-based businesses?

Moreover, the difference in outcomes between Apple and AT&T was certainly not due to dissimilar hiring policies. AT&T's long-standing policy was to hire some of the smartest and most savvy engineers, scientists, and managers in the world. In the same way, Apple founder Steve Jobs once declared: "You don't [systemize it]! You hire good people who will challenge each other every day to make the best products possible...."[3] Hiring good people is, of course, a no-brainer when it comes to sound advice for encouraging innovation, but if it were the key to establishing an ecology of innovation, this strategy should just as well have propelled AT&T to unending success.

We propose, instead, that the key difference is lurking within Job's remarks. What he and others find objectionable in "systemitizing" innovation is its connotation of "routinize." We definitely agree—our call for building an ecology of innovation fully rejects routinization of the processes of innovation in the sense of setting up specific protocols and strict efficiency standards that are designed to streamline resources throughout the organization. Although there are times when this course of action may help, we hold that any efficiency-centric approach to innovation is wrongheaded at its core, since what is demanded instead is the generation of the unprecedented rather than a repetition of routine. This poses a serious challenge to leadership: encouraging the emergence of the unprecedented means venturing into previously undiscovered new territory, an endeavor fraught with all the perils of attempting to achieve something that has never been done before.

COMPLEX SYSTEMS GENERATE NOVELTY

The answer that we have culled from complexity science is embedded in one of its most striking findings: *complex systems possess an inherent capacity to become more adaptable, by generating novelty through natural departures from what is expected. These unexpected events are technically called "fluctuations."* Local experiments arise from unexpected conditions—like the many Chicago deviations from the Seattle norm that we described at Starbucks in the last chapter; an ecology of innovation sees these as not exceptions, but rather a pervasive quality of well-functioning complex systems. Unfortunately, these fluctuations often go unrecognized or are downplayed, and as such they often remain unexploited.

One reason for this missed opportunity is that leaders are neither trained nor expected to notice these *experiments in novelty.* Even if they do, this recognition is usually followed by a reluctance to reinforce them, precisely because such experiments depart from the norm, whereas the entire goal of management is thought to reside in developing a "norm" and sustaining it through routines, standard operating procedures, and other means of control. In stark contrast, complexity science supports the instincts of savvy executives and generative leaders who not only notice the positive novelty that arises from among daily deviations from the "norm," they also go on to clarify, reinforce and amplify the ones that appear to have broad innovative potential. Generative leadership encourages a sense of ownership and accountability in organizational members that is directed at promoting and sustaining active experimentation—especially in the face of rapid change and unexpected situations. It was this type of generative leadership that was prevalent at Apple but absent at the old AT&T.

Furthermore, as we described in Chapter 3, *critical periods* can be a particularly fecund time to initiate experiments in novelty; these periods provide a heightened potential to leverage naturally occurring novelty. And as we described in Chapter 4, these experiments in novelty can become the seeds for emerging system-wide innovations and transformations. Of course, we are *not* advocating that generative leaders simply wait around for a critical period to take advantage of the natural stream of experiments in their organizations! Instead, the goal of this chapter is to show how experiments in novelty are continually occurring throughout organizations even if they are unnoticed. The difference—the key to generative leadership—is to recognize that novelty, and explore it as a source of new information and possible change. In other words, one of the central challenges of generative leadership is learning how to recognize and focus on novelty even when everything seems to be running smoothly and efficiently. The point is that an experiment might offer something new and even better.

In an important sense, criticalization provides a "big picture" perspective on innovation. In Chapter 3 we defined innovation in terms of *macro*-scale dynamics that lead entire organizations and industries toward transformation. In this chapter we adopt a more *micro*-level perspective that examines the origination of individual experiments. By examining what these experiments in novelty look like in practice, we will describe how individual leaders can recognize them, focus on the ones with greatest potential, and disseminate what is learned. In addition, we will explore how generative leadership can *systemize* experiments in the sense of encouraging, recognizing, amplifying and facilitating their *system-wide* occurrence.

EXPERIMENTS IN NOVELTY: FIVE FACTORS
FOR GENERATIVE LEADERSHIP

Experiments in novelty take place on the *verge* that separates the expected from the unexpected, where new information about the organization or its environment is available through experimentation. Many times this is at the literal *periphery* of an organization— far from the top of the hierarchy, or geographically far away from headquarters, where more isolated work groups can respond to conditions on the ground without interference from headquarters. Initially, most experiments appear to be "marginal" beyond a very circumscribed, "local" region. But as prongs into the *unknown* and the *unconventional*, they are potential seeds of innovation that may grow to system-wide importance.

In this section we provide avenues for generative leadership that can move those experiments in novelty away from their marginal status and toward the very center of organizational life. Specifically, leading-edge research from complexity science identifies five factors that can be used by generative leadership to build ecologies of innovation that generate a stream of experiments in novelty:

1. *Differences and the End of Group Think*
2. *The Ubiquity of Fluctuations and the Power of Power Laws*
3. *The Hidden Strength of Weak Signals*
4. *Leveraging Experiments in Novelty through Intercohesive Networks*
5. *Encouraging the Frequency of Experiments in Novelty*

We explore each of these in turn throughout the rest of the chapter.

1. Differences and the End of Group Think

Exploiting the Value of Difference
Since experiments in novelty represent *deviations from the expected*, they can be defined as the generation of *difference*—a central feature of complex systems (see Chapter 1). Difference is also at the core of information, which was famously defined by Gregory Bateson as "a difference that makes a difference." In this way experiments in novelty provide organizations with new information that can become seeds of innovation by being a difference that makes a difference.

Studies have shown that difference itself drives the creation of new information, and recent research by complexity economist Scott Page has emphasized the great power of those differences—heterogeneity—within and across such business organizations, civic groups, government, schools, and other complex systems.[4] Page has cogently shown how differences in backgrounds, differences in perspectives, differences in heuristics, and differences in mental models are, by far, the most likely way to generate innovative solutions to challenging problems. In fact, Page has found that the right combination of difference trumps higher skill levels in homogenous teams, creating better performance as well as more accurate prediction of trends.

Page found that the degree of differences among members of a social system is equivalent to the degree of novelty that the system will generate. For instance, when grappling with a complex problem, the greater the differences among group members, the more likely it is that individuals will be able to generate new mental maps with a higher capacity for effective problem solving.[5] He even demonstrated that in complex problem solving, a *randomly selected* group of very heterogeneous individuals (i.e., people with a wide range of personal experience and mental models) will outperform a set of the *best* individual problem solvers without such heterogeneity.

Many of us are familiar with how highly cohesive groups can inadvertently tend toward *group think,* in which new information is discounted in favor of a single, prevailing mental map.[6] In the terminology of Chapter 3, this becomes a very strong attractor that is quite difficult to exit without effective generative leadership. Like the "dense cluster" type of social network that we describe in more detail in Chapter 7, everyday jargon and shared worldviews can reinforce group think by making assumptions that go untested, and by eschewing alternative perspectives. In contrast, generative leadership actively seeks differences that will expand the information in decision-making processes.

Page warns that the kind of difference uncovered in his research is *not* parallel to a "portfolio" model of investments, which reflect a blended balance of equities and other instruments (e.g., bonds) from different sectors that provide a hedge against variability in the performance of individual stocks. Instead, he points to differences that can build-off of each other in a multiplier fashion, allowing differences to be amplified rather than balanced. In sum, whereas many of the tenets of traditional management involve the struggle for alignment, consistency, and reduction in variance—in other words, the reduction of "risk"—generative leadership focuses on facilitating, supporting, and harnessing the right kind of differences, and by extension risk, so that something novel and unexpected emerges.

Engendering Difference through "Difference Questioning"

In practice, how can organizational differences engender experiments in novelty, leading to innovative outcomes? A powerful tool is the technique of *difference questioning*, described by one of the authors (Jeffrey Goldstein) in his book *The Unshackled Organization*.[7] This tool consists of a series of directed questions that highlight already existing differences within a work group, or between one work group and others. A good example of difference questioning occurred unexpectedly, as part of a large-scale intervention to improve customer service at a major hospital in New York City that we'll call "Parkside Hospital." I (Jeffrey Goldstein) was brought in to "fix" an aggravated situation that was an unintended result of a push to improve customer service. The approach was to have frontline employees—including nurses, nurse's assistants, and floor secretaries—go through an extensive "courtesy" training program. Although the program was delivered by what was putatively the best training program of its kind on the East Coast, the participants derogatorily referred to it as "charm school." To the person, the participants felt demoralized by having to attend what they found excruciatingly demeaning.

When I (Goldstein) first encountered a representative group of front-employees who had gone through "charm school" I found a crowd of people standing outside the door of a meeting room who just about growled at me when I asked if the door was locked. Later I discovered that they thought I was from the same company that had developed the customer service training program; furthermore, when they saw "Dr." on my name badge they automatically labeled me the enemy, assuming that I was a medical doctor.

After creating "relational space"—a process described in Chapter 2—we applied *difference questioning* by asking questions that highlight differences in outlook and perspective, such as:

- What kinds of patients do you find most difficult?
- How does this type of person affect you personally?
- How do you respond to them?
- How does this cause stress?
- How do you deal with the stress?

It is crucial to note that the answers to specific questions are not what drives difference questioning. Rather, in difference questioning the aim is to highlight already existing differences; thus, the group facilitator keeps asking questions that are intended to surface individual differences—in outlook, experience, perspective, and so on.

For example, if someone expresses their frustration about doctors who deal with group members as if they were servants, another person is asked to rate how much they agree with what the first person just said. If this rating is less than a perfect ten, another person is asked if they agree with the second person's rating. The point is to push the differences that already exist into the open, in order to demonstrate to everyone that the group is less homogeneous than they appeared to be when they were observed to be united against a common enemy.

Difference questioning therefore aims at breaking up the consensual status quo by highlighting the differences that get submerged in the presence of group think. In this way difference questioning comes across as a facilitated series of experiments in novelty. By pushing to identify and surface the differences in perspective and experience that represent deviations from the accepted norm, even if that norm was implicit or tacit, difference questioning surfaces and legitimizes new information for the group to consider as it attempts to solve complex problems. This can lead to solutions that are truly innovative.

As a result of a number of sessions of difference questioning, project teams were set up to design a new program that would actually address the everyday needs of the employees involved. In the same way that Southwest Airlines boasts, with veracity, that employees will treat customers with respect only when the organizational culture treats employees with respect, what emerged from the project teams at Parkside Hospital was a series of innovations for improving employees' quality of work life. Far from the previous focus on "courtesy skills" (consider the demeaning presumption that they didn't already know how to act courteously), these employees developed a program that included stress management techniques, social support skills, and an assertiveness training for saying "no" to patients and their families—this latter being remarkable for its radical novelty compared with the rather lifeless norm of "courtesy."

Difference questioning is but one of many techniques that help highlight differences that already exist but get suppressed, mainly due to the pressures to conform in monolithic organizations. The differences that are highlighted through generative leadership signal to those who recognize them that the potential for experiments in novelty is pervasive, even when experiments are not generally recognized as such. In order to explain how experiments in novelty are embedded in the dynamics of complex systems, we now turn to the complexity science approach called power law analysis.

2. The Ubiquity of Experiments and the Power of Power Laws

In complex systems, differences show up as "fluctuations"—variations or enactments that have an element of unpredictability. The fill-in for an absent employee may invent a simpler way to accomplish a task; an unsuccessful bid may trigger a review that finds a previously unknown process problem; a new department head agrees to an employee-suggested change that had been resisted by the mainstream culture but which, when put into place, increases productivity and improves the overall work culture. The ubiquity of these fluctuations from the expected is well explained by the complexity science technique called power law analysis, which, until recently, existed at the margins of statistics.

Since its discovery and development in the eighteenth and nineteenth centuries, the field of statistics has had a huge impact on management in general, and leadership more specifically. With the goal of gaining control and maintaining efficiency, modern managers are obsessed with finding averages—identifying the mean value for a host of employee and organizational behaviors, for example, average revenues, average cost efficiencies, average errors per million, average employee satisfaction . . . the list is virtually endless. As adults we are constantly appealing to average consumer spending, average prices, average monthly household expenditures, average temperatures for July, average life spans, and on and on. Further, we have been trained to believe that differences across averages, for example, a difference in average household income between two otherwise similar communities, are objectively meaningful if and only if the difference is "statistically significant", meaning that their statistical distributions can be distinguished from one another with an error that is within acceptable limits. Otherwise, the difference is "within the margin of error", a concept defined by the inherent unpredictability of events within the normal distribution—the Bell Curve or Gaussian distribution named after the great mathematician Carl Friedrich Gauss.

One of the common grade school examples to illustrate the normal curve is the distribution of heights of students of the same age and gender in a class. For example, if a high school freshman teacher made a chart on the board with the specific heights of students on the horizontal x-axis, and the number of students of each height on the vertical y-axis, the result looks like a bell—an inverted U shape with the bottom of the U flayed out on both sides, representing the "tails" of the curve. Most male students, for example, would have heights a few inches on either side of an average of about 5'5," that is, most of the male students' heights will fall within the bulge in the middle of the Bell. Of course, one would also find students that were shorter than this average by more than a few inches, say around 5'2" and even shorter, plus some students that were more than a few inches taller, say around 5'8" and even taller. This normal distribution demonstrates that there are a lot more students with close-to-average height than those either much shorter or much taller. The heights of those students that are outside the normal range are accordingly known as "outliers." When the Bell Curve distribution is assumed to represent the values in a data set, *most* of the items in the distribution will be near the norm (hence "normal" distribution) while the outliers, characterized by significant *deviations from the norm,* will be far fewer in number.

One thing that we do know from mathematics is that the normal distribution accurately reflects events that occur independently and that have an element of randomness to them—like the height of students, or average daily temperatures. However, in the real world those assumptions rarely hold; instead, most events of interest are not independent but are *inter*dependent, and most phenomena that matter are not random, even if they may be hard to predict. In fact, complexity science has found that many features of complex systems simply cannot be explained using a Bell Curve. Instead, they conform to what is called a "power law" distribution—a mathematical relationship in which, for example, the size of an event is not linearly related to its frequency. A useful example of a power law is the size and frequency of earthquakes, admittedly a topic that is unusual in a leadership text! Although geologists have long known that earthquakes come in all sizes—from the extremely small to the extremely large—we typically only hear news of the largest ones: those earthquakes that inflict so much damage that they are rendered newsworthy. These tend to be larger than about 6.3 on the Richter scale. For example, the earthquake that triggered the horrible Indonesia tsunami of December 26, 2004 that killed approximately 230,000 people, was a whopping magnitude of between 9.1 and 9.3 on the Richter scale, representing roughly 550 million times the power of the atomic bomb dropped on Hiroshima—a tectonic shift so large that it jolted the earth's rotational axis off-kilter![8]

However, such a large earthquake is extremely rare, in contrast to medium-sized quakes, which are moderately common, and small earthquakes, which happen all the time. A good way to understand this relationship is to plot the size of each earthquake—using the logarithmic scale inherent in the Richter metric—against its frequency (also expressed in logarithms). If one were to produce this plot for all the earthquakes in a particular region (e.g., the San Andreas Fault in California), the result would *not* be a normal

Bell shaped distribution. Instead you would find an approximately straight line sloping downwards from the upper left—representing very few earthquakes of very large magnitude, to the lower right representing a very high number of very small earthquakes. In fact, this relationship between size and frequency remains exactly the same across the entire spectrum: for example, about 10,000 earthquakes of magnitude of four on the Richter scale, 1,000 of a magnitude of five, 100 of magnitude six, 10 of a magnitude seven, and so forth.[9] This descending line is known as a *power law*, because the slope of the line is a specific value *raised to the power* of, for example, -1.[10]

In contrast to the normal distribution in which very small events would have a correspondingly small frequency at the left tail of the Bell curve, small-sized events within the power law distribution are quite frequent, mid-sized events are less frequent, and large-size events are relatively rare. It is important to note that this same power law distribution has been found in many natural and cultural complex systems. For example, one study found a power law explained the relationship between the growth rate and internal structuring of manufacturing firms in the United States: a single ratio explains that relationship in companies with as few as 10 employees, all the way up to firms with more than 100,000 employees.[11] Separately, biologists have found a power law relationship between the mass and the metabolism rate of virtually every organism, a single ratio that holds across 27 orders of magnitude (of mass).[12]

Another phenomenon where a power law can be discerned is in the relation between the ranking of a word (according to how often it was used) and how many times it actually occurs in some body of writing. It turns out that the most frequent word will occur about twice as often as the second most frequent word, which in turn occurs about twice often as the fourth most frequent word, and so on.[13]

Some readers may have noticed a similarity of the power law signature with that of the Pareto distribution (the so-called 80/20 rule), which is indeed a type of power law and is found in many social, economic, scientific, geophysical, and actuarial phenomena. The Italian economist who discovered it, Wilfredo Pareto, was surprised to find that the allocation of individual wealth in a society follows an 80/20 rule—regardless of whether the society was capitalist, aristocratic, or even socialist. In other words, 20 percent of the population owns approximately 80 percent of the wealth, whereas the rest of the population owns ~ 20 percent of the wealth. This 80/20 law is ubiquitous: 80 percent of sales are made by 20 percent of salespeople; 80

percent of all phone calls are made by 20 percent of all callers; 80 percent of the value of oil reserves are found in but 20 percent of all oil fields, and only the 20 percent most devastating forest fires are responsible for 80 percent of the total area burned each year.

As these examples show, those events that occur at the high end of a power law—extreme phenomena—are quite interesting to executives, but so are the multitude of ones that are smaller in size but much more frequent in occurrence. Critical periods are times when these fluctuations are extremely important and have the potential of having outsized impacts. In order to gain insight on these periods of criticalization, complexity science research has explored the fluctuations that occur in natural systems undergoing *phase transitions.* It turns out that complex systems undergoing phase transitions are characterized by the emergence of startling new properties, as exemplified by the growth of snowflakes from water vapor that freezes on a winter's day, or the emergence of "superfluidity" when helium gas "freezes" as it is brought to near absolute zero degrees.

Research into this process has revealed a very important property of criticalization, namely that as a system nears the critical point of a phase transition, these fluctuations tend to *increase in size,* meaning they can be detected across a broader scale or scope in the overall system. Thus, the many smaller fluctuations previously marginal in effect now assume a relevance that may impact the entire system once the critical point is reached and passed. This helps explain why generative leadership is so important, especially during periods of criticalization.

Supporting Correlations

Since organizations are complex systems, we would expect to find a power law distribution of the fluctuations that are observed over time. Since these fluctuations are deviations from the expected, they are expressed as experiments in novelty within the organization's ecosystem. This means that we should expect to observe small experiments as quite frequent and pervasive. However, just because they are ubiquitous, neither all nor even many of these experiments in novelty will become seeds of system-wide innovation since, if that were the case, organizations would be constantly swamped by fluctuations resulting in a morass of confusion and unpredictability. Rather, given what we know about the power law distribution, most of these experiments in novelty will be pervasive but remain inconsequential and irrelevant with regard to system-wide innovation and change. Moreover, most will remain confined to a very small radius of influence and perhaps even die off. The challenge of generative leadership is recognizing that even small fluctuations have the potential to become consequential, exploring that potential, and then, if appropriate, riding them through along a wave of renewal.[14]

But, how can a manager identify those fluctuations that may be consequential. The study of "correlation length" provides a useful metaphor. *Correlation length* measures how far across the system one can find commonality, or "correlation," between aspects of an event that are observed locally but which are correlated to aspects of parallel events across the entire system.[15] Certain patterns of behavior, for example, employee absenteeism rates within a regional franchise, may be highly correlated across the system, whereas others, for example, a high degree of conflict between two shifts, may be caused by local conditions, reflecting no correlation. Although on the surface these two "problems" or fluctuations may appear to be equally important, generative leadership would look underneath the fluctuations to the degree of correlation that can be detected broadly across the system. We propose as a rule of thumb that the more highly correlated the fluctuations, the more likely they can be explored and nurtured as seeds for system-wide innovation.

To pursue this example, a report to store managers may identify a moderate level of absenteeism, but also point to a high degree of internal conflict. At the system level, however, a savvy manager might see that the absenteeism issue is highly correlated across the franchise, whereas the areas of conflict are dispersed and without a clear pattern. In this case, if the manager can identify the drivers of absenteeism, these may act like experiments in novelty that, if carried far enough, could be leveraged to make significant positive change.

As an illustration of this process of distinguishing which fluctuations to focus on, imagine the mirror-like surface of a mountain lake. It is so calm that there is not even a sense of wind against your skin. Looking at the lake's surface you may see blue sky and clouds and trees reflected with no discernible movement in these reflections. You are left with the impression of perfect homogeneity throughout the lake—no fluctuations from what appears to be a system in perfect equilibrium.

But appearances can be deceiving; in this case it is the mirror-like surface that keeps you from seeing deeper into what is happening in the water. A sensitive probe pushed beneath the surface would measure not stillness but rather fluctuations everywhere: various water currents flow due to swimming fish and turtles; and underground streams feed the lake and flow throughout it. These currents, flits and stirs are fluctuations—they are the reality of the lake as an ecological system, even though they depart from what one sees and thus what one expects about the lake based upon the placid "norm" that is implied by its mirror-like surface. Our models greatly oversimplify the reality, and this tranquility can blind us to opportunity. But even once these experiments are identified, the question of where one should focus attention remains. There is too much going on to watch everything.

Fortunately, fluctuations in an ecosystem like a lake—or an organization—follow a power law distribution. Going back to our notion of correlation, most of the fluctuations are isolated in one spot and are therefore irrelevant, for example, a water insect skating on the surface, or a leaf landing with a small splash. Some are correlated more broadly, for example, the action of a few bluegills seeking that water insect as a breakfast treat, or a school of lake trout swimming into the current. In this case, each fish in the school disturbs the water within its own unique fluctuation; however, as these eight or nine fishes move together in a school, their individual fluctuations are inter-correlated and so the lake is disturbed by a correlation across a considerable distance. Sometimes, however, the fluctuations are correlated across the whole lake. This is case when the ambient temperature drops below 0° Celsius and the lake begins to freeze,. In this case there are local fluctuations in the state of the lake as it freezes, but all of these fluctuations occur in parallel across the lake. These situations, and ones like them, are the relevant ones for generative leadership, which seeks to recognize and if called for amplify the broadly relevant changes that the fluctuations might be signaling.

3. The Hidden Strength of Weak Signals

It might seem that because most experiments in novelty, although ubiquitous, are often isolated in local environments, leadership is placed in the position of either having to ignore them because they are so marginal, or to amp them up until they have a much broader presence. There is a third option, however, that we present here, namely, that weakness can be a strength—the weak signals that some experiments reflect may actually generate a stronger signal throughout the broader organizational network. This claim is based on Mark Granovetter's insightful work on the "strength of weak ties,"[16] which focuses on the importance of weak connections and how to capitalize on them to engender an ecology of innovation.

If we contrast the *strong* ties comprising a close-knit group—for example, an extended family or a work group that has been together a long time—with the *weak* ties between people who rarely interact, Granovetter's research showed that innovative ideas were much more likely to be disseminated through weak ties rather than strong ties. The reason for this makes sense upon reflection. The members of a "strong-tie network" are quite familiar with each other: they speak in a common idiom and jargon, reinforce a common mind-set, and operate according to the same strong constraints that typically arise in long-standing groups. As a consequence, differences have also been minimized over time through interaction. Most communication in a strong-tie network will be about things that the members already know and about which they share a common perspective.

On the other hand, connections through a weak tie, that is, communicating with a more distant colleague, an acquaintance met at a conference, or speaking with a distant relative, mean linking to someone who doesn't share the common mind-set of a strong-tie network. Not sharing the common mind-set means the weak tie is much more likely to be a source of new information, since by definition a weak tie doesn't communicate about the same things the strong tie does. In this way, linking to a weak tie is another example of *information differences being the source of novelty.*

Earlier we described Page's research that showed how differences among group members can be the origin of increased problem solving capability; this insight is explained by "the strength of weak ties." For example, in the experiment where randomly selected problem solvers outperform a group of experts, the randomly selected members begin with *weak* ties to each other since they don't know each other beforehand. The fact that they are linked by only weak ties means that their mental models will most likely be different enough in relation to each other, and that the recombining of ideas springing from these different mental models might lead to novel approaches. In effect, the differences in information and experience within such a heterogeneous "weak-tie network" become the source of novelty and innovation. When there is effective engagement at this level, an engagement among confident equals, each interaction is likely to deviate from what is expected for everyone involved. Experiments in novelty will emerge.

Admittedly, it can be very hard to work on a problem when it seems like everyone is talking past each other and like nobody seems to agree, even on what is important. However, when the problem is complex enough that nobody has the answer and a solution requires the synthesis of many perspectives, and when the proper conditions are put in place to facilitate continued interaction, this kind of rich engagement can lead to the unexpected—to novelty.

The "strength of weak ties" idea is borne out in a host of research studies. For example, Granovetter has shown that advances in scientific fields tend to arise from novel ideas diffused through weak ties, rather than through dense, strong-tie networks.[17] Another classic research study showed the strength of weak ties in job search: only 16 percent of job seekers got new jobs through a strong tie, whereas the other 84 percent were able to find a new job through weak- tie contacts they only saw "occasionally" or even "rarely."[18] Here again, the strong ties only identify jobs that are old news; in contrast, the weak-tie connections draw in novel information from the periphery—different information that truly makes a difference. Similar results have been found in the innovation literature, which has studied the relationship between the hierarchical level of an innovation's champion and the success of the invention. It turns out that the lower down in the corporate hierarchy is an innovation's champion—that is, the less strongly tied she or he is to the prevailing mind-set—the more radical the innovation tends to be.[19]

An example of the strength of weak signals can be found at Google Suggest, which started as a peripheral group in the company that was connected to more powerful units through only weak ties. Google Suggest forecasters believed that most Internet users around the world would not be sitting at their desks using a full keyboard but instead would be operating non-PC devices like PDA's or cell phones. Here again, the weak ties were strong: the claim led to an internal research project at Google in which ethnographers following non-PC users around all day to see exactly how they used their devices. Back in the lab they spread a multitude of post-it notes all over the walls that were covered with notes about their observations and stories. In their analysis they found that Internet users on portable devices did not want to enter full phrases for searches. In response to these novel insights, Google Suggest was devised to predict what the searches are for and thus avoid having to type in entire cumbersome search terms.

Another example of utilizing the strength of weak ties can be seen in how Hewlett-Packard's printing operation was deliberately set up far from corporate headquarters.

Stanford University Professor Robert Sutton describes how Hewlett-Packard's chief of their printing business, Richard Hackborn, consciously set up shop in Boise, Idaho, far away from HP's headquarters, since the HP tradition was to make computers, not printers.[20] Moreover, Hackborn wanted them to make printers for all personal computers not just HP's since HP only had a small percentage of the market at the time. The long term result of that experiment was that today, printers and those incredibly expensive but necessary ink cartridges make up 50 percent of HP's business.

Information about the experiments in novelty that arise in a complex system is conceptually similar to information that comes across weak ties in a social network that includes contacts outside the organization. These are weak signals because their impact tends to remain local. Thus, the information about most internal experiments can be characterized as being *weak signals* about the internal workings of the organization. The challenge is for leaders to recognize these weak signals that are difficult to notice in the midst of other stronger signals and the background noise associated with day-to-day activity. However, as we've repeated throughout this book, the responsibility for noticing experiments in novelty, and then selecting and disseminating the most promising ones does *not* rest solely on the shoulders of top managers. Instead, this process is shared within a particular social network structure, which we describe next.

4. Leveraging Experiments Through Network Intercohesion

Relying on the "strength of weak ties" alone as the source of novel ideas is too passive a strategy and also places too much burden on the usually surface-level and one-way communication channels typifying links to weak ties. Indeed, simply being the recipient of new ideas by way of a weak tie doesn't insure there will be enough understanding to enable the recombination of disparate ideas that Schumpeter famously trumpeted through this heuristic: "As a rule, the new combinations must draw the necessary means of production from some old combinations ... development consists primarily in employing existing resources in a different way, in doing new things with them."[21] But to do this, one must first understand them deeply.

Such an understanding has been gained by social network experts Balazs Vedres and David Stark. In a groundbreaking study of the social network structure that expedited the rise of new businesses in Hungary after the fall of communism, Vedres and Stark identified a novel network structure that facilitated the creation and successful implementation of innovation.[22] They call this network structure "intercohesion" because it involves a rich interaction between initially separate but internally cohesive social groups. Intercohesion occurs when the membership of these groups overlaps and interpenetrates in ways that capture Granovetter's "strength of weak ties" in the context of strong, cohesive teams that can take new ideas and run with them. Intercohesion supplies a kind of "creative tension" that enables members of these overlapping social networks to share mental models, resources and practices while at the same time attempting experiments in novelty, so as to nurture them into seeds of innovation. Intercohesion across groups, therefore, makes up for the deficiencies of relying entirely on either the strength of weak ties or the power of cohesive groups.

One powerful aspect of intercohesion identified by Vedres and Stark is its ability to facilitate the recombination of ideas resources across sector boundaries. Here they point to the work of Richard Lester and Michael Piore on new product innovations in three seemingly disparate categories: cellular telephones, medical devices, and blue jeans.[23] These products are curiously similar in that they each cross traditional industry boundaries: cellular phones are hybrids of radio and telephone technologies, medical devices stem from the connection between biological science and clinical need, and the blue jeans they studied were at the interface of traditional work clothing and hospital/hotel laundry methods. Each of these innovations involved separate cohesive groups that had to interact deeply, intercohesively. Recombining capabilities in all three cases required both openness to new ideas that initially came across weak ties, plus a high level of mutual understanding, coordination, cooperation and respect that is found in cohesive work groups.

Intercohesion is therefore much more than the interchange of information across weak ties; it is all about the quality of the *interactions* within and across those weak ties. Thus, intercohesion requires *interaction resonance*, one of the key enablers for creating ecologies of innovation (as we described Chapter 2). What is required in these cases is a much higher requisite "bandwidth" than normally associated with contact through a weak tie. The quality of interaction that is contemplated here must be much more than might be suggested by the common images of weak-tie exchanges—crossing a bridge that connects disparate regions, or transmitting information through a conduit. Instead, the interactions that generate intercohesion reflect a "structural folding together" of otherwise separate cohesive groups; the emphasis is on the interactive practice, the interaction resonance, of the overlapping and intersecting elements of the groups. Intercohesion is the network description of what is happening when differences are confronted, experiments in novelty emerge to address them, and these innovations are spread through cohesive action in their local regions. The interactions that create these networks, enabling the emergence of novelty and its diffusion across the organization, are a key element of the nexus of leadership.

In practice social network intercohesion can be extremely successful—and profitable. Research conducted by Brian Uzzi and Jarrett Spiro on Broadway musicals[24] explored the impact of intercohesion on the success of Broadway shows. They measured intercohesion in terms of the continuity of team membership from one musical to the another, combined with the diversity gained through new members joining previously cohesive teams. Their findings show that the higher the intercohesion, the more likely a show became a "hit". In other words, when the stability garnered by cohesion among members who have worked together before was integrated with the novel affiliation of the diversity generated by "weak ties" from reshuffling and new membership, the teams were more innovative and more effective at implementation. Team members at the intersection of the intercohesive networks are "multiple insiders" in that they participate in the familiarity of the strong ties, and in the diversity or differences engendered by the reshuffling and new membership.[25]

From this perspective, innovation does not require leaders to possess a special proficiency for detecting experiments in novelty in isolated locations. Instead, the job of generative leadership is to develop and nurture an intercohesive social network structure, in which silos of specialized expertise are broken down, and closely knit teams from prior projects are reconfigured in ways that challenge shared assumptions but retain hard-won trust and learning from experience. Intercohesive networks serve this function, and as we describe in more detail in Chapter 7, these sophisticated networks, together with interaction resonance, are integral building blocks when creating ecologies of innovation.

5. Increasing the Frequency of Experiments in Novelty

In addition to intervention tools that can be used to enable organizations to capitalize on experiments in novelty, a complementary task for generative leadership is to increase the *frequency* of these experiments and to extend the breadth of influence—the "correlation length"—of the important ones. We alluded to this issue earlier when we described how criticalization can lead to phase transitions in organizations. These periods are characterized by certain experiments having increased correlation length and thus having the potential to influence activities across the organization rather than remaining locally isolated. This raises the question of what leaders can do to increase the sheer volume of new ideas and experiments that are going on and to extend the reach of the really important ones.

Generative Leadership can institute policies that encourage micro-level experiments. This is the driver for the social innovations created by the *micro-finance* industry, introduced by Nobel Laureate Muhammad Yunus in Bangladesh. Micro-finance creates small ripples in the economic system by making many, tiny financial investments to individuals who use the money to develop small "businesses" that would be self-sustaining for themselves and their families. Each investment has the potential to engender a new business, and even an entire ecology, as the ideas that are supported catch on and, through positive feedback, are amplified to transform the financial circumstances of entire villages, even entire countries.[26] Each tiny micro-finance investment (indeed, they are as small as several U.S. dollars!) from Muhammad Yunus's inspiring Grameen Bank can be said to prompt an experiment in novelty. For example, a woman might buy a goat whose milk can be sold in a neighboring village. Or she might expand her basket weaving craft into a viable business model. These experiments then prompt further experiments: her brother might acquire a cell phone that they take to the villages when they sell their milk or baskets. The cell phone itself may be a key resource to generate thriving businesses in these villages, which are too rural and poor to have any telephone landlines.

In each of these cases, the micro-finance investment exploits the informational differences that are inherent in these communities and supports the nascent experiments in novelty that these imply. The results are unpredictable in each individual case. This is the nature of deviations from what is expected after all, but in the aggregate, the success of this approach has been spectacular. In corporate settings, generative leadership involves exactly this process. By supporting differences and fostering experiments that exploit the new information that arises from those differences and then extending good ideas across the organization, your results can also be spectacular.

One company that has been mastering this approach right from the outset is Google, Inc.[27] One way they generate innovation throughout the company is to allow employees to spend at least 20 percent of their time working on whatever they're interested in without worrying how it will help the company—a practice invented at 3M many decades ago. This focus on the periphery—their 20 percent of experimental time—has yielded rich innovations and important new products. One example is Google News, which came about from experiments in using artificial intelligence for designing web crawlers for a different purpose.

An even more far-out example of experimentation at the periphery took place when Google prompted their users to come up with their own experiments—a practice that radically redefines the periphery as outside the company itself! To this end, Google has created an addition to iGoogle that encourages not just its employees but its customer-users to experiment with innovations. Google then lets them spread their innovation to other users. And then there is Google Gadget Maker, which allows users to make a program and send it to other users. One example product that was developed in this way was a photo montage gadget that takes photos of the same child at different ages and juxtaposes these photos so that the parents and family and friends can watch the child grow up. The scale of these experiments starts out at the micro-level, one customer at a time; as these experiments in novelty start to involve other customers, the innovations can quickly spread through the entire global community of Google customers. All corporations have a customer base to which they have a close relationship. It therefore is not such a problem to connect customers to each other and to the communities to which they belong. We live in an age when nonlinear affects are everywhere in the sense that small changes over here can lead to enormous changes over there!

Recognizing that organizational differences are the part and parcel of experiments in novelty and thereby innovation, generative leaders can do many things that prompt more difference and thus more experiments in novelty. One unique approach is described by Robert Sutton: at St. Luke's Communication, an advertising agency in England, every morning the offices are completely rearranged so that you never know, when you step into your building in the morning, exactly where or next to whom you'll be sitting.[28] This means that throughout St. Luke's, everyday there are contacts made through weak ties in the sense that the new day's seat mate will be a weak tie in relation to the strong ties developed by workers who are always sitting next to one another. Each day at St. Luke's is an experiment novelty, in communication, and in working together. Although it may be disconcerting to have a new place to roost every morning, nevertheless this method of rearranging the seating is an explicit and intentional way to break up habitual thinking, something that is not only necessary in the high originality atmosphere of advertising but demanded for every organization today if it is to thrive in today's wildly changing business, social, and governmental environment.

Ways to increase the amount and strength of differences are only limited by the imagination of leadership. Indeed, coming up with these new ways is itself an experiment in novelty on the part of leadership!

CONCLUSION: VALUING EXPERIMENTS IN NOVELTY ON THE VERGE

Generative leadership moves innovation into the center of how the organization does business. Within the ecology of innovation that generative leadership creates, new practices, structures and programs emerge that both build upon past and current elements and reposition these building blocks into new combinations and configurations. In doing so, these experiments also potentially create solutions that are entirely new. New solutions often emerge from the edges of the organization where people with different backgrounds and experience engage the environment daily. Generative leadership recognizes that these new ideas, although originating from weak ties at the periphery, are in fact closer to the opportunity and are therefore better positioned to address the challenges to the organization presented in the marketplace.

An ecology of innovation is certainly not likely to emerge from following prescribed and conformist work practices or processes. Instead, novelty and innovation originate from activities on the edges of what is expected, on the edges of the "bell curve" for example; some for good and some for ill. Indeed, establishing an ecology of innovation requires generative leadership that allows for mistakes since something new and important can be learned from them. Since experimentation and thus the potential for mistakes are sources of new information for the organization, encouraging these activities is a critical organizational capacity; generative leadership encourages and rewards employees who step outside organizational norms and try something different. Newness almost always starts at the edges since that is where new situations in the environment can prompt novel organizational responses, if those working at the verge are given the space to develop new solutions and grow them. Many organizations discourage this, and in so doing they compromise their future. Thus it is often from these edges that organizational members learn what they *should* be doing differently when they get to the office tomorrow morning, rather than continuing to do what those at headquarters *think* they should be doing.

There is a powerful social and organizational intervention that presumes that successful organizational experiments in novelty are already occurring. These experiments are already either solving long standing organizational problems or are finding ways to take advantage of opportunities. However, these successes often go unrecognized beyond their local environment. This intervention, called Positive Deviance, or PD, is a systematic method for finding and reinforcing the very best solutions at work within an organization. PD is a way of tapping into the experiments in novelty that are being tried within a community or an organization and then identifying those that positively deviate from what is expected elsewhere in the community, those that have better, sometimes much better results than what had previously been the accepted norm. The next chapter presents the essential nuts and bolts of the PD method.

NOTES

1. The "old" AT&T refers to the period before 2005, when it was acquired by SBC Communications.
2. AT&T lists dozens of major inventions on their website: http://www.corp.att.com/attlabs/reputation/timeline/.
3. Jobs quoted in Voices of Innovation: Steve Jobs. (2004). *Business Week. The Innovation Economy—The Promise of Innovation.* October 11, 2004. Available at: http://compuserve.businessweek.com/magazine/content/04_41/b3903408.htm.
4. Page, S. (2007). *The difference: How the power of diversity creates better groups, firms, schools, and societies.* Princeton: Princeton University Press. 2007.
5. Ibid.
6. Janis, I. (1972). *Victims of groupthink.* Boston. Houghton Mifflin Company, p. 9.
7. Goldstein, J. (1994). *The unshackled organization.* Portland, OR: Productivity Press.
8. 2004 Indian Ocean Earth Quake. *Wikipedia.* Available at: http://en.wikipedia.org/wiki/2004_Indian_Ocean_earthquake.
9. Bak, P. (1996). *How nature works: The science of self-organized criticality.* New York: Springer, pp. 12, 13.
10. "Power" refers to the slope of the descending diagonal line which is notated as K^{-1}, the -1 being the power the variable is raised: see Anderson, C. (2006). *The long tail: Why the future of business is selling less of more.* New York: Hyperion.
11. Stanley, M., Amaral, L., Buldyrev, S., Havlin, S., Leschhorn, H., Maass, P., et al. (1996). *Scaling behaviour in the growth of companies. Nature* (letters), *379,* 804–806.
12. West, G. B., Brown, J. H., & Enquist, B. J. (1997). A general model for the origin of allometric scaling laws in biology. *Science, 276,* 122–126.
13. Power Laws. *Wikipedia.* Available at: http://en.wikipedia.org/wiki/Power_law.
14. Hazy, James K. (2010). Innovation Reordering: Five principles for leading continuous renewal. In Schloemer, S. & Tomaschek, N (Eds.). *Leading in Complexity: New Ways of Management.* Heidelberg: Systemische Forschung in Carl-Auer Verlag, 40–56.

15. For example, in ferromagnetism, correlation length measures how far the fluctuations of magnetic spin go out in influencing other spins in the system. See Thouless, D. (1989). Condensed matter physics in less than three dimensions. In P. Davies (Ed.), *The New Physics*. Cambridge, UK: Cambridge University Press, pp. 209–235.

16. Granovetter, M. (1983). The strength of weak ties. *American Journal of Sociology, 78*(6), 1360–1380. Granovetter, M. (2004). The impact of social structure on economic outcomes. *Journal of Economic Perspectives*, 3309, *19*(1), 33–50.

17. Granovetter, M. (1983). The strength of weak ties: A network theory revisited. *Sociological Theory, 1*, 201–233.

18. Buchanan, M. (2002). *Nexus: Small worlds and the groundbreaking theory of networks*. New York: W. W. Norton.

19. Granovetter, M. (2004). The impact of social structure on economic outcomes. *Journal of Economic Perspectives*, 3309, *19*(1), 33–50.

20. Sutton, R. (2002). *Weird ideas that work: 11 ½ practices for promoting, managing, and sustaining innovation*. New York: The Free Press.

21. Schumpter quoted in Vedres, B., & Stark, D. (2009). "Opening Closure: Intercohesion and Entrepreneurial Dynamics in Business Groups" MPIfG Discussion Paper 2009 (3) Max-Planck-Institut für Gesellschaftsforschung http://www.personal.ceu.hu/staff/Balazs_Vedres/research/PartB1_INTERCOHESION.pdf.

22. Vedres, B., & Stark, D. (2009). "Opening Closure".

23. Lester, Richard K., & Michael J. Piore. (2004). *Innovation: The missing dimension*. Cambridge, MA and London: Harvard University Press.

24. Uzzi, Brian, & Jarrett Spiro. (2005). Collaboration and creativity: The small world problem. *American Journal of Sociology, 111*(2), 447–504.

25. Hebbert, W., Keast, R., & Mohannak, K. The strategic value in oscillating the strength in technology clusters. *Innovation: Management Policy and Practice*. Available at: http://www.innovation-enterprise.com/archives/vol/8/issue/4-5/article/1657/the-strategic-value-of-oscillating-tie-strength.

26. Yunus, M. (2009). *Poverty: Creating a world without poverty: Social business and the future of capitalism*. New York: Public Affairs.

27. Ferenstein, G. (2009). The Obama and Google Management Style. *Fast Company*. FC Expert Blog, July 20, 2009. Available at: http://www. fastcompany.com/blog/gregory-ferenstein/fastminds/obama-and-google-management-style-eerily-similar.

28. Sutton, R. (2002). *Weird ideas that work*.

CHAPTER 6

THE INNOVATIVE POWER OF POSITIVE DEVIANCE

In this chapter we begin to describe the specifics involved in creating an ecology of innovation in your organization or community. Thus far we have focused on the workings of complex systems, and we have shown how advances in complexity research over the last quarter century can inform one's thinking about innovation and adaptation in organizations. In particular, we have pointed to the importance of a kind of leadership that enables change and adaptation in organizations, what we call generative leadership. Earlier chapters described how such conditions can and do encourage individuals throughout the organization to experiment with novel approaches, either in an effort to capitalize on opportunities or to solve problems. We also described how these simple ideas can, under the right conditions, extend and expand a wave of change that spreads across the entire organization. At the same time, we have insisted that these things don't happen by themselves. Generative leadership is needed to create the conditions that enable success. In this chapter and in the next, we describe specific ways in which generative leadership enables innovation-led success even under difficult and challenging conditions.

As we discussed in the last chapters, a key challenge is sifting through organizational activities to find which projects of innovation should be nurtured and disseminated. In a sense, this process is the "Holy Grail" of successful innovation programs because it is in this nexus of leadership that individuals, doing the right things in the right way, really can make a big difference. However, this is not a silver bullet brought about by leaders operating alone from their hierarchical position, a temptation to be sure since "leaders" are typically looked to in order to provide the answers and the appropriate "push." Instead, we begin by describing an intervention around experiments in novelty that is essentially leaderless yet is a well defined and disciplined process that has succeeded in situations where common wisdom would have thought impossible. Although the case we describe next took place in a non-Western environment and focuses on non-business outcomes, it reveals powerful lessons for innovation in every context.

In the early 1990s Vietnam was suffering from wide-scale child malnourishment, with 60–70 percent of the children in villages suffering from this life-threatening condition.[1] Since at that time Vietnam was still not on very good relations with the United States—the war had been over for less than twenty years—the Vietnamese government was not disposed to ask the United States for help with their social problems. Nevertheless, village leaders working with government officials did turn to Save the Children; despite the charity's connection to the United States; the organization did have a very good record in dealing with this particular malady. Save the Children, in turn, asked for help from the late Jerry Sternin and his wife, Monique Sternin, both of whom were long-time non-governmental organization (NGO) specialists, and Jerry was fluent in Vietnamese (and a remarkable host of other languages). The situation was dire enough that results addressing the serious problems were expected in only six months.

From his many years working in underdeveloped and poor countries, Sternin knew that the causes of malnourishment are systemic: ineffective food distribution systems; poor sanitation; lack of potable water; low yielding agriculture; ignorance about new technologies that could improve farming as well as food production; and others. He also knew the limitations of the usual approach to alleviating malnourishment, the *developmental aid* model, in which wealthy nations, foundations or agencies provide money and other resources to purchase and distribute food. Although these approaches can offer immediate relief, their successes are usually temporary because when the funding gives out, the problem remains behind and often even gets worse since expectations have been raised only to be smashed down. Moreover, aid-based solutions are effectively 'owned' by the aid workers rather than the people or communities who are suffering; thus, aid-based interventions typically de-energize the people being affected, reinforcing a passivity that reduces resolution to work on the required improvements. Such trying circumstances are an appropriate test to see how the tools coming out of complexity theory can be effective. This is because the tried and true methods of the past, the things that work in normative times and in equilibrium situations, are proving powerless to effectuate constructive actions in non-equilibrium contexts.

It was in this atmosphere that Sternin and his wife applied a social intervention program they had been developing—"Positive Deviance," or PD. The Sternins adapted their PD approach from research on childhood malnourishment in developing countries originally conducted by Marian Zeitlin of Tufts University.[2] Zeitlin had discovered something surprising: a small minority of the children in the communities studied were not malnourished but were instead doing much better than the rest of community. Using these exceptional cases as role models, she labeled them *positive deviants*—"deviants" since they deviated from the vast majority of other families, and "positive" since they were in fact doing better than the rest. Drawing on this idea, the Sternins created a social intervention that actively sought out the Positive Deviance practiced by the positive deviants in the community. Specifically, in the Vietnamese situation of childhood malnourishment, the Sternins worked with government officials and village volunteers to identify a minority of community families who had in fact deviated from the normal practices of their village in terms of the way they produced, gathered, cultivated, or ate their food. In other words these positively deviant families were practicing what we called in the last chapter "experiments in novelty" or deviations from the norm, that resulted in raising children who were not undernourished.

Overall, the results of this simple intervention were exhilarating. In Jerry Sternin's words:

> It was wildly successful. We saw malnutrition drop 65% to 85% throughout the villages in a two-year period. But that's not all that's thrilling: The Harvard School of Public Health came to the four original villages and did an independent study. They found that children who hadn't even been born when we left the villages were at the exact same enhanced nutritional levels as the ones who benefited from the program when we were there. That means that the behavior sticks.[3]

The program eventually reached 2.2 million Vietnamese in 265 villages. Since then and over the past decades, Save the Children and other NGOs have applied the Positive Deviance model to help solve malnutrition in more than 20 countries, including Bangladesh, Bhutan, Bolivia, Cambodia, Egypt, Ethiopia, Haiti, Myanmar, Nepal, and Sri Lanka. Further, Positive Deviance has been applied in all sorts of social systems in which novel experiments are utilized to bring about striking resolutions to long-standing problems, even ones that were thought to be intractable[4] in neighborhoods, communities, small firms, and even multinational corporations.

The success of Positive Deviance can be understood through a complexity science – based, nonlinear model for leading constituencies through uncertain and changing environments by leveraging internal innovations into system-wide change. This approach to leading innovation is decidedly different than traditional views. It does *not* place the leader in the role of a visionary who looks out on the situation confronting the organization, envisions a different future, and then effectively designs a new kind of business model that positions the firm for that future. Moreover, Positive Deviance does *not* inculcate laissez-faire leadership in which "self-organization" is supposed to come about if only enough hierarchical command and control infrastructures are dismantled, one of the misunderstandings of complexity science that appeared in organizational literature of the past.

Instead, the leadership model for Positive Deviance posits an *active* leadership role in creating and facilitating the conditions for an ecology of innovation. This is a practical leadership tool that has been proven to work in a manner that is unlike benchmarking or best practices, which often don't produce the results claimed for them precisely because they lack a contextually rich complexity science foundation.

POSITIVE DEVIANCE, POSITIVE DEVIANTS, AND EXPERIMENTS IN NOVELTY

On the surface the themes in this chapter—"Positive," "Deviance," and "Leading"—reflect a paradox. "Deviance" has pejorative connotations since it points to behavior that is generally considered socially noxious, yet it is juxtaposed with the term Positive, and linked to our view of innovation. Moreover, what could "Deviance" have to do with "Leading," except in the need to *eliminate* deviance from the social nexus of a well-functioning organization?

Yet again, the science of complexity offers a unique view on social innovation, which, as we've said before, comes about neither through stronger top-down pressure nor stronger pressures for group conformity. Instead, the generation of novelty is first initiated by *deviances* from the mainstream functioning of an organization; these deviances can go on to play a very *positive* role but only *if* they are recognized, reinforced, and disseminated through generative leadership.

In the previous chapter we presented how experiments in novelty, the very life blood of an ecology of innovation, come out of the rich nexus of differences and micro-level diversity that constitute a complex system—whether a large corporation, a small start up, an NGO, or a social venture like the SEED project that we described in Chapter 4. Research has shown that these experimental deviations are ubiquitous, reflecting a power law distribution of fluctuations that characterizes dynamic, complex systems. These pervasive experiments in novelty are considered to be "on the verge," because due to their minority status, signals about them are typically too weak to be recognized as the seeds of innovation that they potentially are. However the very weakness of these signals makes them a serious challenge for leaders not just to notice but, once noticed, to be amplified into something useful for the purpose of innovation. It was in response to the difficult challenge of recognizing weak signals, that we proposed the "intercohesion" social network structure in Chapter 5. As we further clarify in the Chapter 7, the requisite network structure consists of the right mixture of strong-tie and weak-tie elements that are conducive to identifying and then acting on these deviant experiments in novelty.

In this context, Positive Deviance presents a powerful intervention precisely because it incorporates all of these features of experiments in novelty; moreover, it addresses the specific challenge of how to identify, encourage and disseminate these deviations from the norm, especially in light of their marginal status. Generative leadership has a key role to play here since because of their marginal status, positively deviant experiments in novelty are up against strong pressures in every organization or community that seek to dampen the voice (or signals) of the minority. As pointed out by the organizational innovation researchers Ryan Mathews and Watts Wacker, although many businesses may pay lip service to the need to transgress the norm, when it really comes down to it, leaders "are terrified at the idea of deviating one degree away from the formula that earned them past success."[5] But who is to blame them, according to conventional wisdom, since if something worked in the past, then it seems to be a good enough bet that it will work again in the future.

In contrast, innovation precisely means going beyond the norm, an implication embedded into the center of the word innovation—*nova*—which means doing *new* things rather than repeating what worked in the past. From a complexity science perspective, innovation often begins at the peripheries of the mainstream, through departures away from the reigning conventional wisdom in an organization. And, the novelty generating potency of Positive Deviance lies precisely in its initial marginal status. The goal, as we describe next, is to find a way to listen to these marginalized, weak signals, especially when these deviations from the norm may be revolutionary in their implications.

THE PROGRAM OF POSITIVE DEVIANCE

ASSUMPTIONS AND OBJECTIVES

At the core of a Positive Deviance intervention is the recognition that significant innovation cannot come through reliance on *outside* experts who, from their hierarchical command and control position, tell the *insiders* what to do. Such a tactic in no way evokes the natural capabilities of the system in leveraging the already effective practices of positive deviants within the system. In contrast, the most fundamental tenet of Positive Deviance, drawn from its focus on the emergent capabilities of complex systems, is that innovative solutions to long-standing problems may *already be present* within the community or organization but remain hidden from key decision makers. Also, because those involved in generating these solutions typically have only a marginal status, their solutions are often not recognized by the rest of the social system. Sternin encapsulated this core element of Positive Deviance in the following principle:

- In every community there are certain individuals ("positive deviants") whose special practices, strategies or behaviors enable them to find better solutions to prevalent community problems than their peers who have access to the same resources.

This principle translates into the radical assumption that a small minority of individuals—"positive deviants"—have the capacity to solve intractable problems or engage unprecedented opportunities in original and resourceful ways without recourse to special methods or external resources. What makes these individuals *deviants* is the manner in which their practices *depart from* organizational norms and conventional wisdom; what makes them positive is that their practices offer constructive solutions that the majority of members in the community have not been able to solve. In other words, Positive Deviance represents experiments in novelty occurring at the "fringe" of the mainstream but capable of being appropriated by that same mainstream.

Since the solution exists within a small minority of members, leading by using Positive Deviance begins by gathering key players from the groups affected by the problem who then inquire into their current practices as well as the problems or opportunities they are facing. In the Vietnam example, villagers themselves needed to be involved from the start—individual families and local leaders—and not just governmental officials or outside aid workers. In other words, what Jerry and Monique had to do first was facilitate meetings between this diverse set of key players, including villagers and their representatives, government workers, and aid experts. For example, to ensure that there would be local ownership of the program, village health committees (VHCs) were established, composed of members from the Women's and Farmer's Union, the People's Committee, and other village health interested parties. The VHC then selected female volunteers who were willing to make a commitment to the aims of the Positive Deviance program. Without this sense of ownership all the positive outcomes could be attributed to "outside" experts, or in corporate lingo, "top management" intervention.

In the case of Vietnam, the general problem was already known, *viz.*, malnourishment of children. But what about the details? What were the crucial elements of the problem? How did they manifest in this system? The goal at this stage is to collect as many facts as possible about the problem. In Vietnam this meant compiling health records that could show current data on degree of malnourishment, criteria for malnourishment, who exactly should be classified as malnourished, and so forth. Again, the issue need not be a problem *per se* but could be an opportunity that is not being recognized or taken advantage of by the majority of community members.

Next comes identifying the *outliers*, that is, the small minority of children and their families who are not malnourished. The villagers did this by carefully measuring the positive deviants who were not malnourished and comparing that with careful measurements of the majority, that is, the children who were. Rigorous measurement in this particular case would include tabulating weights and heights and comparing these observations with health standards, as well as measuring body fat using the same sort of calipers found in health clubs across the developed world, plus other metrics of nourishment. The positive deviants would be defined as precisely those children whose measurements indicated were *not* malnourished.

Note how different this move is when compared to the kind of traditional analysis that is taught in business schools. As we described in the previous chapter, common statistics focus on the averages of a population, using the Gaussian "normal distribution" as the model. Even our language of looking for "outliers" reflects the negative view that most statistical analyses have of cases that are not within the most common range of the distribution. In contrast, Positive Deviance works in the context of power law distributions—the complexity science measure of dynamic systems that we described in Chapter 5—which highlights the very few cases that are extremely high in a certain dimension, in this case, childhood nutrition (as well as the great multitude of smaller manifestations). Those few cases can be distinguished from the 80–90 percent of cases that are malnourished. Hence, instead of following Bell curve statistics that would put the onus on the average performers, Positive Deviance doesn't focus on this 80 percent bulk in the middle, but rather finds the real leverage point in minority cases, for example, 10–20 percent or less of the cases.

In Vietnam, this analysis sparked keen curiosity about what was responsible for these children staying nourished, even though their families have the same access to food and other resources as the others in the village. This question reflects another key tenet of Positive Deviance, namely, that things must be essentially equal among these Positive Peviants compared to their larger communities. That is, if a family were receiving "care" packages of food from a rich uncle in Ho Chi Minh City, they would not be included in the program. A community member is only a genuine positive deviant if they have they same access to resources as all the persons in the social system that are touched by the problem or situation.

Once genuine positive deviants are identified, the focus shifts to uncovering what specific practices are responsible for the lack of malnourishment of these positively deviant children. This is accomplished the old fashioned way: by spending long periods of time with the positively deviant children and families to discover exactly how their food and eating practices may differ from the mainstream villagers. Here again, the intervention relies on villagers talking to villagers rather than on ethnographic studies by outside experts on nutrition or food cultivation or in statistical analysis by officials within the governmental hierarchy.

Over time, these committees gain sufficient information to understand the practices that differ from the norm, and how these differ from other community members. Next, attention shifts to how these novel practices can be disseminated—not just in the village where the intervention is initiated but to all the villages who are facing a similar problem of malnourishment. The end result must be the dissemination of practices that previously were "deviant" but now become models of "positive" behaviors that can—and should—be taken up by others in the social system, thereby replicating the approach and amplifying the deviance to solve the problem for the greater community.

Thus, not only is the solution already present within the system, it is disseminated via the same villagers who were involved in the project. This is the key point: the practices making up this solution are spread from the minority to the majority of the system's members by way of the villagers themselves. It is for this reason that Jerry could emphasize how Positive Deviance does *not* provoke an "immune reaction" or the kind of resistance to change that is common when a "foreign" or external practice encroaches into a system. In Vietnam, this stage of Positive Deviance had village families spending time with the Positively Deviant families in each village, learning about the particular behaviors that make up their successful resolution of the problem of malnourishment.

In Vietnam, the specific practices identified as the key resolvers of the problem of malnourishment included the following experiments in novelty (note that the reasons why they provided more nutrition were only accessible after the fact):

1. When cultivating rice off the patty (the primary staple of agriculture for these villagers is rice cultivation), some of the sweet-potato greens around the rice were retained with the rice as well. The greens provided extra minerals and vitamins as well as carbohydrates that are critical for balanced nutrition.
2. Some of the small crustaceans (tiny shrimp and crabs) living in the water around the rice plants were also included with the greens and the rice. These supplied extra protein and calcium.
3. Note that the majority did not retain the greens nor the crustaceans since (a) the greens were considered "low class" food, and (b) it was thought to be an inefficient way to cultivate rice.
4. Another crucial element of positive deviant behaviors was that mothers tended to feed their children more times per day. Accordingly, although the total amount of food for a family was the same between the Positively Deviant families and the majority, the practice of being fed more often during the day meant the children were on the whole eating more food relative to others since, if they were fed only once or twice a day, they simply couldn't ingest that much each time. As Jerry concluded from this finding, "... using exactly the same amount of rice, spread out over an additional two or three meals, the PD kids were getting more food and twice the calories as their neighbors who had access to exactly the same resource!"

EIGHT LEADERSHIP RULES FOR HARNESSING POSITIVE DEVIANCE

In an interview with *Fast Company*, Jerry Sternin emphasized eight crucial rules that leaders can follow to ensure a successful Positive Deviance program.[6] These rules also make up a good list of guidelines of how generative leadership following complexity science insights can harness the power of experiments in novelty toward furthering the creation of an ecology of innovation.

1. *Don't presume that you have the answer.* Of course, this presumption goes against nearly all the conventional wisdom of leadership in which a sense of one's own competence as a leader is bound up with believing you do indeed know the answer, or at least can get to someone in the hierarchy or an outside expert who does. But with Positive Deviance, it is critical to assume the very opposite—indeed, your own answers wouldn't be accepted because of your very status as an outside "expert." The key to Positive Deviance is that it has to emerge naturally out of the community or organization and not be imposed from the top or from the outside.

2. *Don't mix people from different communities, organizations, or departments.* Again, we see a major departure from the current leadership push for cross-functional teams that is heard so loudly these days in corporate America. Of course, as we discussed in Chapter 5 in the context of intercohesion networks, cross-functional teams can have great benefit in connecting across separate fiefdoms in corporations and other large organizations. But in Positive Deviance, according to Sternin, at the outset you are not at the point where generating a lively creative-solving interchange would be of much help. Later on, however, this could prove beneficial in coming up with ways of amplifying the weak signal and distributing it through the community.

   Instead, leadership needs to create a condition in which everyone is able to identify with the others in the group because they are facing the same challenges and relying on the same set of resources. This is also related to the critical point made above that everyone has to have equal access to the same resources, meaning that all other things must be equal for all the parties concerned. Furthermore, this situation specific like-mindedness of the groups' participants will make it more probable that the Positively Deviant practices will be accepted and then repeated by all social system members, and not just by some differently motivated or skilled individuals with a different set of expertise.

3. *Let the groups do it all themselves.* Of course to get the thing rolling, leaders need to play a role in clarifying the problem or opportunity being faced by the organization/community as well as laying out the available tools. Then they must encourage and let the group itself decide how they will go about gathering information on the problem or opportunity, and then let the group identify the positive deviants and their effective practices. In addition, guidelines for how these activities will be accomplished need to be established from the group members themselves. As Sternin said, when the intervention in Vietnam began, the Positive Deviance team only went into four villages where local women were trained to compile growth charts of age, weight, and height. It was these same village women who were then asked if they knew of any children under three years of age who came from the same poor families but were not malnourished. If they indeed know of such cases of well nourished children they were asked, "You mean it's possible for a very poor family to have a well-nourished child in this village?" The village women were not only amazed by their discovery, they were eager to immediately go find out what it was that these positively deviant families were doing that was so different and more efficacious around nutrition than the majority.

4. *Identify conventional practices.* Before positively deviant behaviors can be identified, you first have to know what the current, accepted practices are. In the Vietnam case, Sternin suggested that the volunteers observe how all the mothers in the village fed their children as well as what attitudes the mothers had to eating that they were passing down to their children. In this regard, for example, the village volunteers came up with the very interesting and important fact that certain foods were considered too low class or common although they were in fact nourishing. They also found that, because of fear of diarrhea (a common cause of death by dehydration among children in underdeveloped countries), some mothers tried to keep their children from eating very much at all. In addition, the villagers described how, because the parents were so busy, food was often just lying around for children or they were fed only once or twice a day since it was too time consuming. Remember, that as described above, in contrast the positive deviant

children ate small portions many times a day, which enabled them to actually eat more food because "there's only so much rice that a starving child's stomach can hold."

5. *Identify and analyze the deviants.* This stage is easier than may have been thought at first impression since as the villagers tracked how all the community members went about their food gathering, processing, and eating, a list of all the behaviors held in common as well as the positive deviants and their Positive Deviance practices could naturally be seen. Moreover, at the very same time, it became obvious that the small minority of positive deviants had to be doing something better since they had spontaneously solved the problem of malnourishment: their very results proved it! In many cases, however, even the positive deviants did not know why they succeeded where others failed. Asking them how they did would do no good. But in the end, because it was the villagers themselves who found out all of this on their own, they didn't need an outside solution to be imposed on them. It was the villagers who accomplished all this and not the government officials nor the outside experts. At one point, Sternin described how a successful Positive Deviance project plays out, saying that, eventually, "[t]hey will have discovered a new way of doing things themselves, making it their discovery, not yours. Analyze and list the set of behaviors that the deviants have in common. Single out exactly what makes them successful."

6. *Let the deviants adopt deviations on their own.* According to Sternin, rule six is critical for it is quite different than the traditional approach to transferring knowledge. In particular, disseminating positively deviant behavior is not about importing "best practices" from elsewhere (we'll say more about what distinguishes Positive Deviance from best practices later in the chapter), nor is it a matter of reporting on new information. Instead, knowledge transfer in Positive Deviance is about disseminating new *behaviors* and new *practices.* As Sternin liked to say, it is new behavior, not knowledge that is the source of innovation. Instead of *teaching* new knowledge, Positive Deviance encourages new behavior. "Let the people who have discovered the deviations spread the word in their group. Don't require adherence to the new practices, but do offer incentives for it." For example, in Vietnam, a volunteer would invite eight mothers into her home, but the price of entry would be that the mothers were required to bring a contribution of shrimp, crabs, and sweet-potato greens. Then they would all

cook with these ingredients along with the rice. This gathering would continue for about two weeks; thereafter the mothers would do this in their own homes.

7. *Track results and publicize them.* Publicize the results in multiple ways including information broadcasts that highlight the specific targets required and how they were achieved, in order to let other groups develop their own curiosity. Re-observe and post the new results on a periodic basis and track the results quantitatively to demonstrate that the benefits that come with doing things differently.

8. *Repeat steps one through seven.* Here we can see evidence of the recursive operations so crucial in complexity science. As Sternin pointed out, by repeating the whole thing in a cyclical manner, "Chances are that they've discovered new deviations from the new norm. The bell curve of performance keeps moving up, as long as you disseminate the best deviations across the curve and continue to discover new examples of positive deviance among the next group of best performers." Note how here the goal is not based on eliciting average performance that a Bell curve would suggest but instead moving the whole curve upward to yet uncharted measures of performance.

CORPORATE EXAMPLES OF POSITIVE DEVIANCE IN ACTION

Positive Deviance not only has been successful for dealing with long-standing and what had previously been thought to be intractable problems; PD appears to change the very culture of the organizations or communities in which it has been applied. As Jerry Sternin once heard from a Bangladeshi village woman following on the heels of a Positive Deviance program: "Let us tell you about the changes in our lives. We were like seeds locked up in a dark place, and now we have found the light."[7]

These sentiments are not uncommonly spoken by participants in this kind of social or organizational intervention. And lest it be thought that Positive Deviance is only effective in dire situations found in poor countries, in this section we describe two examples of Positive Deviance and its principles being applied in corporate settings. These examples concern two experiments in novelty at Merck Pharmaceuticals, certainly one of the premier companies in the world. The first of these examples has to do with a spontaneous emergence of novelty at the periphery that was not spearheaded by an explicit Positive Deviance intervention. However, the second example concerns an intentional use of Positive Deviance at Merck's Latin American headquarters in Mexico, which Jerry Sternin worked on along with the Chairman and the President of the Plexus Institute in New Jersey, Henri Lipmanowicz and Curt Lindberg, respectively. The Plexus Institute is dedicated to the application of the sciences of complex systems to improving health care throughout the world, in terms of both organizational and health related issues (one of the authors of this book, Goldstein, is a member of the science advisory board of the Plexus Institute). Once we have gone over these examples, we will come back to more guidelines of how generative leaders can use the principles of experiments in novelty in general and Positive Deviance in particular.

POSITIVE DEVIANCE AT MERCK: ERADICATING RIVER BLINDNESS

Merck, of course, is known for many medical breakthroughs as well as a recent bout having to do with well-publicized problems with certain of its medicines. About 30 years ago, the parasitologist Dr. William Campbell, then working at Merck, identified a substance effective against worms in livestock called ivermectin. The drug quickly became the most successful animal medicine in history. Not only did it kill gastrointestinal worms in a single dose, it also killed the biting insects that caused weeping sores on livestock. It had other uses as well; monthly heartworm medication for dogs usually contains ivermectin.[8]

When Campbell first described the invention to Dr. Mohammed Aziz—the primary infectious disease specialist at Merck, they both quickly recognized the unique attributes of ivermectin. Aziz had worked in Africa for the World Health Organization and had seen many cases of river blindness in humans, a very painful and disfiguring ailment found in various regions in the developing world. The disease is caused by parasites growing under human skin, causing painful sores. When these parasites bore through the eyes, blindness occurs—hence the term "river blindness."

It turned out that ivermectin was effective on a related parasite in horses. Campbell and Aziz approached Roy Vagelos, Merck's future CEO who, at that time, as head of research at Merck had established a reputation of openness and support for novel ideas and methods. We have described other aspects of Vagelos' complexity style of leadership in Chapter 2. The two scientists asked Roy for further funding in order to develop and test a human version of ivermectin for treating river blindness, and Vagelos agreed.

However, because river blindness is mostly confined to the developing world, the top management at Merck realized they could not make up for their expenses by distributing the drug for actual use. Also, there was the distinct possibility of side effects, which might harm the drug's eventual reputation for use as a veterinary agent. Nevertheless, Vagelos, by then the CEO, and the other senior leaders at Merck developed the drug at the firm's own expense. In 1987 as the drug was being perfected and readied for distribution, 18 million people around the globe were identified as having river blindness.

But how can a public company serve 18 million non-paying customers? After exhausting governmental and global agency channels, Vagelos decided that Merck would act on its own, significantly departing from the norms of the pharmaceutical industry. Merck chose to make and distribute the drug for free to anyone at risk for river blindness anywhere around the world, and Vagelos pledged to do this for as long as it was necessary. The result significantly contributed to the near eradication of this disabling disease, and continues to make important inroads against related parasitic diseases such as Guinea worm. We see here Positive Deviance in full force: positive outcomes emerging out of significant departures from the norm. And, of course, it didn't hurt Merck's professional and public reputation!

POSITIVE DEVIANCE AT MERCK'S LATIN AMERICAN SALES HEADQUARTERS

The second application of the idea of experiments in novelty at the periphery includes an intentional intervention of Sternin's program of Positive Deviance for the Latin American sales division at Merck. The highlights of this story are told by Roberto Saco as part of his master's degree dissertation at Oxford University.[9] Mr. Saco had access to Jerry Sternin, the previously mentioned representatives from the Plexus Institute, as well as the personnel at Merck involved in the program including their leader Grey Warner.

Operating in Mexico since 1932, the Latin America group has a long-standing reputation for both profitability and innovation. Indeed, Merck is known as one of the 20 best companies to work for in Mexico. Under Grey Warner's leadership, the Latin American Division had been working at *cultural transformation* for a decade. One important ingredient of this objective is called the "Living Dialogue," which aims at better understanding the varied communities of healthcare practice using Merck's products and services. This has also included a commitment to community engagement through establishing close collaborative relationships among the members of these communities of practice, various NGOs whose mission dovetails with these communities, as well as academic and governmental leadership in the geographical areas affected.

Warner Grey avows, "... companies that want to succeed in today's competitive environment need much more [than product innovation]. They need innovation at every point of the compass, in all aspects of the business and among every team member.... Fostering a culture of innovation is critical to success." Grey's points about innovation, to pursue it "at every point of the compass," parallels our complexity science viewpoint that generative leadership supports experiments in novelty and these in turn support an ecology of innovation. Thus, it was within Merck's vision for innovation that the Positive Deviance program in the sales division was inaugurated in 2005 when Jerry Sternin first visited Merck in Mexico.

The first product they examined was Fosamax, a medication opposing osteoporosis. Fosamax is one of Merck's giant products worldwide as well as in Mexico. However, a survey of the sales records in Mexico revealed that only 22 out of the 180 sales representatives were gaining better-than-average sales. Now, 22 divided by180 is only 12 percent; this small percentage should alert the leader to one of the hallmarks of Positive Deviance, namely, that some deviation in terms of experiments in novelty is likely to be at play when a small minority is doing much better than the majority. These statistics, of course, prompt the question of what the successful minority is doing differently than the rest. To be sure, in the application of Positive Deviance all other factors must be equal or it wouldn't be a revealing statistic; for example, the top 12 percent of sales reps might be focusing on wealthy neighborhoods with a high percentage of aging women, or on unique government accounts. In this case, however, the target population and other elements were parallel.

So with these statistics in place, the next step was for a bottom-up identification on the part of the sales representatives themselves of what was different in the sales practices of the positively deviant 12 percent of the Fosamax sales force. First, the usual practice (indeed, this seems to be universal in the pharmaceutical industry) is to have sales representatives visit doctors' offices on a regular basis. This face-to-face aspect is crucial to pharmaceutical sales, but it can be irritating to doctors' busy professional lives. However, in Mexico, the sales representative themselves actually do not close the sale. Instead, the product is actually bought and stocked by a pharmacy. All the rep can do is influence the physician to prescribe the drug. The sales rep is trained to "hit" each target or doctor several times per year with face-to-face selling but the doctors find it time consuming and annoying.

This "design team" of sales employees did not come up with earth-shaking revelations but they did find the following practices that were deviant, that is, were only practiced by the successful minority "at the periphery":

- Although many doctors only considered sales reps as mere vendors, the positively deviant reps were instead perceived as "equals" by the doctors.
- Moreover, these same minority sales representatives had taken the time to build solid partnering relationships with the docs by sharing information beyond simply product specs, that is, they were listening more than selling and selling their knowledge of the product and not the product itself.
- They went deeper into pharmacy purchasing patterns including pharmacy prescription audits to validate the doctors' prescribing patterns.
- They localized their sales pitch.
- They made it a habit to call the physicians on their birthdays and other important events.
- They kept up to date on local current events to facilitate good conversations with the docs.
- They made use of company resources for arranging visits and other logistics.
- They used satisfaction surveys at events.
- They checked pharmacy stocks pre- and post-events in order to gauge the impact of presentations.
- They used visual aids to communicate the product's advantages.
- They constantly repeated the product name as well as the word "new."

By implementing many of these suggestions across the entire sales team, very strong results were gained. Within a year Fosamax showed a 17 percent increase in sales; with a market growing at 13 percent, the entire division managed to reverse its trend of losing market share. Andres Bruzual, the head of one of Merck's three business units in Mexico, spoke highly of the Positive Deviance intervention: "A lot of learning is taking place across the board." Furthermore, in a testament to the power of the bottom-up process itself, Andres has warned that he would *not* initiate a Positive Deviance program if the following conditions held: if managers felt they were the only problem solvers; if the groups were too small; if the circumstances were highly politicized; or if internal competition was too high (which is certainly true in many sales situations).

Other overall learning coming out of the series of Positive Deviance interventions are also relevant. Participants realized that Positive Deviance should not be considered a one-shot program, but rather a Positive Deviance intervention must be part of a long-range and wide-spread initiative to foster an innovative internal environment. This is precisely our point about systematizing novelty and adaptation by establishing an ecology of innovation. Participants were also somewhat concerned that changes were too sparse, an issue that Sternin himself complained about in terms of fragmented effort. In that context, there was talk about the dangers of being too connected with only one product. As a result they decided on "de-Fosamaxing" the process, that is, encouraging novel practices with other products and services.

IT IS EASIER TO PRACTICE THAN TO THINK YOUR WAY TO A NEW BEHAVIOR

One of Jerry Sternin's favorite sayings about Positive Deviance interventions is that it is easier to practice than think your way to a new behavior. This was confirmed in Vietnam, at Merck, and at the many other organizations and communities that have realized that novel practices at the periphery can sometimes contain the seeds of innovation for an entire complex system. However, those seeds take root only when they are harvested and planted—through new behaviors—rather than simply being talked about by the positive deviants. Note how both of these innovations at the periphery—the health practices in Vietnam and the sales practices at Merck—are parallel to the process a complex system undergoes in the emergence of new order. Fluctuations or perturbations in a system can generate unexpected novelty that represents a significant departure from the norm. What begins as only an outlier effect can eventually become the seed that changes the whole system. Whereas a management of control typically dampens or ignores such innovations, generative leadership sees these deviations as a potential logic for a new order. This new logic, if it can become embedded in the rest of the system, can make the entire organization more effective and adaptive.

HOW POSITIVE DEVIANCE DIFFERS FROM BENCHMARKING

It might seem that by highlighting specific practices that work better than others and then disseminating these practices throughout the system, Positive Deviance is just another form of the best practices approach to benchmarking. However, from both a complexity science perspective and Jerry Sternin's own insights, Positive Deviance differs significantly in many respects to benchmarking. Certainly, benchmarking has proven a very useful tool for improving organizational performance; our aim is not to criticize it in general. Rather, by pointing to the important differences between Positive Deviance and best practice implementation, we believe a surer grasp of the complexity aspects of Positive Deviance can be had.

Simply put, the implementation of best practices takes a work process or practice found effective in one environment, and then transplants it (often with customization) to another environment—in the belief that what worked in one place will also work in the new one. However, as Sternin put it, this transplantation does not pay enough heed to the *contextual* details of the place where the practice was initially developed. In contrast, the Positive Deviance approach focuses precisely on those very details *within* the same social system.[10] The importance of context is a key finding within complexity science, with its concern on how complex systems exhibit adaptability to their changing environments. What "context" means is precisely these variations in environments, which are always changing and thus confronting the system with the need to stay abreast and adapt. Organizations are not only unique, possessing different weaknesses and strengths so they shouldn't be treated the same, their contextual environments are also unique, changing according to their own patterns and rhythms. Best practices in particular and benchmarking in general fail to acknowledge this crucial fact about the interrelationship between systems and their contexts.

Furthermore, whereas benchmarking tends to focus on identifying the best and most effective process or approach with efficiency as the highest value, Positive Deviance does not assume that efficiency is the most appropriate guide for adaptation to environmental change, especially when efficiency is defined in terms of lower costs or higher production rates. Instead, experiments of novelty at the periphery are all about *new results*, not ones measurable by some preset standard of what the costs or time of production should be. Thus, whereas benchmarking is about repeating what has previously proven successful, Positive Deviance is about innovations that face toward a new future. Such innovations are inherently idiosyncratic and hence are not amenable, when they first appear, to analysis via efficiency considerations.

Whereas benchmarking brings ideas and concepts from outside to inside an organization, Positive Deviance, as a method of identifying experiments in novelty at the periphery but within the organization or community, assumes that innovation is already emerging *inside* the organization. Bringing something from outside and imposing it on others will virtually always bring some measure of resistance to change; therefore leaders using benchmarking must be ready with all sorts of tactics to overcome this resistance to change. However, positive deviants are members of the same group as the majority, and therefore their practices do not have to be imported. As we described before, Sternin pointed out that the innovative practices discovered and disseminated by the positive deviants have the advantage of not provoking an immune reaction from the host, since they are part of the very host's "body." Experiments in novelty at the periphery are inherently accessible to everyone in the social system because it is members of the same social system who came up with the idea in the first place.

Sternin has pointed out that best practices face such a strong challenge of replication that benchmarking often fails. Positive Deviance focuses on replicating the *process*, not the solution:

> [Solutions are] context-specific and contingent on resources, local conditions, politics, and the like, and are therefore not universally adaptable. You cannot transplant a model grown in one soil to another and expect it to flourish. Externally identified solutions might require specific conditions that your business or organization does not offer. Simply transferring the technical solution will not be sufficient.

While benchmarking is about replicating outcomes, Positive Deviance is about replicating the process of learning new approaches. The respect and ownership generated through this "process of discovery" by those inside the problem and thus owning the solution is irreplaceable.

CONCLUSION: A GENERATIVE LEADERSHIP OF POSITIVE DEVIANCE

In a conversation with Roberto Saco, Jerry Sternin clarified how he saw the role of leadership in the utilization of Positive Deviance: the emphasis is on facilitation from the perspective of a participant/observer and not on prescription.[11] Indeed, for Positive Deviance to work successfully, the leader/facilitator must in a sense blend into the background so that the group members have an opportunity for learning within the community. In this capacity,

Jerry liked to quote from the Chinese sage Lao Tzu in his classic Tao de Ching:

> Learn from the people
> Plan with the people
> Begin with what they have
> Build on what they know.
> Of the best leaders
> When their task is accomplished
> The people all remark
> "We have done it ourselves."

With this style in mind, let's close the chapter by recapitulating the six "D's" of Positive Deviance, which also apply to leading experiments in novelty in general as part of the strategy of creating an ecology of innovation:

Define what the problem is, exactly, and determine the desired outcome. This relates to what we have been calling opportunity tension. The leader identifies the natural stress on the system that comes about when an opportunity is recognized in the environment by the members of an organization, but they also realize that, as currently configured, the system is unable to realize its potential. Generative change is required.

Determine the individuals and groups of individuals who are already exhibiting the desired outcome within the common behaviors in the community. These are the persons or groups who represent the kind of novelty outside the norm that if replicated can change the system. This confers on them the status of being positive deviants within the system.

Discover those unique practices or behaviors that enable the positive deviants to find better solutions. This means carefully investigating exactly how and through what differences in practices their novelty bestows advantages on those who practice them.

Design and implement social interventions whereby the majority have access to and learn the new practices inherent in the novel successes of the positive deviants.

Discern the ongoing pulse of the organization by implementing mechanisms that provide continuing monitoring and evaluation of the emergent novelty, initiatives, and other experiments across the organization.

Disseminate the successful innovations on as wide a scale as possible throughout the organization. As changes to practice diffuse widely, system wide change, and emergent order at a new level becomes possible as we described in chapters 3 and 4.

Intriguingly, most of these elements reflect action across an entire social system—throughout the social network. Understanding how social networks are structured can therefore support the process of Positive Deviance, as well as further all the elements of an ecology of innovation. Thus, in the next chapter, we explore the nature of social networks, and reveal key insights about the structure and formation of networks for generative leadership.

NOTES

1. One of the authors of this book, Jeffrey Goldstein, had the good fortune of learning Positive Deviance while working as a co-consultant with Jerry and Monique Sternin in 2006. Much of the material on PD in this chapter is culled from the time Jeffrey spent with the Sternins on this project. The chapter is supplemented, however, from other sources containing information about PD as indicated in the endnotes. Sadly, Jerry Sternin passed away while this book was being written.

2. Saco, R. (2005). *Good companies: Organizations discovering the good in themselves by using Positive Deviance as a change management strategy.* MSc Dissertation, HEC Paris, Oxford Executive Education, Oxford University.

3. Dorsey, D. (2000). Positive Deviant—Jerry Sternin. *Fast Company,* December. Available at the Plexus Institute website: http://www. plexusinstitute.org/ideas/show_elibrary.cfm?id=270.

4. See the website devoted to PD: http://www.positivedeviance.org.

5. Mathews, R., & Wacker, W. (2002). *The Deviant's Advantage.* New York: Random House, p. 240.

6. Dorsey, D. (2000). Positive Deviant—Jerry Sternin. *Fast Company.*

7. Ibid.

8. Vagelos, R., & Galambos, L. (2004). *Medicine, science, and Merck.* Cambridge: Cambridge University Press.

9. Saco, R. (2005). *Good companies.*

10. Bertels, T., & Sternin, J. (2003). Replicating results and managing knowledge. In *Rath and Strong's six sigma leadership handbook.* Hoboken, NJ: John Wiley and Sons, pp. 450–457.

11. Saco, R. (2005). *Good companies,* p. 19.

CHAPTER 7

LEADING THROUGH SMART NETWORKS

A key theme throughout this book, one that sharply distinguishes it from other works in the genre of leadership/management/ organizational theory, is that complexity is not something to be avoided or somehow damped down but instead is capable of yielding great dividends if it is embraced in the appropriate manner. In this chapter, we offer many insights from burgeoning research into social networks, one of the most intense and promising areas of complexity science, in order to show how leaders can reap benefits through transmuting their organizations' complex social networks into *smart* networks that play a inimitable role in constructing ecologies of innovation. Smart networks contain this potential since it is through them that the identification and dissemination of experiments in novelty can become the requisite seeds of innovation. At the same time, smart social networks enable rapid adaptation to a relentlessly changing environment.

One might think that network approaches are only workable on a small scale since they are tricky to control as an organization grows. But as our example demonstrates, this impression is simply not the case: networks have become the linchpin in nothing less than the US Military in its radical revision of modern warfare. This shift toward network-centric warfare can be readily seen in the revised interpretation of two of the traditional standbys of military doctrine, namely, economy of force, and concentration of mass, as found in the U.S. Army's most recent *Field Manual*.[1]

Economy of force was understood by the great German military strategist Carl von Clausewitz as not allowing troops or weapons to remain idle during a battle. Instead, every aspect of the military system should be geared toward the objective of winning the battle and the war. Historical exemplars of economy of force are easy to find; for example, contemporary military strategist Clark Murdoch describes why, during the American Civil War in the 1860s, General Robert E. Lee's Confederate army was able to defeat the far more numerous forces of General Joseph Hooker's Union army: over half of Hooker's troops were never engaged during the battle! Another example occurred at the decisive Battle of Midway in WWII when Japanese Admiral Yamamoto's suffered a defeat by Admiral Nimitz's command which comprised less than half as many warships since many of the Japanese ships were thousands of miles away (some of them trying to lure the U.S. fleet toward the Aleutian Islands).[2]

The idea of concentration of mass in military strategy refers to a *massing* of combat power to "disrupt, divert, delay, or destroy" enemy resources. Murdoch points out that it was precisely this kind of "massing" that was *not* done in WWI when the German General Erich Ludendorff frittered away his mass of combat power on the "line of least resistance" by repeatedly changing the objectives of his offensive, and in so doing, disconnecting with his operational design. "Mass" in this sense means knowing both where and when to attack as well as where and when not to attack. A positive example was General Douglas MacArthur's strategy in the Pacific theater in WWII to bypass Japanese strongholds, and instead seize more loosely defended airfields and harbors such as on New Guinea and the Admiralty Islands.

These two stanchions of military strategy have undergone a dramatic reorientation due to the vast increase and accessibility of information that has become available on and off the battlefield. Technological advances in information processing and communicational networks have led to the emergence of "network centric warfare" [NCW]. As David Alberts, John Garstka, and Frederick Stein have emphasized, "In essence, NCW translates information superiority into combat power by effectively linking knowledgeable entities in the battle space."[3]

The architecture underlying NCW is the integration of three layers of networks: (1) a "sensor grid" made up of highly interconnected satellites, radar, optical devices, acoustic systems (sonar), as well as people-based intelligence gathering (somewhat similar to the inter-cohesion network described in Chapter 5); (2) an "information grid" consisting of communication linkages, data transmission pathways, and computerized command centers; and (3) a "transaction grid" drawing upon the information generated from the first two grids to galvanize and align troops and weapons where they are needed at any particular phase of a battle. The information revolution is allowing for real time sensing and action in relation to enemy positions and capabilities. With these new information capabilities, a geographically dispersed force can operate as a single integrated system, able to focus on tightly defined and precisely specified micro-level targets. NCW leverages new degrees of information and connectivity through a network of troops and other military resources, resulting in a fulfillment of military goals to maximize connectivity, capability, and parallelism, while minimizing serial chains.[4] At the core of this enhancement is a deep and novel understanding of social networks to which we now turn.

A WORLD OF SOCIAL NETWORKS

It is not just the military, of course, that is benefiting from the vast new social networks connecting all parts of the world. Indeed, a striking sign of our time is the flurry of social networking taking place through Facebook, Myspace, LinkedIn, Twitter, Second Life and all the other forums. Not only teenagers and young adults are caught up in this frenzy of virtual socializing. It has also become an indispensable mainstay for business, commerce, and social action involving people of all ages. In concert with the internet, the ubiquity of these new technologically enhanced social networks have truly made our planet a much smaller world.

In fact, social networks constitute the underlying social structure of all of our organizations rendering them thereby as the means through which leadership operates in communicating, influencing, and allocating resources. Building effective social networks is critical for furthering business alliances, developing collaborations, and pursuing new opportunities.[5] Research shows that many benefits accrue from establishing more effective professional social networks:[6]

- Work teams with better linkages to other teams inside and outside the organization finish their assignments faster.
- Teams with heightened social connectivity discover better ways of getting their jobs done and then are more able to effectively transfer their newly discovered knowledge.
- Managers with "better connections" both inside and outside the organization are able to spot and then develop more opportunities for both their departments and their organization as a whole.
- Project managers with better network connections are more successful in reaching project goals within time and financial parameters.

But these are just a few of the advantages coming from an intelligent establishment of strong social linkages. To better appreciate how social network connectivity can be utilized by generative leadership, we need to get a handle on the dynamics and structure of social networks.

MULTIPLIER EFFECTS AND THE IMPORTANCE OF DIFFERENCES

The basics of social networks are quite simple: the fundamental unit consists of a node, also known as an agent, which is connected to other nodes by edges or links. Already connected nodes/agents are then connected to other nodes/agents, a process iterated many times in order to constitute the full connectivity characterizing a particular social network, and ultimately, our entire modern world. There are many factors involved in this connectivity that can significantly enable or impede the flow of information and resources within a social network.

Certainly, from simply visualizing one or even several nodes connected to one another, even when this process is iterated, it's still not easy to appreciate what is so important about social network connectivity. But underneath these apparently lineal connections is a multiplier effect—a significant disproportionality that can only be described using *nonlinear* mathematics. In particular, the high degree of nonlinearity in networks is exemplified by what is known as Metcalfe's Law of Network Utility which describes how the utility of a network increases with the *square* of the number of nodes in the network. Thus, whereas 10 nodes permit 100 possible connections (100 being 10^2), 100 nodes allow for 10,000 connections![7] Imagine the utility of a network consisting of 10,000 or even 10 million nodes, which are no longer uncommon figures pertaining to network connectivity. Such a nonlinear multiplier effect is even augmented many times over when we take into consideration all the information possibilities opened up by attached documents, photos, videos, artwork, diagrams, blueprints, spread sheets, games, and on and on. Indeed, it strains the imagination to even consider the immensity of this connectivity.

Along the same lines as the discussion in Chapter 5 concerning Scott Page's research into the key role of *differences* in complex systems, it is important to recognize the importance of differences among nodes to the flow of information through a network, a dynamic analogous to how the flow of electric current requires a difference in polarity, positive and negative. Here again Gregory Bateson's definition of information comes into play—information is "a difference that makes a difference." Without difference within a social network, there is only a paltry amount of new information generated or transmitted, just more of the same. As Page proved, differences are an indispensable ingredient for more effective problem solving and decision making, as well as for making more correct prediction of trends.[8]

Consider, for example, the kind of dense social network called a "cluster" such as a group of friends who get together every Saturday night. These friends are likely to share likes and dislikes, and they primarily talk about what they are familiar with. Thus, the chance that *differences* will be expressed is low, and consequently any new information flow that comes from sources internal to the cluster will be low. If new information is needed, however—if the group has to fulfill a unique task or wants to pursue something they've never done, they will have to expand their network connections to include one or more nodes with substantial differences. Likewise, recall the insight around the strength of weak ties, which we described in Chapter 5: dense networks of strong ties are simply ineffective for finding a new job. Specifically, research has found that only 16 percent of employed persons got their jobs through a "strong" tie network, that is, from within the kind of friendship cluster structure described earlier, whereas the other 84 percent were able to find a new job through "weak tie" contacts that they only saw "occasionally" or even "rarely."[9]

THE LENGTH OR "DEGREES OF SEPARATION" IN SOCIAL NETWORKS

Another important characteristic of a social network is the "length" of connectivity, that is, the number of nodes that exist *between* any other node or agent. The average *length* of a particular network, otherwise known as the *degree of separation*, is the basis of the well-known "Six Degrees of Separation" idea at the center of John Guare's play and movie. This whimsical expression also relates to the "Six Degrees of Kevin Bacon" game, the object of which was to guess how connected Hollywood stars are with each other. In this social network game, the popular actor Kevin Bacon is used as the intermediary node from which all other degrees of separation are calculated. For example, if one star acted directly with Kevin Bacon in a movie, they would have zero degrees of separation with him, but if they were in a movie with someone who had acted with Kevin Bacon, then they would have one degree of separation from Kevin Bacon. It's hard to know how Kevin Bacon became the target for this game but probably it had to do with his having acted in a large number of movies of very varied types. The aim of the Kevin Bacon game is to determine how "small" the network "world" is that connects Hollywood stars to one another. It turns out that it's quite hard to identify actors with more than four degrees of separation from Kevin Bacon.[10]

The origin of the idea "six degrees of separation" (and that of a small world) goes back to research conducted by Stanley Milgram, otherwise known for his powerful social psychological experiments on conformity and the proclivity to violence.[11] Milgram researched "small world" networks by investigating the network path lengths in acquaintance-based social networks, that is, how closely connected people were to each other in their social networks. Remember that network length refers to how many other agents are *between* one agent and another. Participants in Milgram's experiments were asked to pass a letter to one of their first-name acquaintances in order to get the letter to an assigned target. Although most of the letters never reached the target, about a quarter did, passing through only an average of six intermediaries on the way, hence the expression "six degrees of separation." This might seem hard to believe but in many rounds of playing a "small-world" game with friends and colleagues in workshops, one of the authors of this book (Goldstein) managed to find even fewer than six intermediaries linking a farmer in the middle of China with a politician in South America, two nodes that would presumably be vastly separated from each other.

FILTERS IN SOCIAL NETWORKS

The information that is transmitted in a social network can be understood in terms of three dimensions: relevance, accuracy, and timeliness.[12] If one of these dimensions is low, then the value of the information is questionable. For example, imagine a sales focused corporation whose information about consumer spending patterns is 98 percent accurate, yet this information is six months out of date. In general, the longer a social network, that is, the greater the number of intermediary nodes along the pathways, the less relevant, accurate, and timely the information tends to be.

The inverse relationship between network length and value of information is magnified by the existence of *filters* at each node by which the agent modifies the content of what's being transmitted. This is played out in many ways. Traditional bureaucracies, for example, typically reduce the quantity and quality of information being sent up and down the organizational hierarchy. Thus we have the well-known "mum effect" whereby employees lower in the organization are reluctant to speak truthfully to those in higher level positions for fear of the consequences resulting from honest communication. In this context, one of the authors (Goldstein) had once started working in an executive position in a corporation, three layers down from the CEO. About two weeks into the job he was standing outside his office door when the CEO passed by and asked him how everything was going. During this brief conversation, the CEO asked Goldstein if he had yet spoken to the head of a certain department. Since he hadn't, he guilelessly replied "not yet but I've left a message." Five minutes later, after Goldstein entered his office, he received a phone call from the department head about whom the CEO had asked. This department head asked Goldstein why he told the CEO that he couldn't be reached! Never again did that CEO receive anything resembling the truth!

Because of the rampant "mum" effect that such encounters with the CEO engendered, Goldstein wasn't that surprised a couple of years later (and in a new job) when he heard about a scandal at this same corporation involving a $7 million embezzlement by a senior manager who had created an entirely fraudulent outside company that was selling nonexistent and very expensive equipment to the firm. The "mum effect" was no doubt one of the reasons that this kind of larceny had not been detected earlier!

AN OVERVIEW OF SOCIAL NETWORK STRUCTURES

One of the most important features of a social network is its structure, also called its topology, which refers to the specific patterns by which nodes are connected to each other. A network's topology has significant influence on how information is shared and acted on in a social ecology. For example, a very simple network structure or topology is the "line" in which the links between one agent and the next are connected like the cars of a commuter train. In a "line" structured social network, information can only flow through each intermediate agent, from one end of the "line" to another. In contrast, a particularly dense type of network is called a "mesh" in which every node is directly connected to every other node. Obviously, in a fully connected mesh, the network structure makes it much easier and faster for each agent to reach every other agent directly with new information. Email, of course, has facilitated movement in this direction, not only in otherwise very large corporations or government bureaucracies but just about across the whole span of the planet where a *virtual* kind of connectivity can link agents in an incredibly fast manner. On the other hand, not only is such deep connectivity unlikely in any social ecology, the vast amount of information circulating around in a mesh would overwhelm virtually all of its agents.

Thus, the typology of a network can explain a lot about how information—differences—can be utilized in appropriate ways. Here we examine six common social network structures as to their advantages and disadvantages, dense clusters, hub networks, random networks, scale-free networks, small world networks, and smart networks. Later we suggest ways they can be shaped, influenced, and utilized by generative leadership.

DENSE CLUSTERS

A common type of network topology is the dense cluster—we've mentioned this already in the context of close knit friendship groups, work teams, or neighborhood-based ethnic groups. The density of such clusters stems from the large number of direct, within-cluster connections from each agent to others in the network. The extreme example of this kind of structure is the completely connected mesh topology. As we just described, this kind of dense cluster can approach Metcalfe's Law, where the total number of links is equivalent to the *square* of the number of other nodes in the network. For example, a dense cluster with 100 military personnel, could generate nearly 10,000 links connecting these 100 nodes. Such a rapid increase in complexity allows for a huge increase in information, flexibility, and innovation, but it also introduces the risks associated with cognitive overload and competing influences that must be overcome if timely decisions are to me made and acted upon.[13]

Even in very dense clusters it is rare that every member is directly linked to every other member. Rather, there are smaller clusters within larger ones, so that a member in one small cluster is linked to a member of another small cluster through intermediary nodes of others in either small clusters. An intriguing example of how subclusters can emerge within a dense cluster was reported by anthropologist Paul Tapsell and organizational researcher Christine Woods,[14] in their study of the Maori indigenous community in New Zealand. Although the Maori as a whole are a very dense cluster network, Tapsell and Woods found two competing subgroups among them—the older generation and the younger generation—each with differing views on a range of issues that the community was facing. Tapsell and Woods argue that such intergenerational division into smaller subgroup clusters can be found in the wake of many political systems that were originally colonial. Although leadership within such smaller dense clusters may have originally been established to counter colonial rule, collective influence can become diluted by this intergenerational divisiveness. Because dense networks can be self-reinforcing, the very density of the network structure of these smaller subgroups can be counterproductive in restoring the viability of larger ethnic and cultural goals such as more equitable resource exploitation or improvements in urban development.

HUB NETWORKS

Another type of social network structure is the *hub* network, in which certain nodes or agents play a centralized role amongst all the links connecting the nodes. A clear example is the traditional airline hub network. Delta Airlines has a hub in Atlanta. U.S. Air has hubs in Philadelphia and Charlotte NC. American Airlines has a hub in Miami. Usually, the geographical placement of a hub reflects the dominant air travel routes of the airline. Thus, Miami is an important hub of American Airlines because American has a brisk business connecting the United States with Central America, the Caribbean, and South America, with Miami being geographically advantageous stepping-off cite for traveling south. A hub network has the positive outcome of reducing costs because smaller, more cost-effective airplanes can be used to fly passengers from less populated areas to hub airports first before transferring them to other aircraft that are bound for other destinations. The hubs also offer the convenience and efficiency of centralized maintenance facilities.

A drawback to a hub network is that the "hub" nodes actually increase the length of the network, which decreases efficiency in two key ways. First, since so many routes pass through the hub, increased length means that information and resources take longer to move around the network. Second, hubs lead to increased information distortion due to the presence of more filters that come along with more intermediary nodes. In addition, since a hub network structure requires that some nodes have a very large number of linkages—technically called "high degree" nodes—hub networks are especially vulnerable to breakdown. Even if only one of these high degree nodes in a hub is taken out of commission, a large part of the network becomes nonfunctional. That is why hubs in a hub network are prime targets for terrorism.

RANDOM NETWORKS

Perhaps the longest studied network is the *random* network, a structure in which the nodes and links are laid down in a random fashion, with the degree of each node distributed according to a normal statistical distribution.[15] Examples of the random social network structures can be seen in the connections among people who are randomly mingling in a large party (i.e., without the host intentionally introducing guests to each other), or in the grid system of highways in the rural United States that link cities and towns of different sizes. One important feature of the normal distribution of degrees for various nodes in a random network is that most agents have a similar number of links (the median), while, a few nodes have either a very high or very low number of connections (a very high or very low degree). One might note that a random network is associated with little or no allowance for individual preferences and interdependence. In a random network, each choice to connect is assumed to be independent of all others, a situation that is uncommon in human experience. Even at a large party people tend to connect with others based upon personal preferences and their prior experience with connections.

SCALE-FREE NETWORKS

Most of the social networks studied in depth in recent years have not been random (and normally distributed) but rather are "scale-free" networks, so called because the patterns of connection are similar across multiple scales. In contrast to the random network with its normal distribution of degree across all nodes, a scale-free network reveals a characteristic *power law* distribution, with many nodes having only a few links, a moderate number of nodes have a moderate number of links, and a few nodes have very many links. Power law distributions, like the ones we discussed in Chapter 5, have been found in many diverse types of systems, including genetic networks, metabolic networks in *E. coli* bacteria and other living forms, scientific collaboration networks, e-mail messages, human sexual contacts networks, electronic circuits, and the distribution of the number of cities with a particular population.[16]

One very important property in the build up of scale-free networks is that the nodes with the most links are the ones most likely to gain more links. This is due to what's called "preferential attachment" or "cumulative advantage;" in network terminology, the highest-degree nodes grow much more rapidly than the nodes with lesser degree. This "rich-get-richer" dynamic has been called the "Mathew Effect" by the preeminent sociologist Robert King Merton after *Matthew* 25:29, "For unto every one that hath shall be given, and he shall have abundance: but from him that hath not shall be taken away even that which he hath"; or as Billie Holiday memorialized in *God Bless the Child:* "Them thats got shall get. Them thats not shall lose . . ."[17]

A host of scale-free networks appear to exhibit the Matthew Effect, including the World Wide Web (consider the growth in degree of nodes like Google, Yahoo, Facebook, and YouTube), the Internet in general (although this is a subject of hot debate among computer scientists), protein interactions in certain kinds of yeast, and so forth. This property is very important for leadership, since, according to complexity science research, innovations are more likely in scale-free collaborative networks that reflect "cumulative advantage."

Further, some argue that many natural, spontaneously growing networks, ones typically thought of as emerging through self-organization as discussed in Chapter 4, grow through this dynamic of preferential attachment. For example, a webpage with many incoming links will tend to attract more links than a webpage with fewer incoming linkages. Cities also seem to have this property since once a settlement begins, more and more people prefer to settle in the same area because of the increase of services, protection, and other resources available at this site. But to the extent that cities possess scale-free social network structures, we would also expect to find in them the "poor get poorer" dynamic, which gets exhibited as an increasing impoverishment of the already marginalized subpopulations.[18]

Another feature of scale-free networks is their great resilience against systemic failure: even if a huge number of nodes are (randomly) eliminated, the networks tend not to exhibit degradation. This property follows from their power law distribution; since scale-free networks contain a huge prevalence of nodes with few linkages, eliminating any of these nodes will not have much effect on the network as a whole. Thus, even if some terrible computer virus wiped out a very large number of nodes the overall structure of the web would remain. Studies suggest this would be true even if the virus destroyed nodes with huge degree such as Google, Yahoo, and Facebook.

SMALL WORLD NETWORKS

Another type of social network that has gained considerable attention is the *small-world* network, in which linkages between nodes have as few intermediaries as possible. The result is a kind of "small-world," as in the "six degrees of separation" social network described earlier.[19] The links that tend to make networks "smaller world" are typically "weak tie" links that connect dense "strong tie" networks with one another. Below we'll look at how leaders can begin to construct smart networks by first creating "smaller worlds" within their organization. Adding just a few links can greatly improve social network connectivity and in the process bring great benefits to the entire organization.

SMART NETWORKS—A NEW MODEL OF ORGANIZING

In some of the most remarkable scientific success stories of the last decade, neuroscientists have recently been classifying many of the network structures that connect neurons within the human cerebral cortex. In one case, using the latest in advanced brain imagery technology and cutting-edge network analysis techniques, Hagmann and his colleagues discovered that neuron activation activity is transmitted across the cerebral cortex through a unique kind of network structure shown in figure 7.1.[20]

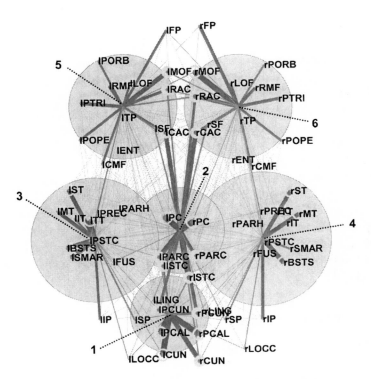

Figure 7.1   Network Structure of the Human Cerebral Cortex

This diagram is a map of actual neuronal networks in the human brain: the grey circles identify six key *modules* or operating centers; the much smaller circles are nodes where the thick nerve transmitting lines meet linking anatomical sub-regions of the cerebral cortex; and the thickest lines represent the major linkages connecting the modules with the outlying nodes. As we will see in this chapter, the specific network structure (or topology) of the human cerebral cortex implied by this model can be classified as a combination of a *hub* network connecting six main modules or centers of linkages along with additional strong connections to more peripheral regions. Hagmann and his colleagues call this unique structure a "smart" network, since the human brain represents the epitome of natural intelligence.

The particular details of this structure need not concern us here, except in so far as they indicate that Hagmann and his colleagues have in effect discovered a uniquely complex structure that characterizes a particularly *smart* network, the one that appears to operate within the human brain. Because human intelligence represents the best natural example of evolved information gathering and use that has been identified, there is ample reason to consider the potential benefits of this structure as it might apply to organizations. The potential for this network to facilitate intelligent choices and to organize complex actions can be better appreciated by contrasting it with the *social* network structure that is typically implied by a company's organizational chart.

In the main, traditional organizational designs demonstrate several salient features of a *not-so-smart* network. First, in highly centralized companies, unidirectional top-down decision making means that information must pass through many intermediary nodes as it cascades from top to bottom. This serves to both slow down the flow and to filter or distort the content of the information as various layers absorb and filter it. Not only does this degrade performance directly, it also leads to political behaviors that exploit information asymmetries to further personal ambition, often at the expense of the organization's goals.

Although the use of new technologies means that in practice few organizations are completely dominated by such a network structure today, many organizations still maintain this model of information flow in their formal structure. Many even guard it in an effort to retain control. This means that some members of the organization think the system operates one way, while the informal system actually gets things done in quite a different way, often with different priorities and objectives. Because the formal hierarchy is maintained as a façade, there is actually very little understanding of how information actually flows through the organization's social network. No wonder it is so difficult to change, to innovate and to adapt. No one really knows how the system works.

In this kind of not-so-smart social network structure there is also the serious drawback stemming from what can be called the *bottleneck* of complexity. If complexity is defined in terms of differences and variations, a bottleneck structure can form between the information-rich agents at the edges of the organization and the top-level decision makers. It's a "bottleneck" because there is simply too much information trying to squeeze through too small an opening. Very few individuals on the top rungs of the hierarchy have access to the fertile differences within the system. This leads to less innovation and adaptation as compared to what might be perceived to be both needed and possible by people lower in the organization. Where does this nascent innovation potential go? Unfortunately, it is neither realized, absorbed nor processed. Rather it is ignored. As we describe throughout this book, adaptation requires matching the organization to the environment. By failing to recognize requisite complexity, not-so-smart-network structures impose fatal barriers to information flow that block change and adaptation processes.

In contrast, as figure 7.1 shows, the brain's network structure shows evidence of a scale-free structure, with hub clustering, peripheral clustering, and linkages between core hub modules and peripheral clusters. To the extent that this particular network structure reflects the evolution of human intelligence, it presents a striking picture of a *smart* network, more specifically a network structure that favors *distributed intelligence* among its different sub-regions. Indeed, networks that combine scale-free, hub-type, and clustered periphery networks tend to be associated with naturally growing, "self-organizing" complex systems that are constrained by system-level demands from the environment. Within these systems, "like attracts like" and linkages reflect the pathways within which a kind of network intelligence is embodied.[21] One may notice that this topology hints at a departmental structure common in organizations. However, smart networks avoid degenerating into silo structures or fiefdoms by also enabling intercohesion among sub-regions (or "departments") as we described in Chapter 5.

ORGANIZING SMART NETWORKS—EXAMPLES

The smart network of the human brain discovered by Hagmann and his colleagues is quite similar to the "smart" social network that social entrepreneur June Holley advocates for organizations aiming at ongoing innovation. Over the past 20 years, June Holley has become well known for developing economic and social capital across Appalachia, in ways that have enhanced individual lives and revitalized whole communities. With her relational innovations she has established richly resonant social networks among home and cottage industries, and taught community leaders the skills that she calls "networkweaving."[22] By connecting fledgling home-based and cottage industries into larger viable (smart) networks, she reinvigorated whole communities that had previously been relegated to intractable poverty. Holley's networkweaving increases the density of existing clusters, and more importantly she helped connect these clusters to previously isolated agents or groups such as home-based businesses, outside suppliers, manufacturers, distributors, and customers.

The social networks that Holley helped create are "smart" in the sense that they combine the scale free topology that results from preferential attachment with structural intercohesion across highly connected expert clusters such as marketing, distribution, manufacturing and so forth. By enabling interaction resonance both within and across clusters, smart networks like these promote cooperation, openness to innovation, and adaptability.[23] As figure 7.1 shows, these networks are comprised of a group of centralized high-degree nodes in the "middle". These are connected together to form a core of hubs (corresponding to the yellow modules in the human cortex). The hubs are then each connected outwards to lesser degree nodes that exist away from the center, closer to the environment. In short an effective smart network within a human organization, shown in figure 7.2, looks a lot like the human brain.

Smart social networks favor the development of viable and sustainable communities. A core of multiple hubs can easily connect scores of scattered clusters in a way that avoids bottlenecks since decision making is distributed across the centralized hubs as well as among the clusters at the periphery.[24] This reflects a *heterarchical* structure that, in contrast to the hierarchical structure of classic bureaucracy, combines the best of both organizational worlds: the most informed aspects of centralized decision making exist side by side with openness to informed decision making close to the action. This approach reinforces innovative ideas that are bubbling up across the organization. The smart network structure in turn "feeds" these new ideas into the core hubs.

A smart network structure that is also characterized by strong interaction resonance allows for bidirectional influence and information flow and avoids costly bottlenecks. As we described in Chapter 2, interaction resonance enables the expression and sustain

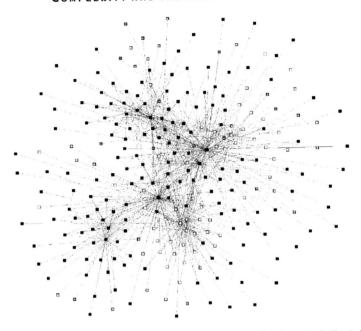

Figure 7.2 A Version of Holley's Smart Network-Multi-hub/Periphery Networks

of relevant informational differences, and promotes a rich reciprocity between the core hubs and the peripheries. In this powerful nexus of information flow, innovation and ultimately adaptability flourish in the organization. It is through this nexus that investments in generative leadership pay their dividends. By bridging differences across the hubs and among the peripheral networks, information and resources flow freely so that patterns can be recognized, tested and reinforced without losing or ignoring the complexity that is resident inside the organization's own network or within that of its ecosystem.

This feature of innovation is based on the "strength of weak ties," which is a part of the underlying structure of *smart* networks as well as the intercohesion networks described in Chapter 5. As we've presented before, the strong ties that comprise dense networks generally reinforce those members' existing store of information, beliefs, and experiences. In contrast, links to acquaintances outside the cluster, that is, connections from a node within a cluster to a node outside of it, tend to be weaker than the strong ties within the cluster. Novelty arises because there is a greater probability that information received through weak ties is going to be different than what already exists within a cluster or clique. Interaction resonance, across the weak ties and within the cluster, sustains and clarifies these differences until effective experiments in novelty can emerge as was described in Chapter 5.

As we pointed out earlier, it's been shown that advances in scientific fields are more likely to be found through the importation of new knowledge acquired through weak ties rather than strong ties.[25] Moreover, there are vastly more weak ties than strong ones in very large networks, for example, making up a city. This means that although most of these weak links carry insignificant information, the ones that do indeed carry significant information are prevalent due to their large number.

Thus, the key for increasing the likelihood of innovation lies in being connected by weak links to the outside and, equally important, in being open to and being able to sustain and even amplify the "weak" signals carried along the weak ties. These weak signals are what Jacqueline Novogratz, the founder of the "The Acumen Fund" who we quoted earlier in the book, is getting at when she describes the social entrepreneurs with whom her fund invests. In many areas, government and large NGOs are failing to deliver essential services like affordable health care or clean water. Thus, instead of focusing on those centralized networks, the Acumen Fund looks for entrepreneurs who are "in the trenches" so to speak—close to low-income community members who are at the edges of society's social network. From the periphery come innovative approaches— Novogratz describes "what can happen when an entrepreneur looks to the market as a listening device, tailoring services and products to the preferences of low-income people who are viewed as consumers, not victims."[26] At the same time, with the strong ties that Acumen has with larger institutions and investors, those social ventures gain necessary resources and attention that helps them flourish.

The "strength of weak ties" in innovation parallels the well-known research by Everett Rogers who found that innovators make up only a very small percentage of a social system. In our language, this percentage should be understood as inhabiting only the farthest limit of the tails in a normal distribution curve.[27] The implication is that novel ideas are more likely to stem from otherwise "marginalized" employees who are sources of creative differences in the organization, and are better placed to break away from established, standard practices. This is because they are only loosely connected to those who enforce the norm. This notion, that the source of innovation within an organization is with the marginalized and the hierarchically lowly, is a key aspect of the Positive Deviance method that was discussed in the previous chapter. Methods like PD, when embedded in smart networks, are ways for generative leadership to enable the potentials unleashed through experiments in novelty.[28] Likewise, enabling intercohesive networks like those described in Chapter 5 are also a way that generative leadership can intervene at many levels in the organization to combine the best of weak tie linkages that introduce and recognize experiments in novelty, with the best of strong tie linkages that support group stability and focus as well as provide access to resources.[29]

CONSTRUCTING SMART NETWORKS

Earlier in this chapter we surveyed the essential components of social networks: *length* refers to the number of intermediate nodes in a network, *degree* measures the number of links that extend from any given node, *directionality* refers to the influence or flow of information, *filters* reflect how information can be modified at each node, and *structure/topology* refers to the specific configuration of connections that link nodes to other nodes. We also looked at the integration of weak ties and strong ties in smart networks and in intercohesion. Now we lay out some of the ways that generative leadership can strengthen ecologies of innovation by constructing and enhancing different types of network structures.

Creating smaller worlds

One of the insights about information diffusion across networks has to do with path length, or the number of intermediary nodes through which information has to flow to get from the initial sending agent to the eventual receiving nodes. A powerful implication of this, which we hinted at above, is the role of small-world networks in producing ecologies of innovation.

A key feature of small world networks is their shorter path lengths when compared to some other topologies. Shorter average path length results when there are fewer intermediate nodes along a path because some direct links bypass some of the nodes. The presence of fewer intermediate nodes leads not only to faster information flow, but it also limits the impact that filters will have on that flow. If an organization's members at the periphery or at lower levels face long path lengths, then adding links to make a smaller world is a relatively low cost way to deepen the organization's ecology and enhance innovation. As a first step, an organization's innovative potential can be quickly enhanced simply by connecting the inner circles with the outer circles over shorter path lengths.

Creating smaller worlds is not as hard as it might seem—we demonstrate this in the next two figures. Figure 7.3 is a stylized

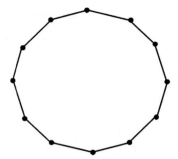

Figure 7.3   Stylized "Large Network"

drawing of a network that is "large" because its longest path length is 6.0, and its average path length is of 3.36 (i.e., this is the average number of links between any two nodes in the network). By adding just four new links to this "large network" we can turn it into a "small world"—an outcome shown in figure 7.4. The resulting new longest path length is only 4.0 (equivalent to one-third less than the large network) and the average path length drops to only 2.11 (again about one-third less than that of the large network).

Of course, figures 7.3 and 7.4 are highly stylized, simplistic diagrams of actual social networks that are much larger and far messier. The question remains as to where generative leadership should start an effort to decrease the length of their social networks. Which nodes should be bypassed? Where should one add new links? More generally, how does one determine the best way to make the network smaller and, accordingly, more effective for information sharing, resource allocations, and ultimately for innovation?

Fortunately, a pertinent finding from the study of networks demonstrates a kind of phase transition like those described in

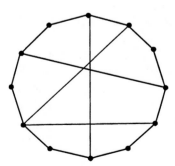

Figure 7.4   Making the "Large" World "Smaller"

Chapter 4 can take place in networks. It turns out that no matter how many nodes are being connected in a network, a relatively small percentage of additional random links will suffice to connect nearly all nodes along some path. Furthermore, this percentage actually decreases as the number of nodes increases![30] For example, in the case of a social network of 300 nodes, even though there are close to 50,000 possible links among these nodes, only about 2 percent, that is, only about 1,000 linkages are required to insure that nearly all 300 nodes will be connected to each other.

As links are added, there is a point where quite suddenly nearly all nodes are connected to each other. This transition point is called the emergence of a "giant cluster or component." Essentially, by having marginalized zones brought into the fold of the giant cluster, the novel information now flows from the weak ties in the more marginalized nodes and becomes directly accessible to the more central—and resource-rich—modules or hubs where these innovative ideas can be reinforced. However, generative leadership needs to walk a fine line here, because although collapsing weak ties into the center of the network may, in the short run, bring the innovative ideas closer to where they can be implemented, in the long run, this same making of a smaller world may *destroy* the novelty nurturing potency of the weak ties throughout the system. Instead, generative leadership can construct smart and cohesive social networks that simultaneously employ both the strengths of the strong ties and the strengths of the weak ties. We now turn to an example of how this was done successfully in the highly complex healthcare industry.

CONSTRUCTING SMART NETWORKS TO FIGHT PENICILLIN RESISTANT BACTERIA

The value of constructing smart and intercohesive networks can be seen in a program designed to reduce the spread of infections caused by the antibiotic-resistant bacteria MRSA. There are 100,000 cases of MRSA infection in the United States each year, and 20,000 people die of the disease each year. Furthermore, 84 percent of the infections are associated with transmission from health care workers to patients.[31] As a means of reducing this shocking number, a program of Positive Deviance, overseen by the Plexus Institute mentioned in an earlier chapter, was enacted at a large hospital to take advantage of successful experiments in novelty that were already producing positive outcomes.

This highly successful program was conducted at a consortium of hospitals in the Pittsburgh area under the mentorship of

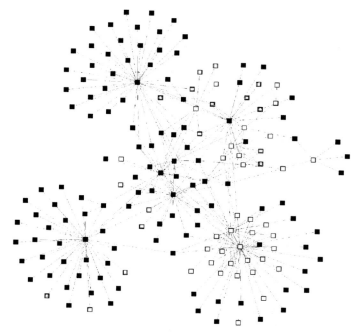

Figure 7.5 Social Network of Hospital Units before the Advent of a PD Program to Inhibit the Spread of MRSA

networkweaver June Holley and her colleagues, with key input from members from the Plexus Institute, a nonprofit group devoted to the application of complexity science to health care and health care administration. In the program, health care workers on certain nursing floors were trained in Positive Deviance and in engendering rich information flow through smart social networks. Figure 7.5 depicts the original dense network clustering with very weak links outside the clusters that existed before the program was initiated.

Note the social network topology of clustering and the weakness of interconnection among the clusters (the gray links are barely noticeable). This network topology means that even if the various units or the executive staff (presumably acting in part as "gate keepers" to retrieve relevant information from outside sources) did come up with innovative methods to halt MRSA infections, they did not possess a social network structure that was sufficiently pervasive to disseminate their innovations.

However, after the Positive Deviance program was initiated and the "network weavers" started reshaping the topology of the social networks involved, the resulting interconnection had much greater efficacy in transmitting and acting on the innovative measures that

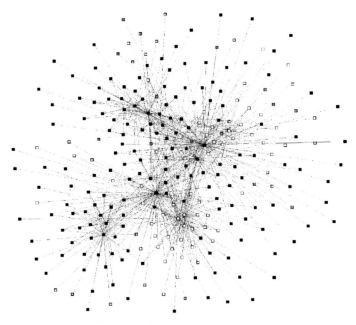

Figure 7.6   The More Connected Network Topology after the PD Intervention

helped to halt the spread of MRSA. This novel topology is depicted in figure 7.6.

The hospital unit denoted by the cluster of nodes in the upper right of figure 7.6 is now not only the most strongly connected cluster to other nodes and other clusters outside its boundaries, it also has the lowest transmission rates for MRSA across the hospital. The unit consisting of the array of nodes in the lower left of figure 7.6, which is the least connected outside the cluster, has the highest transmission rates. This strongly suggests that something about the new connectivity had helped to disseminate the useful innovations that were identified in the Positive Deviance intervention and had thus helped to slow the spread of MRSA. In our analysis this difference relates to the higher degree of interconnection and richer interactive resonance that now characterized the connections.

Holley calls the hospital's progress a move toward a "smart network," since the resulting network had stronger simultaneous connections among hubs and with peripheral nodes—in fact, its topology does resemble the network of the human cerebral cortex shown in figure 7.1. As a result of enhanced connectivity (and other aspects of the Positive Deviance intervention), a metric that the team developed called *awareness*, which measures how well people in one part of the network know what's happening in the other units, went up by a multiple of four when compared with its original level. Indeed, another metric, the *connector score*, which measures overall connectivity, was now 26 times greater than before!

According to Holley, mapping out the social networks when implementing this kind of intervention has several benefits. First, it can identify where in the organization innovative ideas are being imported by network linkages. That is, if several people in particular are linked more to individuals in other separate areas, then more information about successes and failures would flow around the network. Moreover, possessing an actual visual map of the various social networks in which they are working encourages greater collaboration and cooperation. Furthermore, utilizing *awareness* as a metric of social network capacity can reveal the aspects of the network structure that could be enhanced. An example would be in making networks more robust by adding additional redundant pathways connecting the nodes so that if certain nodes or links become less effective, other avenues would continue to exist for the flow of information.

From Holley's work and other sources, we suggest that the following questions be used to help focus attention on the construction of more effective and adaptable networks:

- What must the networks accomplish?
- Who need to be connected to whom and for what purposes?
- What linkages can you construct to reduce the average length of pathways in the network?
- How will the network be maintained? That is, how can the organization keep its networks robust?
- How will you enhance interaction resonance across the network?

Although network research can provide insights into how connectivity can add to or detract from effective information and resource flows, it is also important to include the reality of political and economic "power" differences among individuals due to management level and other factors. Consequently, we propose that generative leadership must thoughtfully add linkages to an organization's internal social network, as well as between the organization's members and the member's of other systems in its ecology, taking power relationships into consideration. Imaginative and careful thought needs to go into questions about where, how and with whom to make these connections.

In particular, generative leadership must take into consideration where the high-degree agents—those with many strong and weak tie connections—should be, which individuals can bring the requisite talent and experience to these positions, and where decision making authority should rest. Other considerations relate to the assignment of power and authority over resource distribution as well as how these choices are to be implemented within a smart network context. Finally, it is critical to avoid constructing *more* linkages without also focusing on their *richness*. In the end, it is both the structure of the network and the level of *interaction resonance* throughout the network that makes the difference by supporting the reciprocity and the bidirectionality of information and influence throughout the organization.

CONCLUSION: GENERATIVE LEADERSHIP FOR INNOVATION-FRIENDLY SOCIAL NETWORKS

Although social networks and their scale-free power law distribution appear to result from "self-organizing" processes, this appearance is deceiving for this reason: human organizations and human networks do not organize on their own, nor do social systems of any consequence "self-organize" absent significant managerial support.[32] Our point is that managerial influence on networks can be either positive and enabling, or negative and stifling to innovation and adaptation. Generative leadership seeks to thoughtfully use complexity ideas to maximize the former where innovation is needed and minimize the latter when it operates against the organization's purpose.

One of the key themes in this book is that complexity science has gone far beyond some of the naïve interpretations of complexity in earlier times where authors implied that a laissez-faire style of leadership was all that was needed for people and whole organizations to "self-organize." This naïve but highly marketed line of reasoning suggested that, "if only those pesky command and control Neanderthals would get out of the way, we could self-organize ourselves into paradise." In retrospect, this attitude was silly at best, and dangerous at worst. In stark contrast, we contend that it is not good enough for leadership to wait around hoping that innovation-friendly network topologies will somehow emerge "spontaneously." It won't happen. Complex organizing in human systems requires that the right context and the right substrates be in place to begin with, and that these are continually nurtured and maintained in order to support the emergence and growth of useful and innovative structures. This is what generative leadership is all about.

Indeed, we are suggesting that there is a very active role for generative leadership. Among other things described elsewhere in the book, this involves *constructing* and *sustaining* innovation-friendly social networks like smart and intercohesive networks, and enabling *interaction resonance* across all of these connections. Similarly, in this context we are proposing the construction of heterarchies consisting of distributed networks which have both reciprocal flows of information and also clear accountability and decision making authority. To be sure, clear authority and responsibility for decision making remain important; it's just not all concentrated at the top.

Complexity science shows that heterarchies should be established as an integrated complement to the more traditional hierarchies that are already in place. Like the premise of "network-centric warfare," such an intentionally constructed heterararchy enables the emergence of innovation and of adaptability, since the strengths of strong tie networks and those of weak tie networks are brought together to facilitate rich, bidirectional information flow. These broader flows serve to maintain rather than diminish the relevant differences across the system.

In an important sense what we are proposing in this chapter is to take very seriously all the buzz about "social networking." We hear about this regarding job searches, finding new customers, and generally expanding one's circle of work and personal relationships. Today, web-based social networking vehicles such as Twitter, Facebook or LinkedIn stand at the ready to help, and to be exploited. It's not just hype. "Networking" is a cogent strategy for finding novel opportunities whether that opportunity is a job or a new client. As anyone who has been involved in an earnest and intense job search knows, success in such endeavors often comes down to *who* you know as much as or even more than *what* you know.

The power of social networking was clearly demonstrated in one workforce development initiative that served predominantly low-income women in the United States with a high-school diploma or equivalent. The study found that among those who were recently unemployed, 74 percent, reported having fewer than five social connections they could turn to for help in finding a job![33] Even more striking, 40 percent of the participants reported job networks that consisted of only two, or one, or even no contacts! Research in this area has found that between 40 and 50 percent of new jobs in the United States are found through connections via social networks. Furthermore, research has shown that quit rates are lower for those who enter a new job through the bridge of a social network connection, even taking into consideration other factors such as ability or quality of the work.[34] As the economist Robert Putnam has put it: "Whereas physical capital refers to physical objects and human capital refers to properties of individuals, social capital refers to connections among individuals—social networks and norms of reciprocity and trustworthiness that arise from them".[35]

Mark Granovetter, the same economist who put forward the thesis of the "strength of weak ties" offered the following thought experiment.[36] Imagine the constituents of one's social network as red and white balls in an urn. Assume that those contacts with useful information are the red balls and the others with no useful information are the white balls. Now draw a ball from the urn. If the ball is white, draw again, no loss no foul. However, if the ball is red, relevant information is received, and there is the very real possibility that this new connection will add more red balls to your urn. Thus, the next draw out of the "urn" is more likely to be red and so on. The more one networks, the greater the benefit. This is the idea behind the notion of cumulative advantage that is so ubiquitous in innovation studies. Thoughtfully building networks in this way begins (but only begins) the process of building a smart network.

Granovetter goes even further, however. He points out that the proportion of red balls also depends on whether the agents with whom you have become newly connected have themselves been making new links along the course of their work lives. If so, then the enhancement of their own social networks will in turn feedback to your advantage further increasing the number of "red balls" in your own "urn." The point is that when social networks are enhanced by, for example, constructing smaller worlds or linking more agents on the periphery to core hubs, these enhancements can change the network structure itself. A stronger network augments future social networking opportunities.

Success builds upon success. More begets more. This is what it feels like to leverage nonlinear science. Each individual across the organization, from the trenches to the corner office, contributes his or her energy and resources to form and maintain connections and to build, improve and constantly maintain interaction resonance. It takes time, and it takes work. Everyone has a part to play, and everyone shares responsibility for success. It is within this nexus of high bandwidth information exchange that generative leadership is critical, and it is here where it is most powerful. This nexus empowers each of us, and it empowers all of us. By using this potential wisely, we can create ecologies where innovation flourishes, and we can build a sustainable world to pass on to our children, a world that they, their children, and their children's children can comfortably, and safely, use and enjoy.

NOTES

1. The U.S. Army Field Manual for 2001 edition of 3-0. Operations, cited in Murdock, P. (2002). Principles of war on the network-centric battlefield: Mass and economy of force. *Parameters, 32*(1), 86–95.

2. According to Murdock other factors were intelligence advantage and sheer luck. Furthermore, according to Bernard Brodie, an expert on military strategy, quoted in Murdock, economy of force is also meant "to suggest shrewd husbandry or usage" of military forces. This means to employee all available combat power, that is, to mass all the forces to achieve the primary objective while allocating minimum but necessary power to secondary tasks. The "economy" is meant to suggest discrimination in use of military force, not leaving any elements without a purpose, for example, General William T. Sherman's strategy of placing the enemy on the horns of a dilemma" by simultaneously attaching at several places and thereby obliging the enemy to defend them all.

3. Alberts, D., Garstka, J., & Stein, F. (1999). *Network centric warfare: Developing and leveraging information superiority* (2nd Rev. Ed.). Washington, DC Department of Defense/CCRP, pp. 16, 20.

4. Kopp, C. (2005).Understanding network centric warfare, *Australian Aviation*, January/February 2005. Available at: http://www.ausair power.net/TE-NCW-JanFeb-05.html.

5. See, for example, Gulati, R. (1999). Network location and learning: The influence of network resources and firm capabilities on alliance formation. *Strategic Management Journal, 20*(5), 397–420.

6. Krebs, V., & Holley, J. (2002). Building Sustainable Communities through Network Building. Available at: http://www.supporting advancement.com/web_sightings/community_building/community_ building.pdf; and Krebs, V., & Holley, J. (2002–2006). *Building smart communities through network weaving*. Available at: http://www.orgnet.com/BuildingNetworks.pdf. See also Ancona's research on externally focused teams: Ancona, D., & Caldwell, D. (1992). Bridging the boundary: External activity and performance in product development teams. *Administrative Science Quarterly, 37*, 634–668.

7. Metcalfe's Law, available at: http://en.wikipedia.org/wiki/Metcalfe% 27s_law, states: as the number of nodes increases linearly the potential value or effectiveness increases exponentially as the square number of nodes, that is, for every n node there are n-1 possible interactions between the nodes; hence the potential value-creating interactions is $n(n$-1) or n^2-n for large values of n; this is effectively n squared.

8. Page, S. (2007). *The difference: How the power of diversity creates better groups, firms, schools, and societies.* Princeton: Princeton University Press. On differences see also Eoyang, G., & Olsen, E. (2001). *Facilitating organizational change: Lessons from complexity science.* New York: Wiley (Pfeiffer).

9. Buchanan, M. (2002). *Nexus: Small worlds and the groundbreaking theory of networks,* New York: W. W. Norton.

10. Adamic, L. (1999). The small world web. In Abitebous, S. & A. M. Vercoustre (Eds.), *Research and advanced technology for digital libraries.* Heidelberg: Springer-Verlag,

11. Newman, M. (2003). *The structure and function of complex networks,* Available at http://wwwpersonal.umich.edu/~mejn/courses/2004/cscs 535/review.pdf.

12. Murdock, P. (2002). Principles of war on the network-centric battlefield. *Parameters,* 86–95.

13. Carley, K. M., & Ren, Y. (2001). Tradeoffs between performance and adaptability for C3I architectures. In Proceedings of the 2001 Command and Control Research and Technology Symposium. Conference held in Annapolis, Maryland, June, 2001. Evidence Based Research, Vienna, VA.

14. Tapsell, P., & Woods, C. (2009). A spiral of innovation framework for social entrepreneurship: Social innovation at the generational divide in an indigenous context. In J. Goldstein, J. Hazy, & J. Silberstang (Eds.), *Complexity science and social entrepreneurship: Adding social value through systems thinking* (pp. 471–485). Litchfield Park, AZ: ISCE Publishing.

15. Newman, M. (2003). *The Structure and Function of Complex Networks,* Available at http://wwwpersonal.umich.edu/~mejn/courses/ 2004/cscs535/review.pdf.

16. Csermely, P. (2006). *Weak links: Stabilizers of complex systems from proteins to social networks.* New York: Springer.

17. Cited in Newman, M. (2003). *The structure and function of complex networks,* Available at http://wwwpersonal.umich.edu/~mejn/ courses/2004/cscs535/review.pdf.

18. Gregory Todd Jones, G.T. (Forthcoming) Heterogeneity of degree and the emergence of cooperation in complex social networks. *Emergence: Complexity and Organization.*

19. Watts, D.(1999). *Small worlds: The dynamics of networks between order and randomness.* Princeton: Princeton University Press.

20. Hagmann, P., et al. (2008). Mapping the structural Core of the human cerebral cortex. *PLOS Biology,* 6(7-e159), 1479–1493 (Open Access).

21. Csermely, P. (2006). *Weak links,* pp. 18ff.

22. Holley, J. (n.d.). *Network Weaver.* Available at: http://www.network weaving.com/june.html.

23. Holley, J. (2007). *Networks and evaluation.* Available at: http://www. networkweaving.com/june_files/NetworkMetricsOverviewPaper.doc;

and Krebs, V., & Holley, J. (2002–2006). *Building smart communities through network weaving.* Available at: http://www.orgnet.com/ BuildingNetworks.pdf.

24. Holley, J. (n.d.). *Weaving smart networks to support healthy communities: Introduction.* Available at http://www.networkweaving.com/june_ files

25. Granovetter, M. (1983). The strength of weak ttties: A network theory revisited. *Sociological Theory, 1,* 201–233.

26. Novogratz, J. (2009). *The blue sweater: Bridging the gap between rich and poor in an interconnected world.* Emmaus, PA: Rodale Press, p. 2.

27. Rogers, E. (2003). *Diffusion of Innovations,* New York: Free Press.

28. According to Csermely, earlier research found that information spread much more by way of "weak ties" among students in a junior high school. Yet, strong ties are more relied upon by people from lower levels or at the margins, presumably closely related or friendship clusters. Csermely, P. (2006). *Weak links: Stabilizers of complex systems from proteins to social networks.* New York: Springer.

29. Besides directionality and influence, those practicing generative leadership must also be aware that there are other possible rules of interaction at work in a network including what I. Trofimova has called *compatibility* and *sociability.* Compatibility of nodes indicates how amenable each agent is to cooperative agendas on the part of other connected agents. This is related to both *interaction resonance* and the *emergence of cooperation.* If we are talking about social exchanges across differences, it might seem at first impression that compatibility as such could be quite hard to attain given the fact that nodes can be very different in interests, traits, and so on. However this need not be the case within the context of the *differences* framework we are adopting in this book—it is in precisely *the bridging across differences* that networks possess the capacity for enriched decision making and problem solving. That is, compatibility as a local nodal rule can and does coexist with differences among the nodes in a social network. *Sociability* of nodes has to do with the constraints on the number of possible links each node can have with other nodes—in other words, each node cannot have the same level of contact with every node in the world. A deficit of contacts may lead to agents choosing less adequate types of linkages, a situation that can lead to marginalization of sizeable populations in either an organization or a community. But this is something that leaders can definitely do something about as we'll be discussing later in this chapter. The fact is that people will naturally form social linkages but the purposes to which such linkages are put are determined in large measure by what opportunities for social connectivity exist. Trofimova, I. (2001). Principles, concepts, and phenomena of ensembles with variable structures (EVS). In W. Suls & I. Trofimova (Eds.). *Nonlinear dynamics in the life and social sciences* (pp. 217–231) (NATO Science Series). Amsterdam: IOS Press.

30. Buchanan, M. (2002). *Nexus: Small worlds and the groundbreaking theory of networks*, New York: W. W. Norton.
31. Buscell, P. (Abridged Version of) Singhal, A., & Greiner, K. (n.d.). Do what you can, with what you have, where you are: A quest to eliminate MRSA at the VA Pittsburgh healthcare system. *Deeper Learning, 1*(4), 1–13.
32. McKelvey, B., & Lichtenstein, B. (2007). Leadership in the four stages of emergence. In J. Hazy, J. Goldstein, & B. Lichtenstein (Eds.), *Complex systems leadership theory* (pp. 93–108). Boston, MA: ISCE Press. Chapter 5.
33. Spaulding, S. (2005). *Getting connected: Strategies for expanding the employment networks of low-income people*, New York: Public Private Ventures.
34. Fernandez, R.M., Castilla, E.J., & Moore, P. (2000). Social capital at work: Networks and employment at a phone center. *American Journal of Sociology, 105*(5), 1288–1356.
35. Spaulding, S. (2005). *Getting connected.*
36. Granovetter, M. (1985). Economic action and social structure: The problem of embeddedness. *American Journal of Sociology, 91,* 481–510.

CHAPTER 8

APPLYING GENERATIVE LEADERSHIP TO YOUR ORGANIZATION

Throughout this book we've described and exemplified how generative leadership informed by complexity science can work successfully in organizations large and small. Each example has drawn out one or more key insights into how complexity science can be leveraged to create ecologies of innovation. For example, we saw how:

- Netflix grew through "ecological" partnerships that often constrained them at the same time
- IBM successfully navigated a period of criticalization
- The SEED program in Indonesia emerged in unexpected ways that were more effective than could have been planned
- Starbucks's move into Chicago was facilitated by a four-phase process of emergence
- Apple, Inc., and Parkside Hospital found ways to "systematize" experiments in novelty
- Jerry and Monique Sternin identified "positive deviants" in Vietnamese villages, and reframed their marginal behavior into shared knowledge that virtually alleviated malnutrition there and in dozens of other countries
- June Holley constructed smart networks that dramatically decreased hospital infections, and the U.S. Army now pursues warfare through information networks
  The list goes on.

One critical step remains: how can individuals like you begin to apply generative leadership in your own organization? We tackle this question by summarizing the takeaways from each chapter with a focus on how each idea can be turned into a tangible expression of generative leadership. In the final section we offer a vision of what it might be like to work in an organization where an ecology of innovation is the norm.

HOW TO CREATE AN ECOLOGY OF INNOVATION

INCREASE ENERGY FLOW ACROSS BOUNDARIES

What enables Netflix to succeed is a creative and adaptive understanding of its role in the ecology of home entertainment. As we cited in Chapter 2, Netflix pursued a strategy of increasing the size of the market through unlikely partnerships, collaborating with its immediate competitors, and even eliminating successful revenue streams in favor of a symbiotic relationship within the industry. In each case, Netflix applied a powerful insight from ecology: innovation is sparked when increased energy and resources can be directed *across* apparent boundaries in the ecosystem.

Whenever Netflix found itself constrained by large-scale market forces—for example, the lack of households who owned a DVD player, the onslaught of a huge competitor like Amazon into its domain, or its lack of power in the entertainment business—it used generative leadership to reenvision the source of those constraints, turning constraint into opportunity. In the face of a paucity of DVD players Netflix reached across organizational and industry boundaries to form unlikely partnerships with DVD manufacturers, and in so doing increased the total amount of energy—in the form of money and information—and resources that flowed through this newly redrawn ecosystem. In the face of competition from one of the fastest-growing Internet firms in the world, Netflix permeated boundaries that seemed sealed by making a deal with Amazon to gain high-visibility promotion for its DVD rentals while in exchange Netflix accepted constraints on its own business model by agreeing to pull the plug on DVD sales as a promotional tool. Both moves served to increase the sales and revenue of the two former competitors. Likewise, in the face of being a virtually unknown player in the movie distribution business, Netflix permeated the boundaries of the Independent film world by sponsoring individual movies, creating new industry awards, and entering into unprecedented sole distribution rights that resulted in much higher exposure for the films, and more customers within more very small film niches.

In each of these ways, generative leadership started by identifying the boundaries within the ecology that already existed, and making a clear-minded assessment about the actual flow of energy and resources within and across those boundaries. Then, by relaxing the perceived solidity of certain boundaries, a series of possible innovations were found that might expand the overall flow of energy through the newly redrawn ecosystem. In this expression of generative leadership, an ecology of innovation is created through new perceptions that literally redistribute the boundaries of an ecosystem—whether internal to the organization or across its environment. When stable boundaries become semipermeable, "micro-diversity" can flourish, allowing for the creation of innovative ideas in unlikely places.

ENACTING AN ECOSYSTEM

As we described in Chapter 2, researchers have found seven facets of all ecosystems that, when enacted together, lead to a thriving ecosystem. At the same time, complexity science suggests that these interdependent facets are like dishes in a feast: one or two alone aren't enough to satisfy, but by the time three or four of these are put on the table, something memorable can start to happen. Then, adding more, one by one, can lead to a truly great party. We take this approach in describing how generative leadership can enact each of these features: Start with two or three and build on their success in the creation of an ecology of innovation. To facilitate this approach, we have combined similar facets to reduce the complexity of the effort.

Increase and amplify differences in the ecology

Every good manager recognizes the positive role that heterogeneity can play, especially in project groups and cross-functional teams. Generative leadership pushes this view farther, by recognizing the importance of how diversity—across informational differences—generates seeds of novelty leading to highly innovative organizational ecologies. Diversity in this sense does not just mean a broad range of demographic differences but includes differences of perception, difference of mental models, difference in perspectives. Variations in organizational functioning are the spice of difference and are sparked through fluctuations or departures from group norms that lead to both creative and pragmatic solutions working within existing constraints.

Ecosystems thrive on diversity because diversity provides a wide range of possible responses to any given situation. The wider is the range of variations, the more likely it is that (at least) one will become viable in furthering the adaptability of the whole. By enacting a stream of differences and variations, the potential for innovation is increased even in the face of rapid environmental change. For this reason, generative leadership pays attention not just to the degree of diversity at any one time, but to identifying and encouraging a diversity of ideas over time, never allowing a comfortable quiescence of standard operating procedures to settle over the ecology. As we described in chapters 5 and 6, finding and amplifying differences is a driver for an ecology of innovation.

Generative leadership can spark an ecology of innovation by highlighting differences, especially giving voice to those who do not represent the dominant majority. This also holds for amplifying those departures from the norm that improve overall adaptability, even if the innovations (may appear to) contrast with widespread assumptions and cultural beliefs. As Netflix's value statement says: challenge prevailing assumptions when warranted, and suggest better approaches. These differences are fuel for an ecology of innovation.

Find the nexus of interaction and give it resonance

Generative leadership lives in the *nexus* where the webs of the social networks of individual contributions coalesce, that is, the entire concept is based on the influence that arises *between* people, not *from* a person. An ecology is sustained and thrives through this nexus of exchange, when interactions between two or more actors bring more energy/resources to each of them. Further, growth and development happens *in* this nexus, in interactions that expand the conceptual frames of the actors such that an improvement in one feeds back to reciprocally improve the other, and so on.

According to complexity science, generative leadership can encourage this reciprocal interaction by increasing the depth and quality of communication and information flow throughout the network. As we mentioned in Chapter 2, meaning is increased when there is a resonance between people—when each person can listen for a sympathetic vibration in an interchange, and be given the tools to focus on amplifying that vibration. These tools include but go beyond the "Management 101" advice of being an engaged and active listener. These tools for creating a "relational space" involve expanding the capacity of these communication channels, and developing a culture in which difference and novelty are encouraged and allowed to amplify.

Thus, generative leadership actively engenders a culture of engagement and respect, especially in areas of difference, for example, between managers with high degrees of power and employees with few sources of power, between more extraverted members and those who are marginalized and/or less vocal, between middle managers across different functional areas, between customers and product development engineers, and so on. Likewise generative leadership finds ways to increase the capacity of information flow—in some sense to expand the "diameter" of the conduit of exchange, perhaps through slowing down the pace of certain exchanges, or providing different avenues for engagement that can personalize or enrich any given interaction. By improving interaction resonance across every nexus of exchange an ecology of innovation can begin to flourish.

Pursue coevolution through symbiotic relationships

In contrast to the go-it-alone mentality of traditional business, generative leadership sees successful strategic growth as a *co*evolution where the development of one entity is intimately tied to the development of other entities in the ecology. Netflix provided many examples of this strategy of coevolution, through which its evolution was dependent on and at the same time supported the evolution of its partners, many of whom were its competitors. In ecology the name of the game is coevolution, for any change anywhere in the network will necessarily have an impact on the range of options available to its neighbors, and thus on the total capacity of the niche.

Generative Leadership strives for this degree of integration and even fusion of parts to a greater whole, in ways that retain the integrity of each element but increase their combined capacity to achieve specific goals. In strategic terms, generative leadership is always searching for ways to coevolve with other members of the ecology. In organizational terms this is a focus on the coevolution of sole employees and of work groups. For example, can individual contributors be paired with peer mentors to encourage the coevolution of both? Can members of work teams be incentivized to coevolve with each other through more applied learning that accrues to the individuals and the group? Finally, creating an ecology of innovation is only possible when you practice generative leadership and coevolve with others in the process, expanding your own personal and professional development in concert with the development of the ecology.

Be prepared for a disequilibrium, multileveled ride!

Complexity science shows that innovation and emergence are not feasible in stable conditions; instead, rapid change and significant imbalance provide the necessary energy to begin the process. Disequilibrium is not a condition to be avoided but the precursor to coevolutionary change. Thus, generative leadership finds and embraces disequilibrium, as well as the uncertainty and unpredictability that it brings.

In a similar way, generative leadership takes a wide-angle view of an ecology, seeing as many levels of an ecosystem as possible, all at the same time. In other words, rather than focusing the level of interaction that is most stable or common, diversity and innovation are sparked by viewing the entire range of levels, from the particular words and gestures used by a manager in their interaction with another employee, to the set of interactions between these two and others over time, to the pattern of exchange between your department and other units, to the culture and process of interchange between your organization and corresponding entities in your value chain, your industry, your sector, and so on. Each degree of resolution offers new information, the aggregation of which can increase the disequilibrium throughout the system. Further, as we saw in Chapter 3 on the Cusp of Change, experiencing disequilibrium can be a very powerful impetus for positive innovations of all kinds.

HOW TO LEVERAGE THE CUSP OF CHANGE

Complexity science shows that a moderate degree of disequilibrium can support an ecology of innovation without initiating any kind of major shift in the organization as a whole. However, as we saw with IBM and with the entrepreneurial start-up of Targeted Marketing Solutions, Inc., every once in a while an organization faces a critical period that portends unprecedented change. In Chapter 3 we called this "criticalization," and showed that during a critical period the organization has the opportunity—and the need—to shift from its current mode of functioning into a mode characterized by nonlinearity, unpredictability, and lack of control. What worked before is simply not working now, and predictable, linear relationships no longer hold, a fact that IBM had to face when the more salespeople they hired the *fewer* profits were realized as their margins went negative.

Generative leadership can leverage a critical period into a Cusp of Change, by enacting insights gained through complexity science research. First, it recognizes two parameters that measure the underlying drivers of criticalization: opportunity tension, and informational differences. Opportunity tension occurs when a situation in the organization's ecosystem presents an opportunity and those in the organization respond with an entrepreneurial drive to push the venture to a new level of functioning. Generative leadership can move an organization into a Cusp of Change by linking an external opportunity with internal passion (pressure) for action. When members of the organization respond by enacting an approach that makes the opportunity more tangible, this further reinforces the need to respond, driving the system into higher and higher degrees of disequilibrium—further into the Cusp of Change.

At the same time, in order for the presence of opportunity tension to engender criticalization in the ecology, there must also be a requisite level of informational differences that are identified or shared among its people and across its network. If everyone is using the same information, no change will commence, and if there are differences in information but these are not explored or shared with one another, there won't be a recognition that the opportunity is present, and there will not be enough momentum to spark a shift. In Chapter 7 we described ways to expand the capacity of a social network, and below, we review those insights. Suffice it to say that criticalization begins when opportunity tension is high, and the potential outcomes and concurrent actions are not visible to everyone in the field, that is, when there is a moderate degree of informational differences. However, these differences are visible to many people, and enough of those people are well enough connected to have begun to share their ideas. When there is opportunity tension, and there are constraints on information flow in the organization such that no one has the complete picture but at least some people are talking about it, the organization is in a Cusp of Change.

The Cusp of Change is an abstract model based upon complexity ideas that describes a very tangible experience: when opportunity tension and informational differences both increase, there is a point where there emerges a split between the stability associated with the current "old way" of operating, and the emerging stability of a "new way" of conceiving the organization. In complexity science this is explained as a shift in the organization's attractor, which is the dominant logic that guides all of an organization's action (see Chapter 3). In the Cusp of Change the organizational attractor literally splits: on one "side" of the cusp is the old way of doing things, and on the other side is a new way. Between, within the cusp, both attractors compete for the hearts and minds of the people in the organization. This is when generative leadership is particularly important. As the two attractors pull in different directions more and more people question the previous model, and as informational differences are exploited to a greater and greater degree, members are increasingly challenged with greater indeterminacy and ambiguity. There are literally two answers for a while.

Generative leadership can help resolve this tension and encourage the movement from one attractor to the next. For example, sometimes a clear commitment by one key player can be enough to shift an entire work group or organization. In other cases, as shown in the Stag Hunt game in Chapter 3, when groups are incentivized to work together, a critical mass can emerge that encourages the transition to a new, more robust attractor. In still other cases, the small minority who want the change can find small-scale ways to incorporate it into the prevailing strategy, essentially using symbiosis to retain the innovation and gradually modify the attractor in stages rather than transforming the organization from one attractor to another in one giant leap of faith.

In addition, generative leadership can help choose the pace of transition. In some cases, once a Cusp of Change is reached the pursuant shift can occur very rapidly, as it did at Targeted Marketing Solutions, Inc. In other cases, the shift can proceed over a much longer period of time, by continuing to hold the opportunity tension and its constraints over many months while encouraging a more patient movement across the organization. IBM, for example, achieved this more moderate paced change through disaggregating the corporation into modules that were linked through a strong network. By engaging generative leadership within each separate group, the entire organization was able to unfold into a new, more adaptive attractor.

Overall, these insights provide a conceptual framework for understanding the dynamics of changing from one attractor to the next. We put these together in our description of *emergence*, highlighting how generative leadership can enact new organizing structures, often with unexpected properties. The emergence process is enabled through four phases, leading ultimately to a more sustainable organization that is better able to adapt to its changing ecology.

HOW TO LEAD EMERGENCE

In nearly all complexity books, the process of "emergence" has been shrouded in the mystique of "self-organization"—but neither term has been well defined and virtually no rigor has been brought to these presentations. The result has been an unfortunate belief that emergence is merely brought about spontaneously, somehow self-generated and thus outside the active reach of managers and executives.

Complexity and the Nexus of Leadership changes all of that, by offering a more accurate understanding of emergence in complex systems, and showing how it unfolds as a fourfold process. Formally, emergence is the coming into being of new structures, practices, and processes that result in the birth of new ventures or the renewal of organizations in whole or in part. Both a top-down and a bottom-up process, emergence integrates the strategic vision of top managers with the day-to-day working knowledge of line employees. Complexity science has shown how emergence proceeds through phases of (1) disequilibrium conditions, (2) amplifying actions, (3) recombinations, and (4) stabilizing feedback. The artful use of generative leadership can facilitate these processes and support positive emergent outcomes.

Disequilibrium conditions

Generative leadership can spark disequilibrium conditions by "turning up the heat" or "shakes things up" in the ecology. This can be done through knowledge creation, extending social networks, or unlocking technological advances that may be uncovered through experiments in novelty, as we described in Chapter 5. Opportunity tension can also be a driver of disequilibrium tension, whether the opportunity is directed at a change within any size work unit or even the creation of a start-up venture. As mentioned, disequilibrium can be sparked by diversity, as we saw with origin of the SEED program whose founders represented a great diversity of cultural/ethnic backgrounds, education levels, frames of reference, and differing relationships to the community. Whether through shaking things up, opportunity tension, or diversity, generative leadership can push the system out of its normal comfort zone, setting the first conditions for emergence.

Amplifying actions

The second phase of emergence, can also be enacted by generative leadership. As disequilibrium increases, the sense of impending organizational crisis, and the uncertainty that comes with it, can lead to high amounts of tension, stress and interpersonal conflict. Generative leadership recognizes that with this tension comes a stream of experiments—potential solutions that would increase the capacity of the system in a real way. Any of these experiments can become the seed of change; thus, generative leadership encourages these experiments while embracing and easing the discomfort and ambiguity that comes with them. Whereas the typical response is to dampen these departures from the norm, generative leadership seeks to amplify them, seeking to gain a momentum for a potential shift to a new attractor.

Recombinations

In the third phase, recombinations occur when resources and ideas—some new, many already existing—are reaggregated in a way that increases the capacity of the system to operate. Generative leadership supports this process by nurturing one or more of the seeds for change, drawing people and attention toward the one that seems to catalyze a broad base of support. Recombinations are more successful when they draw on the rich relationship structures within the ecology of innovation rather than relying on outsiders or experts to make unilateral moves, which will rarely be integrated into the entity as a whole.

Generative leadership also appreciates the "nucleation" process of emergence: the seed of novelty represents only the first step in an iterative sequence of dissemination. Once the new structure takes hold in one place, it has much greater likelihood of spreading to additional areas, potentially reconfiguring the entire attractor. Here again, by going against the typical response of reinforcing current stabilizing order, generative leadership facilitates subtle emergence processes such as reducing the number of parts in the new organizational entity while increasing its functionality. In both cases the key is to balance the top-down urge to facilitate emergence with the bottom-up messiness and uncertainty that are inherent in recombinations that work.

Stabilizing feedback

In the fourth phase, stabilizing feedback leads to sustainability, as generative leadership helps institutionalize the new structures, practices and processes that have emerged. In complexity science this means finding the appropriate parameters for the new attractor—identifying the "order parameter" that arises in the system. Generative leadership catalyzes this process by increasing the feedback loops within the system. It does this by feeding the outputs of the system—for example, marketplace success, supply agreements and partnerships as we saw in the Netflix case in Chapter 2—back upon to the various emergent structures within the organization to change and improve them.

In an organizational sense, generative leadership can stabilize emergence by developing new and effective routines, and by creating partnerships and coalitions that increase the legitimacy of the emergent entity. In addition, these emergent processes can be stabilized by giving incentives not just to innovators but equally to the implementers of an initiative, based on their ability to effectively embed it into the organization's ecology.

In sum, emergence is a well-documented process that moves through four phases of activity. Generative leadership can facilitate each one of these phases, and thus support the positive outcomes of emergence while avoiding dead-ends and negative spirals. Moreover, in the same way that generative leadership can encourage the creation of an ecology of innovation by pursuing a range of system-wide interventions, so emergence can be encouraged through a system-wide view of the process rather than a single-minded focus on any one of the phases. Creating the conditions for emergence, and innovation, is at the heart of generative leadership.

At the same time, the heart of emergence—the seed of change—is innovation that becomes amplified in a disequilibrium system. We turn now to the tools for enhancing these experiments in novelty—the "coin of the realm" in an ecology of innovation.

HOW TO GENERATE EXPERIMENTS IN NOVELTY

Generative leadership takes a broad systemic view on most aspects of organizing, but not so in the arena of experiments. Instead, generating experiments in novelty requires a very close attention to detail, an ability to notice and then confidently interpret even the most subtle of signals, and to amplify those ideas that may seem marginal or that depart from organizational norms or even depart from the leader's own strategy. None of this is easy, but complexity science reveals five factors that can generate experiments in novelty.

EMPHASIZE DIFFERENCES AND END "GROUP THINK"

As we noted in the first chapter, certain themes—like this one— are important enough to be mentioned multiple times throughout the book. Earlier in this chapter we suggested how the value of difference can be a driver of an ecology of innovation; here we extend that claim by reviewing Scott Page's research on heterogeneity in group composition (see Chapter 5). Generative leadership can exploit the power of difference in several ways, each based on findings from his research into team heterogeneity and performance:

- Outcomes are better for a good combination of differences across a team as compared to simply higher average skill levels in more homogenous teams. In other words, higher-skilled but more homogeneous work groups are trumped by lower-skilled groups but with higher diversity, leading to better performance as well as more accurate prediction of trends.

- The greater the differences among group members, the more likely that individuals will be able to generate new mental maps with a higher capacity for effective problem solving.
- In complex problem solving, a *randomly selected* group of very heterogeneous individuals will outperform a set of the *best* individual problem solvers.

Recognizing that diversity includes variations in age, gender, tenure, and expertise as well as a range of personal experience and mental models, team members should be chosen according to a broad set of criteria. At the same time, organizational research shows that too much heterogeneity can make communication less effective within the group, so here again a good balance should be found between heterogeneity and coherence, a balanced gained through experience.

One particularly effective tool for identifying and amplifying group diversity is Difference Questioning, which is an intervention designed to highlight already existing variations in outlook, experience, and perspective. Through an ongoing series of queries, individuals in a task group are asked to reveal differences in opinion and perspective; generative leadership then uses these differences to surface and legitimize new information for the group. The result is more innovative solutions to complex problems.

INCREASE THE FREQUENCY OF EXPERIMENTS

Whether referring to complex systems or ecologies, it is evident that variation—diversity—is a fertile source of adaptive strategies. The more diversity in a system, the more routes the system has to generate innovation and positive change. These findings, which we summarized in the prior section, might lead one to conclude that "more is better"—the more experiments, the more innovation. But this conclusion is not altogether true. That's because the generation of experiments is a nonlinear affair: more experiments are not necessarily better, and small experiments can, in certain cases, be far more influential than large ones. These results are explained by the complexity science of power laws, and generative leadership can learn much from this approach.

Power laws provide a mathematical explanation of why many dynamic systems—such as models that describe experiments, investments, company sales, and even earthquakes—have outputs that are non-proportional to their inputs. Informally related to the more well-known 80/20 rule, this research shows that the majority of events in a dynamic system will have very little influence, but a tiny percentage will create most of the change that is seen in the whole. As an example that was already presented in Chapter 5, the vast number of earthquakes in the world are never felt, whereas a very small percentage end up having a tremendous impact in the earth's environment. In the same way, the vast number of experiments in a dynamic ecology of innovation will have no impact in the organization as a whole. However, a few of them will become the seeds for major positive change. From this perspective, generative leadership is about identifying those few that stand out among the many.

The simplest move here is to increase the total number of experiments, which will, in a nonlinear fashion improve the chances that one of them will be a winner. We gave numerous examples of how generative leadership achieves that goal, including:

- Micro-finance, which makes many tiny investments toward self-sustaining businesses, with the aim that these will help support a locality and in some cases, may expand to transform a regional economy.
- Google and 3M have programs that require employees to devote a small amount of their time to personally enriching projects, with the aim that a small percentage of these will lead to major innovations that the company can benefit from.
- At Google.com, users are encouraged to experiment with gadgets and applications, in the hopes that perhaps one such application will provide a unique avenue for entrepreneurial action.

What does complexity science say about determining which experiments to amplify? The answer is hidden in the notion of "correlations," which we referred to in Chapter 5. Correlations refer to commonalities or resonances between experiments and actions in different parts of the same ecology. According to complexity science, the more an experiment is correlated with similar fluctuations in the ecology, the more likely it will have an important impact in the organization. This provides a key for distinguishing which experiments in novelty to pursue! But it also suggests that generative leadership would do well to "hook-up" various parts of their organizations more effectively by, for example, generating "smaller world" social networks or the social network structure known as intercohesion which we'll describe shortly.

MAKE THE MOST OF WEAK SIGNALS

Generative leadership offers another approach for amplifying experiments, and that is to leverage those that are isolated and seemingly marginal. That's because these so-called weak signals actually have tremendous power. For example, studies show that since closely knit "strong-tie" networks are much less likely to pursue ideas that are different, most innovations are disseminated through weak-tie networks, that is, through distant colleagues and associates with whom one rarely connects. Essentially, the differences in information and experience within these weak-tie networks become the source of novelty and innovation for the larger system.

Thus, generative leadership would be especially attuned to new ideas that spread through weak ties, and experiments that are generated from the periphery—a notion we'll expand upon in a later section.

DEVELOP NETWORK INTERCOHESION

As important as variations are for initiating innovation, an equally critical task is to implement innovation that integrates across the organization. Complexity science research has identified a unique approach that links the power of weak-tie networks to the effectiveness of strong-tie networks, through the model of *intercohesion*. Usually there are strict differences between the strong-tie and the weak-tie forms of network structure in an ecology, but research has found instances in which they can be combined. Making this combination work is a final key to identifying and amplifying the experiments in novelty that have the greatest potential.

Generative leadership achieves this combination in a two-step process. First, a set of internally cohesive groups are identified—work teams that have a strong ability to work together due to their long-time membership in the group or other forms of homogeneity. Then, members of these groups are mixed to a degree, so that these previously separate work teams become linked together in a broader network. This overlapping membership within internally cohesive groups leads to a creative tension that facilitates the recombination of ideas and resources across sector boundaries. The weak-tie aspect of the network provides openness to new ideas, while the strong-tie aspect of the network provides high levels of mutual understanding, coordination, cooperation and respect. Together they create an intercohesion that facilitates innovation and its dissemination, a powerful combination that can be leveraged by generative leadership.

CREATE MORE THROUGH POSITIVE DEVIANCE

Generative leadership offers another method for developing experiments—Positive Deviance. The premise, as we described in Chapter 6, is that certain individuals in every community practice certain unique—"deviant"—behaviors, which allows them to find better solutions to local problems than others in the community. By finding these positive deviants, and spreading their innovation, the entire community can solve problems and achieve goals that were impossible under the normally accepted rules.

SIX STEPS FOR LEVERAGING POSITIVE DEVIANCE

Generative Leadership provides an outline for pursing a Positive Deviance intervention:

- *Define* what the problem is and determine the desired outcome. This relates to what we have been calling opportunity tension. The leader identifies the natural stress on the system that comes about when an opportunity is recognized in the environment by the members of an organization, but they also realize that, as currently configured, the system is unable to realize its potential. Generative change is required.
- *Determine* the individuals and groups of individuals who are already exhibiting a desirable outcome within the common behaviors in the community. These are the persons or groups who represent the kind of novelty outside the norm that if replicated can change the system. This confers on them the status of being positive deviants within the system.
- *Discover* those unique practices or behaviors that enable the positive deviants to find better solutions. This means carefully investigating exactly how and through what differences in practices their novelty bestows advantages on those who practice them.
- *Design* and implement social interventions whereby the majority have access to and learn the new practices inherent in the novel successes of the positive deviants.
- *Discern* the ongoing pulse of the organization by implementing mechanisms that provide continuing monitoring and evaluation of the emergent novelty, initiatives and other experiments across the organization.
- *Disseminate* the successful innovations on as wide a scale as possible throughout the organization. As changes to practice diffuse widely, system wide change, and emergent order at a new level becomes possible, as we described in Chapter 4.

EIGHT RULES OF ENGAGEMENT FOR POSITIVE DEVIANCE

As we describe in Chapter 6, through his many years of effort, one of the founders of the Positive Deviance method, Jerry Sternin, identified eight rules for insuring success in implementing Positive Deviance. We summarize those rules for generative leadership:

1. Don't presume you have the answer. Of course, this already goes against traditional or conventional leadership theory, which presumes that top managers or experts are people "in the know" who by nature have more information than the "natives" they are consulting to. In contrast, Positive Deviance presumes that the best ideas and a full resolution of the problem exist as potential already in the system, and can emerge through experiments in novelty.

2. Don't mix people as is done with cross functional teams. Here again, this goes against the contemporary push for cross functionality. In a Positive Deviance model, "the weak-tie" element of innovation is already present in the system, in "deviants" whose practices form a positive solution to the situation at hand. Thus, generative leadership emphasizes the cohesive quality of groups—the strong-tie networks.

3. Let the groups do it themselves, from information gathering, to measurement, to identification of positive deviants, to dissemination.

4. Identify conventional practices: this has to be done before deviance can be recognized and its mechanisms understood.

5. Identify and analyze the set of behaviors that the deviants have in common. Single out exactly what makes them successful. As Sternin stated, "They will have discovered a new way of doing things themselves, making it their discovery, not yours." This of course contrasts with the "leader with special skills"– view of leadership.

6. Let the community adopt deviations on their own. Far from importing "best practices" from elsewhere, these innovations arise from within the system itself, specifically, from experiments in novelty occurring in the system. Thus, the people who have discovered the innovative practices should spread them themselves. Rather than requiring adherence to the new practice, offer incentives to do so. What is disseminated is new behaviors, and not just one innovation but a new process for encouraging *ongoing* innovation.

7. Track results and publicize them: experiments in novelty will remain marginal if they are not amped up and disseminated. Leadership has a crucial constructional role here!

8. Iterate: an example of the recursive operations so crucial to the nonlinear dynamical systems aspect of complexity science.

With these rules, and in the right situation, Positive Deviance can be a powerful source of innovation in any ecology.

HOW TO CREATE SMART NETWORKS

As we've said throughout, whether building an ecology of innovation, expanding experiments in novelty, or moving through a period of criticalization, generative leadership relies on the creation and expansion of social networks. In the last chapter we described the many different types of networks, including dense clusters, hub networks, scale free networks, small worlds, and smart networks. We also reviewed the research on how beneficial networks can be for everything from team effectiveness, knowledge transfer, opportunity recognition, goal achievement, and so on. Clearly networks matter; the question is, how to build them—and how to build the right kind of networks within and across organizational boundaries.

Generative Leadership answers this question by highlighting a new kind of network structure, namely smart networks. Smart networks are similar to the intercohesion idea, in that they combine the coherence that comes from within densely connected networks, with the innovation that can come from peripheral connections. In formal terms, a smart network involves dense clusters that have extensions to weak links on the network periphery. These networks are robust yet open to new information, and are relatively easy to expand.

Constructing a smart network means adding specific links and deleting other links, in order to shorten the average length of connections across the entire network. The goal is to bring peripheral nodes more into the center, by creating strong linkages between key individuals who have been more marginal and the dense networks in the core. Beyond introductions, this can be achieved by being sensitive to power and status relationships while increasing the membership of certain committees, giving those on the periphery some new responsibility, and finding avenues for interpersonal connection, for example, through shared interests or shared experiences. At the same time, certain people may have become intermediaries between networks; to reduce the risk of counter productive political behaviors, these middle nodes should be eliminated by strengthening the connections across the gap, and perhaps shifting certain responsibilities or interactions.

According to the complexity science research, this restructuring does not have to be extensive: shortening the path length between virtually all the nodes of any network can be achieved by adding merely 2 percent more links than already exist. To make it even easier, these 2 percent new connections could be random—they don't have to be carefully analyzed and decided by some outside consulting firm! After that, generative leadership recommends increasing the robustness of the network by adding redundant pathways to central nodes. A level of redundancy serves to insure that the overall communication flow remains stable even if some key people change their role, leave the organization, or begin to act politically in ways that are at odds with the organization's goals.

This process may take some time, but the benefits are well worth the effort. Shorter path lengths improve the overall quality and quantity of information flow within the network. By making the margins of the network less peripheral, diversity is increased because more unique voices are heard, and novelty that does start at the periphery can be identified and amplified sooner and more easily.

PRACTICING GENERATIVE LEADERSHIP

Generative leadership is a system-wide process that arises by enriching every interaction between organizational members across the entire network. Focusing on "the space between" people, giving more voice to previously marginalized stakeholders, and creating the conditions for the emergence of something new and uncertain—these require the combined commitment of everyone in an organization, from the entrepreneurs and top executives to the middle managers to line personnel and to partner organizations across the value chain. *Complexity and the Nexus of Leadership* is not a quick fix—we never promised a magic bullet—but the long-term effects of building an ecology of innovation are certainly worth the effort.

This systemic view of leadership is indeed a core contribution of complexity science. We have emphasized this again and again, starting with the notion that generative leadership is enacted as an event rather than through a person, and continuing through every theme in the book. We conclude with a few key insights that summarize *Complexity and the Nexus of Leadership*, insights based on rigorous and careful applications of complexity science to the practice of generative leadership.

Generative leadership focuses on the quality as well as the quantity, of interactions. It takes time to enact deeper and richer interactions, and that time—even a few extra minutes—is perhaps the most valuable investment that can be made by any stakeholder in the organizational ecology. Each interaction is an opportunity for *mutual, reciprocal* influence. Thus, every single employee is responsible for generative leadership on an hour-by-hour, day-by-year basis. Although senior and middle managers are accountable for organizational goals, leadership is not *in* these senior managers; instead, leadership is in every interaction throughout the organization.

Complexity science shows that innovation is embedded in heterogeneity, thus the more differences that are present in a system, the more likely it will be that new experiments in novelty will arise. More than demographic diversity, it is openness to differences of opinion and perspective—which usually get squashed in corporate settings—that most increase information flow, meaning, and innovation.

Change is not a problem to be overcome; it is the essence of business success. Within the waves of ambiguity and unpredictability that accompany any significant change are powerful currents of innovation and opportunity. Complexity science shows that innovation will emerge when members continue forward in the face of uncertainty; only by actually feeling the discomfort of ambiguity and lack of control *without* altering the situation too quickly, can a truly novel path be set within any organization.

Establishing generative leadership in your organization is neither easy nor a one shot deal. Instead, it is a systemic process carefully built over time through the shared interactions of many stakeholders. The key is to operationalize the kind of leadership that is able to leverage the insights of nonlinear science to create ecologies of innovation around you. So where does one start? One place that immediately comes to mind is enabling *resonant* interactions that spur micro-diversity. These departures from the norm, or what we are calling "experiments in novelty," can then be sustained and amplified to increase their frequency, range of influence, and potency in galvanizing energies across the unit, department, division, or the entire organization. Generative leadership can provide resonance capacity by setting-up conditions to recognize "weak signals" such as through constructing and supporting the appropriate types of social networks, for example, the *intercohesion* networks described in chapters 5 and 7. This can lead to a striking symbiosis among organizational units and between the organization and its many partners in the environment.

At the same time, it is crucial to resist the temptation to take action aimed at prematurely reducing the disquieting sense of disequilibrium that results. As the environment changes for either good or ill, your organization must likewise change. Any discomfort experienced may be a positive sign indicating that the organization is moving into a *Cusp of Change*. This is when generative leadership manages the tension between two attractors, that is, the way things had been done in the past versus a new and different way of doing things. As we've shown, processes of emergence result in recombinations of existing capabilities that further the aim of innovation. Specific steps at this juncture include the six steps of Positive Deviance and the construction of smart networks.

These constructive changes, supported as they are by the thousands of resonant interactions occurring everyday, lead to a palpable shift in the culture of an organization. One can feel a difference in energy level in offices, in corridors and in online chat rooms. The climate in such a place is palpably different than the normal "office" environment. Conversations about work are frequent, earnest and intense; emotions are visible, but they reflect passion about the project under discussion not personal anxiety. Individuals express their differences freely and proudly, but are also readily willing to bow to a better idea. As interaction resonance between individuals expands across and throughout the organization, information flows more freely and with greater nuance and depth. In time a common language and a unique set of new symbols emerge that further enhance the depth and quality of information exchange. Experiments are encouraged and enacted as a wider range of ideas are expressed by a more diverse set of organizational members, each person challenging others, demanding newer, better, and stronger ideas. New ideas are tried out regularly, and an attitude of "throw it against the wall to see what sticks" prevails. Higher capacity within interactions leads to greater leveraging of informational differences, which then leads to an increase in new ideas and eventually results in a culture of successful innovation. Success builds on success. A sense of potential grows. This is what an ecology of innovation feels like. A positive, creative, and dynamic environment like this can emerge in your organization when you and your team adopt the principles and tools of generative leadership.

Beyond these specific tools, *Complexity and the Nexus of Leadership* introduces a new way of thinking about how work can be organized, a framework that emphasizes connection and creativity, the two keys to innovation. Your organization will become more adaptable, your teams more engaged, and life in your organization will become more rewarding. This holistic and systemic approach is by no means a quick fix. Indeed, observing, reflecting and acting is never easy within the complex nexus of human interaction, but this is where effective leadership is most necessary, where it is absolutely crucial. The good news is that complexity thinking and nonlinear science are powerful and hopeful. By enacting the ideas in this look, you can confidently improve innovation throughout your ecology and provide the leadership that is needed to create and sustain a world-class organisation.

BIBLIOGRAPHY

Adamic, L. (1999). The small world web. In Abitebous, S., & Vercoustre, A. M. (Eds.), *Research and advanced technology for digital libraries*. Heldelberg: Springer-Verlag.

Afuah, A. (2003). *Business models—A strategic analysis*. New York: McGraw Hill/Irwin.

Alberts, D., Garstka, J., & Stein, F. (1999). *Network centric warfare: Developing and leveraging information superiority* (2nd Rev. Ed.). Washington, DC: Department of Defense/CCRP.

Allen, P. (1984). Ecology, thermodynamics, and self-organization. *Canadian Bulletin of Fisheries and Aquatic Sciences, 213,* 3–26.

———. (2004, September). *Micro-diversity in evolution.* Paper presented at the ISCE Conference: Managing or Muddling Through.

Allen, T. H. F., & Roberts, D. (1997). Foreword. In Robert Ulanowicz (Ed.), *Ecology, the ascendent perspective* (pp. xi–xiv). New York: Columbia University Press.

Ancona, D., & Caldwell, D. (1992). Bridging the boundary: External activity and performance in product development teams. *Administrative Science Quarterly, 37,* 634–668.

Anderson, C. (2006). *The long tail: Why the future of business is selling less of more.* New York: Hyperion.

Anderson, P. (1999). Complexity theory and organization science. *Organization Science, 10,* 222.

Arnold, V. I. (1992). *Catastrophe Theory.* Berlin: Springer-Verlag.

———., Goryunov, V. V., Lyashko, O. V., & Vasil'ev, V. A. (1998). *Singularity Theory I.* Berlin: Springer.

Ashby, R. (1962). Principles of the self-organizing system. In Heinz Von Foerster, & George W. Zopf, Jr. (Eds.), *Principles of self-organization* (Sponsored by Information Systems Branch, U.S. Office of Naval Research), pp. 102–126.

Bak, P. (1996). *How nature works: The science of self-organized criticality.* New York: Springer.

Baker, T., & Nelson, R. (2005). Creating something from nothing: Resource construction through entrepreneurial bricolage. *Administrative Science Quarterly, 50,* 239–366.

Baron, R. A., & Shane, S. A. (2008). *Entrepreneurship: A process perspective* (2nd Ed.). Mason, OH: Thomson South-Western.

Beck, Daniela, & Chong, L. Choy (2009). Creative interaction in culturally diverse groups. In Jeffrey A. Goldstein, James K. Hazy, & Joyce Silberstang (Eds.) *Complexity science and social entrepreneurship: Adding social value through systems thinking* (pp. 487–506). Litchfield Park, AZ: ISCE Publishing.

Bénard, H. (1901). Les tourbillons cellulaires dans une nappe liquide transportant de la chaleur par convection en régime permanent. *Annales de Chimie et de Physique, 23*, 62–114.

Bertels, T., & Sternin, J. (2003). Replicating results and managing knowledge. In Bertels, T. (Ed.). *Rath and Strong's six sigma leadership handbook* (pp. 450–457). Hoboken, NJ: John Wiley and Sons.

Bradbury, R. H. & Van Der Laan, J. D., & Green, D. G. (1996). The idea of complexity in ecology. *Senckenbergiana marit, 27*(3/6), 89–96.

Bradbury, H., Lichtenstein, B., Carroll, J., & Senge, P. (2010). Relational space: Learning and innovation in a collaborative consortium for sustainability. *Research in Organizational Change and Development.*

Brooks, A. (2009). *Social entrepreneurship—A modern approach to social value creation.* Upper Saddle River, NJ: Prentice-Hall.

Browning, L., Beyer, J., & Shetler, J. (1995). Building cooperation in a competitive industry: Sematech and the semiconductor industry. *Academy of Management Journal, 38*, 113–151.

Buchanan, M. (2002). *Nexus: Small worlds and the groundbreaking theory of networks.* New York: W. W. Norton.

Bunnell, D., & Luecke, R. (2000). *The e-bay phenomenon: Business secrets behind the world's hottest Internet Company.* New York: Wiley.

Burgelman, R. A. (1994). Fading memories: A process theory of strategic business exit in dynamic environments. *Administrative Science Quarterly, 39*, 24–56.

Buscell, P. (Abridged Version of) Singhal, A. & Greiner, K. (n.d.). Do what you can, with what you have, where you are: A quest to eliminate MRSA at the VA Pittsburgh Healthcare System. *Deeper Learning, 1*(4), 1–13.

Carley, K. M., & Ren, Y. (2001). Tradeoffs between performance and adaptability for C3I architectures. In Proceedings of the 2001 Command and Control Research and Technology Symposium. Conference held in Annapolis, Maryland, June, 2001. Evidence Based Research, Vienna, VA.

Chambers, J. T., & Bryant, A. (2009). Openers: Corner office—in a near-death event, a corporate rite of passage. *The New York Times.* August, 2, 2009, p. 2 Business.

Chiles, T., Meyer, A., & Hench, T. (2004). Organizational emergence: The origin and trans-formation of Branson, Missouri's Musical Theaters. *Organization Science, 15*(5), 499–520.

Csermely, P. (2006). *Weak links: Stabilizers of complex systems from proteins to social networks.* New York: Springer.

Dooley, K. (1997). A complex adaptive systems model of organization change. *Nonlinear dynamics, psychology, and the life sciences,* 1, 69–97.

Dorsey, D. (2000). Positive Deviant—Jerry Sternin. *Fast Company,* December. Available at the Plexus Institute website: http://www. plexusinstitute.org/ideas/show_elibrary.cfm?id=270.

Duve, C. (2005). *Singularities: Landmarks on the pathways of life.* Cambridge, UK: Cambridge University Press.

Elton, C. S. (1955). *The ecology of invasions by animals and plants.* London: Methuen.

Eoyang, G., & Olsen, E. (2001). *Facilitating organizational change: Lessons from complexity science.* New York: Wiley (Pfeiffer).

Ferenstein, G. (2009). The Obama and google management style. *Fast Company.* FC Expert Blog, July 20, 2009. Available at: http:// www.fastcompany.com/blog/gregory-ferenstein/fastminds/obama-and-google-management-style-eerily-similar.

Fernandez, R. M., Castilla, E. J., & Moore, P. (2000). Social capital at work: Networks and employment at a phone center. *American Journal of Sociology,* 1288–1356.

Fiscus, D. A. (2001). The ecosystemic life hypothesis I: introduction and definitions. *Bulletin of the Ecological Society of America, 82*(4), 248–250, October 2001.

Gerstner, L. (2002). *Who says elephants can't dance: Inside IBM's historic turnaround.* New York: HarperBusiness.

Goldstein, J. (1986). A far-from-equilibrium systems approach to resistance to change. *Organizational Dynamics, 15*(1), 5–20.

———. (1994). *The unshackled organization.* Portland, OR: Productivity Press.

———. (1999). Emergence as a construct: History and Issues. *Emergence, 1*(1), 49–72.

———. (2000). Emergence: A concept amid a thicket of conceptual snares. *Emergence, 2*(1), 5–22.

———. (2006). Emergence, creative process, and self-transcending constructions. In K. Richardson (Ed.), *Managing organizational complexity: Philosophy, theory, and application* (pp. 63–78). Greenwich, CT: Information Age Press.

———., Hazy, J. K., & Silberstang, J. (Eds.) (2009). *Complexity science and social entrepreneurship: Adding social value through systems thinking.* Litchfield Park, AZ: ISCE Publishing.

Guastello, S. J. (2002). *Managing emergent phenomena: Nonlinear dynamics in work organization.* Mahwah, NJ: Lawrence Erlbaum Associates, Publishers.

Gulati, R. (1999). Network location and learning: The influence of network resources and firm capabilities on alliance formation. *Strategic Management Journal, 20*(5), 397–420.

Granovetter, M. (1983). The strength of weak ties: A network theory revisited. *Sociological Theory, 1,* 201–233.

Granovetter, M. (1985). Economic action and social structure: The problem of embeddedness. *American Journal of Sociology, 91*, 481–510.

Hagmann, P., et al. (2008). Mapping the structural core of the human cerebral cortex. *PLOS Biology,* 6(7–e159): 1479–1493 (Open Access).

Haken, Hermann (2006). *Information and self-organization: A macroscopic approach to complex systems.* Berlin: Springer.

Hastings, Reed: How I Did It, As told to P. Sauer. (2005). *Inc.* December, 2005. Available at: http://www.inc.com/magazine/20051201/qa-hastings.html.

Hazy, J. K. (2008). Toward a theory of leadership in complex adaptive systems: Computational modeling explorations. *Nonlinear Dynamics, Psychology and Life Sciences, 12*(3), 281–310.

——. (2010). Innovation Reordering: Five principles for leading continuous renewal. In Schloemer, S. & Tomaschek, N (Eds.). *Leading in Complexity: New Ways of Management* (pp. 40–56). Heidelberg: Systemische Forschung in Carl-Auer Verlag.

——., Tivnan, B. F., & D. R. Schwandt. (2004). Permeable boundaries in organizational learning: computational modeling explorations. *InterJournal Complex Systems (Online), Manuscript number 1063,* 1–8

——., Goldstein, J. A., & Lichtenstein, B. (2007). *Complex systems leadership theory: New perspectives from complexity science on social and organizational effectiveness.* Mansfield, MA: ISCE Publishing.

Hebbert, W., Keast, R., & Mohannak, K. (2006). The strategic value in oscillating the strength in technology clusters. *Innovation: Management policy and practice.* Available at: http://www.innovation-enterprise.com/archives/vol/8/issue/4-5/article/1657/the-strategic-value-of-oscillating-tie-strength

Henning, J. (1995). *Model Languages: The newsletter discussing newly imagined words for newly imagined worlds,* 1 (4), August 1, 1995. Available at: http://www.langmaker.com/ml0104.htm#1.

Hirsch, M. W., Smale, S., & Devaney, R. L. (2004). *Differential equations, dynamical systems and an introduction to chaos* (2nd Ed., Vol. 60). Amsterdam: Elsevier Academic press.

Holley, J. (2007). *Networks and evaluation.* Available at: http://www.networkweaving.com/june_files/NetworkMetricsOverviewPaper.doc.

—— (n.d.). *Weaving smart networks to support healthy communities: Introduction.* Available at http://www.networkweaving.com/june_files.

—— (n.d.). Network Weaver. Available at: http://www.networkweaving.com/june.html.

Indian Ocean Earth Quake (2004). *Wikipedia.* Available at: http://en.wikipedia.org/wiki/2004_Indian_Ocean_earthquake.

Janis, I. (1972). *Victims of groupthink.* Boston: Houghton Mifflin Company.

Jobs, Steve (2004). *Business week: The innovation economy—The promise of innovation.* October 11, 2004. Available at: http://compuserve.businessweek.com/magazine/content/04_41/b3903408.htm.

Jones, G. T. (2008). Heterogeneity of degree and the emergence of cooperation in complex social networks. *Emergence: complexity and organization, 10*(4), 46–54.

Jones, A. J. (2000). *Game theory: Mathematical models of conflict.* Chichester: Horwood Publishing.

Katz, D., & Kahn, R. (1966). *The social psychology of organizations.* New York: Wiley & Sons.

Koehn, N. (2001). *Howard Schultz and Starbucks coffee company.* Boston, MA: Harvard Business School.

Kopp, C. (2005).Understanding network centric warfare, *Australian Aviation*, January/February 2005. Available at: http://www.ausairpower. net/TE-NCW-JanFeb-05.html.

Kotter, J. (1995). Leading change: Why transformation efforts fail. *Harvard Business Review* (March–April), 59–67.

Krebs, V., & Holley, J. (2002). *Building sustainable communities through network building.* Available at: http://www.supportingadvancement. com/web_sightings/community_building/community_building.pdf.

——., & Holley, J. (2002–2006). *Building Smart Communities through Network Weaving.* Available at: http://www.orgnet.com/BuildingNetworks.pdf.

Lester, Richard K., & Piore, Michael J. (2004). *Innovation: The missing dimension.* Cambridge, MA: Harvard University Press.

Levi-Strauss, C. (1966). *The savage mind.* Chicago: University of Chicago Press.

Lichtenstein, B. (1997). Grace, Magic & Miracles: A "Chaotic" Logic of Organizational Transformation. *Journal of Organizational Change Management, 10*(5), 393–411.

—— (2000). Self-organized transitions: A pattern amid the chaos of transformative change. *Academy of Management Executive, 14*(4), 128–141.

——. (2010). Moving far from far-from-equilibrium: Opportunity tension and entrepreneurial emergence. *Emergence: Complexity and Organization, 11*(4), 15–25.

——., Carter, N., Dooley, K., & Gartner, B. (2007). Complexity dynamics of nascent entrepreneurship. *Journal of Business Venturing, 22,* 236–261.

——., & Plowman, D. (2009). The leadership of emergence: A complex systems leadership theory of emergence at successive organizational levels. *The Leadership Quarterly, 20,* 617–630.

MacIntosh, R., & MacLean, D. (1999). Conditioned emergence: A dissipative structures approach to transformation. *Strategic Management Journal, 20,* 297–316.

Margulis (Sagen), L. (1967). On the origin of mitosing cells. *Journal of Theoretical Biology, 14*(3), 255–274.

——. (1970). *Origin of Eukaryotic cells.* New Haven, CT: Yale University Press.

Mathews, R., & Wacker, W. (2002). *The Deviant's Advantage.* New York: Random House.

Mayr, E. (1985). *The growth of biological thought: Diversity, evolution, and inheritance.* Cambridge, MA: Harvard University Press.

McKelvey, B., & Lichtenstein, B. (2007). Leadership in the Four Stages of Emergence In J. Hazy, J. Goldstein, & B. Lichtenstein (Eds.), *Complex systems leadership theory,* Chapter 5 (pp 93–108). Mansfield, MA: ISCE Press.

Metcalfe's Law. Available at: http://en.wikipedia.org/wiki/Metcalfe's_law.

Murdock, P. (2002). Principles of war on the network-centric battlefield: Mass and economy of force. *Parameters, 32*(1), 86–95.

Newman, M. (2003). *The structure and function of complex networks.* Available at http://www-personal.umich.edu/~mejn/courses/2004/cscs535/review.pdf.

Netflix Blog, September 2, 2009. Available at: http://blog.netflix.com/2009/09/winner-of-netflix-find-your-voice-film.html.

Netflix Values Statement. Available at www.netflixfindyourvoice.com.

Nonaka, I. (1988). Creating organizational order out of chaos: Self-renewal in Japanese firms. *California Management Review, 30* (Spring), 57–73.

———., & Takeuchi, H. (1995). *The knowledge-creating company.* New York: Oxford University Press.

Novogratz, J. (2009). *The blue sweater: Bridging the Gap between rich and poor in an interconnected world.* Emmaus, PA: Rodale Press.

Okasha, Samir (2006). *Evolution and the levels of selection.* Oxford: Clarendon Press-Oxford Univerity Press.

O'Neill, R., DeAngelis, D., Waide, J., & Allen, T.F.H. (1986). *A hierarchical concept of ecosystems.* Princeton: Princeton University Press.

Page, S. (2007). *The difference: How the power of diversity creates better groups, firms, schools, and societies.* Princeton: Princeton University Press.

Phelps, K., & Hubler, A. (2007). Towards an understanding of membership and leadership in youth organizations: Sudden changes in average participation due to the behavior of one individual. *Emergence: Complexity and Organization, 8*(4), 28–35.

Plowman, D. A., Baker, L., Beck, T., Kulkarni, M., Solanksy, S., & Travis, D. (2007). Radical change accidentally: The emergence and amplification of small change. *Academy of Management Journal, 50,* 515–543.

Positive Deviance website: http://www.positivedeviance.org.

Power Laws. *Wikipedia.* Available at: http://en.wikipedia.org/wiki/Power_law.

Prahalad, C. K., & Bettis, R. (1986). The dominant logic: A new linkage between diversity and performance. *Strategic Management Journal, 7,* 485–501.

Prigogine, I. (1955). *Introduction to the thermodynamics of irreversible processes.* New York: Wiley & Sons.

———. & Glansdorff, P. (1971). *Thermodynamic theory of structure, stability, and fluctuations.* New York: Wiley & Sons.

Prigogine, I., & Stengers, I. (1984). *Order out of chaos.* New York: Bantam Books.

Rogers, E. (2003). *Diffusion of innovations.* New York: Free Press.

Saco, R. (2005). *Good companies: Organizations discovering the good in themselves by using Positive Deviance as a change management strategy.* MSc. Dissertation, HEC Paris, Oxford Executive Education, Oxford University.

Schultz, Howard, & Yang, Dory Jones. (1997). *Pour your heart into it: How Starbucks built a company one cup at a time.* New York: Hyperion.

Spaulding, S. (2005). *Getting connected: Strategies for expanding the employment networks of low-income people.* New York: Public Private Ventures.

Stanley, M., Amaral, L., Buldyrev, S., Havlin, S., Leschhorn, H., Maass, P., et al. (1996). *Scaling behaviour in the growth of companies. Nature (letters), 379,* 804–806.

Strong, D., Simberloff, D., Abelof, L., & Thistel, A. (1984). *Ecological communities: Conceptual issues and the evidence.* Princeton: Princeton University Press.

Surie, G., & Hazy, J. K. (2006). Generative leadership: Nurturing innovation in complex systems. *Emergence: Complexity and organization (E: CO), 8*(4), 13–26.

Sutton, R. (2002). *Weird ideas that work: 11 ½ Practices fro promoting, managing, and sustaining innovation.* New York: The Free Press.

Swenson, R. (1989). Emergent attractor and the law of maximum entropy production: Foundations to a theory of general evolution. *Systems Research, 6*(3), 187–197.

———. (1992). Autocatakinetics, yes—Autopoiesis, no: Steps toward a unified theory of evolutionary ordering. *International Journal of General Systems, 21,* 207–228.

Tapsell, P., & Woods, C. (2009). A spiral of innovation framework for social entrepreneurship: Social innovation at the generational divide in an indigenous context, In J. Goldstein, J. Hazy, & J. Silberstang (Eds.), *Complexity science and social entrepreneurship: Adding social value through systems thinking* (pp. 471–485). Litchfield Park, AZ: ISCE Publishing.

Thom, R. (1989). *Structural stability and morphogenesis: An outline of a general theory of models.* Reading, MA: Addison-Wesley.

Thouless, D. (1989). Condensed matter physics in less than three dimensions. In P. Davies (Ed.), *The New Physics* (pp. 209–235). Cambridge, UK: Cambridge University Press.

Trofimova, I. (2001). Principles, concepts, and Phenomena of ensembles with variable structures (EVS). In W. Suls & I. Trofimova (Eds.), *Nonlinear Dynamics in the Life and Social Sciences* (NATO Science Series) (pp. 217–231). Amsterdam: IOS Press.

Uhl-Bien, M., Marion, R., & McKelvey, B. (2007). Complexity leadership theory: Shifting leadership from the industrial age to the knowledge era. *The Leadership Quarterly, 18*(4), 298–310.

Ulanowicz, R. (1997). *Ecology, the ascendent perspective.* New York: Columbia University Press.

US Army Field Manual for 2001 edition of 3–0. Operations, cited in Murdock, P. (2002). Principles of war on the network-centric battlefield: Mass and economy of force. *Parameters, 32*(1), 86–95.

Uzzi, B., & Jarrett, S. (2005). Collaboration and creativity: The small world problem. *American Journal of Sociology, 111*(2), 447–504.

Vagelos, R., & Galambos, L. (2004). *Medicine, science, and Merck*. Cambridge: Cambridge University Press.

Van de Ven, A. (1993). The development of an infrastructure for entrepreneurship. *Journal of Business Venturing, 8,* 211–230.

———., & Garud, R. (1989). Technological Innovation and industry emergence: The case of cochlear implants. In A. H. Van de Ven, H. L. Angle, & M. S. Poole (Eds.), *Research on the management of innovation: The Minnesota Studies*. New York: Ballinger/Harper & Row.

———. (1994). The Coevolution of Technical and Institutional Events in the Development of an Innovation. In Joel Baum and Jitendra Singh (Eds.), *Evolutionary dynamics of organizations* (pp. 425–443). New York: Oxford University Press.

Vedres, B., & Stark, D. (2009). "Opening Closure: Intercohesion and Entrepreneurial Dynamics in Business Groups" MPIfG Discussion Paper 2009 (3) Max-Planck-Institut für Gesellschaftsforschung.

Viegas, J. (2006). *Pierre Omidyar, founder of e-bay*. New York: Rosen Publishing Company.

Wallack, F. Bradford (1980). *The epochal nature of process in Whitehead's metaphysics*. New York: State University of New York Press.

Watts, D. (1999). *Small worlds: The dynamics of networks between order and randomness*. Princeton: Princeton University Press.

West, G. B., Brown, J. H., & Enquist, B. J. (1997). A general model for the origin of allometric scaling laws in biology. *Science, 276,* 122–126.

Whitman, Meg (2001). Quoted in Table. eBay: Of the People, by the People, for the People. *Business Week/E.Biz,* December 3, 2001. Available at: http://www.businessweek.com/print/magazine/content/01_49/b3760603.htm?chan=sb.

Wiens, J. A. (1984). On understanding a non-equilibrium world: Myth and reality in community patterns and process. In D. Strong, D. Simberloff, L. Abelof, & A. Thistel (Eds.), *Ecological communities: Conceptual issues and the evidence* (pp. 440–457). Princeton: Princeton University Press.

Wolk, A. (2007). Social entrepreneurship and government: A new breed of entrepreneurs developing solutions to social problems. In M. Z. Wu (Ed.), *The Small Business Economy—Report to the President* (pp. 151–212). Washington, DC: U.S. Government Printing Office.

Yunus, M. (2009). *Poverty: Creating a world without poverty: Social business and the future of capitalism*. New York: Public Affairs.

Zeeman, E. C. (1977). *Catastrophe theory: Selected papers, 1972–1977*. New York: Addison-Wesley Educational Publishers.

INDEX

CPSIA information can be obtained at www.ICGtesting.com
Printed in the USA
LVOW08s1344010616

490782LV00003B/99/P